# Apology of Culture

# Apology of Culture

Religion and Culture in Russian Thought

Edited by

## Artur Mrówczyński-Van Allen,
## Teresa Obolevitch,
and **Paweł Rojek**

PICKWICK *Publications* · Eugene, Oregon

APOLOGY OF CULTURE
Religion and Culture in Russian Thought

Pickwick Publications
An Imprint of Wipf and Stock Publishers
199 W. 8th Ave., Suite 3
Eugene, OR 97401

www.wipfandstock.com

ISBN 13: 978–1-4982–0398-2

*Cataloging-in-Publication data:*

Apology of culture : religion and culture in Russian thought / edited by Artur Mrówczyński-Van Allen, Teresa Obolevitch, and Paweł Rojek.

x + 242 p. ; 23 cm. —Includes bibliographical references.

ISBN 13: 978–1-4982–0398-2

1. Religion and civil society—Russia—History. 2. Christianity and culture—Russia—History. I. Mrówczyński-Van Allen, Artur. II. Obolevitch, Teresa. III. Rojek, Paweł. IV. Title.

BR932 .A67 2015

Manufactured in the U.S.A.                                             02/17/2015

# Contents

*Contributors* | ix

Introduction—Apology of Culture and Culture of Apology: Russian Religious Thought against Secular Reason | 1
—Artur Mrówczyński-Van Allen, Teresa Obolevitch, and Paweł Rojek

## Part I: Russian Thought and Secular Reason

1   Man as Spirit and Culture: Russian Anthropocentrism | 15
    —Marcelo López Cambronero

2   The Trinity in History and Society: The Russian Idea, Polish Messianism, and the Post-Secular Reason | 24
    —Paweł Rojek

3   Georgy Fedotov's *Carmen Saeculare:* A Reflection on Culture as a Judgment of Modernity from the Philosophy and Theology of Some Nineteenth- and Twentieth-Century Russian Thinkers | 43
    —Artur Mrówczyński-Van Allen

4   The Polyphonic Conception of Culture as Counterculture in the Context of Modernity: Fr. Pavel Florensky, Mikhail Bakhtin, and Maria Yudina | 53
    —Olga Tabatadze

5   Pavel Florensky on Christ as the Basis of Orthodox Culture and Christian Unity | 63
    —Nikolai Pavluchenkov

6    The Problem of Christian Culture in the Philosophy of Vasily
Zenkovsky | 72
—Oleg Ermishin

7    Overcoming the Gap between Religion and Culture: The Life and
Works of Mother Maria (Skobtsova) | 79
—Natalia Likvintseva

8    Apology of Culture in *The Journals* of Father
Alexander Schmemann | 87
—Svetlana Panich

## Part II: Historical Focuses

9    Catholicity as an Ideal Foundation of Social Life: Gregory Skovoroda
and His Concept of the High Republic | 99
—Victor Chernyshov

10   Religiosity and Pseudo-Religiosity in Russia's Nineteenth Century
Liberation Movement Preceding Bolshevik Quasi-Religiosity | 110
—Katharina Anna Breckner

11   Tolstoy and Conrad's Visions of Christianity | 119
—Brygida Pudełko

12   Nikolai Fedorov and Godmanhood | 129
—Cezar Jędrysko

13   Catastrophism as a Manifestation of the Crisis of Consciousness in
Russian and Polish Cultures | 138
—Natalia Koltakova

14   Nikolai Berdyaev and the Transformations of the Idea of
Humanism | 146
—Ovanes Akopyan

15   Between Idol and Icon: A Critical Appraisal of the Mystery Project of
Culture by Vyacheslav Ivanov in the Context of the Thought of Jean-
Luc Marion | 153
—Marta Lechowska

16   Ivan Il'in on the Foundations of Christian Culture | 162
—Yury Lisitsa

17  Religious Realism and Historical Challenges: Vasily Zenkovsky and Russian Youth Abroad  |  172
    —NATALIA DANILKINA

18  Russian Religious Thought in the Middle of the Twentieth Century: Discursive Strategies in the Philosophical Diaries of Yakov Druskin and Alexander Schmemann  |  180
    —MARIA KOSTROMITSKAYA

19  The Symphonic Unity of Traditions: Sergey Horujy's Synergetic Anthropology and the Interpretation of History  |  187
    —ROMAN TUROWSKI

## Part III: Religion, Politics, and Ecumenism

20  The Roman Question in the History of Russian Culture in the Late Nineteenth and Early Twentieth Centuries  |  199
    —FR. YURY OREKHANOV

21  The Rotten West and the Holy Rus: Ethical Aspects of the Anti-Occidentalism of the Contemporary Russian Orthodox Church  |  208
    —FR. MARCIN SKŁADANOWSKI    208

22  The Universalism of Catholicity (Sobornost'): Metaphysical and Existential Foundations for Interdenominational Dialogue in the Philosophy of Semen Frank  |  218
    —GENNADI ALIAIEV

23  Local Civilizations and the Russian World: Nikolai Danilevsky and the Russian Orthodox Church of the Moscow Patriarchate  |  227
    —OLGA SHIMANSKAYA

24  The Idea of the Antichrist in Russia: From Religious to Political Narration  |  235
    —MAGDA DOLIŃSKA-RYDZEK

# Contributors

**Ovanes Akopyan**, Doctoral Student at the University of Warwick, England.

**Gennadi Aliaiev**, Professor at the Poltava National Technical Yuriy Kondratyuk University, Poltava, Ukraine.

**Katharina Anna Breckner**, Independent scholar, Hamburg, Germany.

**Marcelo López Cambronero**, Professor at the Institute of Philosophy "Edith Stein," Granada, Spain.

**Victor Chernyshov**, Professor at the Poltava National Technical Yuriy Kondratyuk University, Poltava, Ukraine.

**Natalia Danilkina**, Assistant Lecturer at the Immanuel Kant Baltic Federal University, Kaliningrad, Russia.

**Magda Dolińska-Rydzek**, Doctoral Student at the Justus-Liebig-Universität, Giessen, Germany.

**Oleg Ermishin**, Research Fellow at the Alexander Solzhenitsyn Memorial House of the Russian Abroad, Moscow, Russia.

**Cezar Jędrysko**, Doctoral Student at the Jagiellonian University, Krakow, Poland.

**Natalia Koltakova**, Assistant Lecturer at the Interregional Academy of Personnel Management, Donetsk, Ukraine.

**Maria Kostromitskaya**, Doctoral Student at the Russian State University for the Humanities, Moscow, Russia.

**Marta Lechowska**, Assistant Lecturer at the Jagiellonian University, Krakow, Poland.

**Natalia Likvintseva**, Research Fellow at the Alexander Solzhenitsyn Memorial House of the Russian Abroad, Moscow, Russia.

**Yuri Lisitsa**, Professor at the St. Tikhon's Orthodox University, Moscow, Russia.

**Artur Mrówczyński-Van Allen**, Professor at the International Center for the Study of the Christian Orient and Instituto de Filosofía "Edith Stein," Granada, Spain.

**Teresa Obolevitch**, Professor at the Pontifical University of John Paul II in Krakow, Poland.

**Fr. Yury Orekhanov**, Professor at the St. Tikhon's Orthodox University, Moscow, Russia.

**Svetlana Panich**, Research Fellow at the Alexander Solzhenitsyn Memorial House of the Russian Abroad, Moscow, Russia.

**Nikolai Pavluchenkov**, Assistant Professor at St. Tikhon's Orthodox University, Moscow, Russia.

**Brygida Pudełko**, Assistant Professor at Opole University, Opole, Poland.

**Paweł Rojek**, Assistant Lecturer at the Pontifical University of John Paul II in Krakow, Poland.

**Olga Shimanskaya**, Associate Professor at the Linguistics University of Nizhny Novgorod, Russia.

**Fr. Marcin Składanowski**, Assistant Professor at the John Paul II Catholic University of Lublin, Poland.

**Olga Tabatadze**, Assistant Lecturer at the International Center for the Study of the Christian Orient, Granada, Spain.

**Roman Turowski**, Doctoral Student at the Pontifical University of John Paul II in Krakow, Poland.

# Introduction

## Apology of Culture and Culture of Apology

*Russian Religious Thought against Secular Reason*

—Artur Mrówczyński-Van Allen, Teresa Obolevitch, and Paweł Rojek

The secret police which supervised the Church under the various Eastern European communist regimes issued a special questionnaire for informers who spied on priests. According to it, they were to pay special attention to references occurring in sermons, firstly to those pertaining to the Bible, secondly to Church Fathers, and thirdly to general literature.[1] Priests were not considered dangerous when they quoted religious sources alone; the communist regime saw the greatest threat in merging Christianity with general culture.

Surprisingly enough, the same intuition can be found in John Paul II. He wrote: "The synthesis between culture and faith is not only a demand of culture, but also of faith . . . A faith that does not become culture is not fully accepted, not entirely thought out, not faithfully lived."[2] Christianity, understood as an existential Event, remaining within the limits imposed by the artificial concept of "the religious," becomes meaningless, powerless and worthless. To stay alive, religion should embrace and penetrate the whole of

---

1. We owe this observation to Andrey Kurayev, "Kak nauchnyy ateist stal d'yakonom," 341.

2. John Paul II, Address to the Italian National Congress.

human reality, including art, science, politics and economy. It seems very significant that both enemies and defenders of faith alike admitted it.

True religion implies culture, but also culture calls for true religion. A Christian religion without culture is dead, as is a culture devoid of faith. The "deculturalization of faith" is as dangerous as the "desacralization of culture." Catharine Pickstock wrote about "necrophilia," the love of death, of modern culture,[3] which stems from its closeness to religion. We would like to pay attention on the twin phenomenon on the side of religion, which could be labeled "zoophobia," that is a fear of life. Religion too often fears its own manifestation and incarnation in all spheres of human reality. As a result, both the necrophilia of culture and the zoophobia of religion leads to the domination of secular order.

## The Integrality of Russian Thought

Contemporary philosophy and theology are still more conscious of the fact that the model of relations between religion and culture developed in modernity is the key for understanding the current state of the Western world. The processes of the secularization of society, culture, and even religion, are rooted in the dualistic vision of religion and culture introduced in the late Middle Ages. Modern thought, language and practice are deeply affected by this dualism. The division between the sacred and the secular brings about the gradual removal of the sacred and the final triumph of the secular. Christian Events, instead of being the fundamental inspiration of human life, ultimately become a particular private interest of no real importance.[4]

If we seek a way out, we need to explore domains of culture unaffected by Western European secular thinking. We might look for inspiration in past pre-modern Western thought, but we also may investigate contemporary non-modern Eastern thought. Russian thought is remarkably well prepared to formulate an alternative to secular modernity. Indeed, in Russian culture there was neither a Renaissance nor an Enlightenment. Eastern Christianity retained an integral patristic vision of human nature which had not been divided into separate "natural" and "supernatural" elements. These pre- and non-modern visions are now gaining exceptional value in the post-modern reality in which we find ourselves.[5]

---

3. Pickstock, *After Writing*, 105–6.

4. For a concise summary of accounts of the endogenous process of secularization, see Javier Martínez, *Beyond Secular Reason*.

5. See Mrówczyński-Van Allen, *Between the Icon and the Idol*, 80, 104, and Rojek, "Mesjańska teologia polityczna."

We believe that the heritage of Russian Christian thought may serve as a source of inspiration for alternative approaches to religion and culture. In this aspect, Russian thought may be compared with *Nouvelle Théologie*, Radical Orthodoxy and other recent movements in Christian post-secular thought and for this reason it remains astonishingly contemporary. Moreover, perhaps it is even a hidden source of all these intellectual movements; as it was recently argued, Henri de Lubac, their founding father, was deeply influenced by Russian thought.[6]

Russian religious thinkers have provided not only a profound diagnosis of the crisis, but have also searched for ways to overcome it. They desired the "re-enchantment of the world,"[7] the reversal of the process recognized by Max Weber as the core of modernization. Duns Scotus, Thomas Hobbes, John Locke, Adam Smith, and many other fathers of modernity, imposed the modern concept of religion[8] and wanted to delineate the boundaries between such "religion" on the one hand, and the autonomous secular domains of philosophy, politics and economics on the other. Russian thinkers blurred these supposed boundaries. That is why Russian philosophy is so often indistinguishable from theology from the Western point of view. It is not a methodological error, but rather a direct consequence of an alternative approach to the supposed relation between religion and culture. Moreover, the principle of integrity led to the characteristic blurring of genres in Russian culture. Philosophy is not separated from theology, but also from literature, religion life, social and political activity and biography in general. Again, this is not an error, but a result of an integrated approach to culture.

Now we would like to focus on just two examples of the Russian integral way of thinking. Nikolai Gogol (1809–1852), a classic Russian writer, was also a deep Christian thinker who foresaw the coming erosion of religious culture and its replacement with the modern state. He belonged, along with Vladimir Odoyevsky (1803–1869), to the first generation of original Russian Christian thinkers who anticipated all the development of Russian philosophy. The great philosopher Vladimir Soloviev (1853–1900) formulated with a masterly clarity the dialectics of secularization and saw the only way out for religion is creation of its own culture. Soloviev was also a poet and literary critic. Both Gogol and Soloviev constitute the great Russian tradition uniting religion with culture on the one hand, and literature with philosophy on the other.

6. See Dell'Asta, *La teologia ortodossa e l'Occidente.*

7. This term has been coined in German by Michael Hagemeister in his (highly critical) description of Florensky's views; see Hagemeister, "Wiederverzauberung der Welt."

8. Cavanaugh, *Myth of Religious Violence.*

## Gogol on Integral Christian Culture

Russian philosophical thinking goes beyond the formal boundaries of what is understood under the term philosophy in the West. The reason for this is that it undertakes a metaphysical reflection, that it has never ceased to pose questions on such fundamental issues as evil, that it has never lost its existential character. "The Russian thinker," wrote Siemion Frank,

> from a simple pilgrim [*bogomolets*] to Dostoevsky, Tolstoy, and Vladimir Soloviev, always seeks "*pravda*"; not only does he want to understand the world and life, he strives also to grasp the main religious and moral principle of the universe, so as to transform life and the world, to be cleansed and saved. He longs for the unconditional triumph of truth, in the sense of "true being," over falsehood, over untruth [*nepravda*] and over injustice [*nespravedlivost'*].[9]

This is why the Russian tradition has a propensity to obliterate the boundaries between philosophy and literature, between thought and art. The common goal is the discovery of man and the truth revealing itself in him. In this way all elements participate in, co-create and become saturated with the all-unity of common experience, namely tradition, and culture created by it.

"Gogol was our first prophet of the return to a holistic religious culture—the prophet of Orthodox culture," wrote Vasily Zenkovsky.[10] Gogol's genius is in his understanding of the significance of the ability to create Christian culture and tradition as well as in his deeply thought out interpretation of the dechristanization processes of Western culture. At the core of this dechristanization lies the expulsion of Christ as the center of human life, and in this way the loss of everything that is truly human. The advancing diminishment of community and alienation prevents the formation of culture originating from perichoresis, inseparably binding beauty, good and truth.

The author of *Dead Souls* aptly remarks that the processes constraining contemporary Europe stem from the presence of "empty spaces" that appeared in the relations between people who became individuals and citizens. Modern Western European countries try to fill these "empty spaces" with complicated laws and regulations, want to transform them into something new of absolute moral value, in something that, according to the prophetic words of Gogol, will lead Europe to "bloodshed."[11]

9.  Frank, "Essence and Leading Themes," 36.

10.  Zen'kovskiy, *Russkiye mysliteli*, 55

11.  Ibid., 58, 59.

According to Zenkovsky, what was only a vague symbolic construct in *A City without Name* by Odoyevsky[12] became in Gogol an expression of life experience resulting from a deep relation of soul, heart and mind. This is the axis, the extremely important foundation in the tradition of Russian religious thinking of Odoyevsky's and Gogol's followers, a precious source of inspiration for a Christian West increasingly consciously searching for answers to questions posed by postmodernism.

## Soloviev on the Dialectics of Secularization

"Religion"—as Vladimir Soloviev wrote at the beginning of his fundamental *Lectures on Divine Humanity*—"must determine all the interest and the whole content of human life and consciousness."[13] This straightforward claim briefly summarizes the account for the problem of the relation between religion and culture in Russian religious thought. Soloviev clearly saw that the abandoning by the religion of its central place led to the process of secularization:

> For contemporary civilized people, even for those who recognize the religious principle, religion does not possess this all-embracing and central significance. Instead of being all in all, it is hidden in a very small and remote corner of our inner world. It is just one of the multitude of different interests that divides our attention. Contemporary religion is a pitiful thing.[14]

In other words, dualism at first leads to secularization, then to privatization and, finally, to the annihilation of religion. The current pitiful state of religion in the modern world is a direct consequence of the conceptual division between religion and culture in past. The resumption of the integrality of the sacred and the secular is the only way to overcome the current cultural and religious crisis.

Religion, if it is supposed to be something at all, must be everything. It must penetrate all domains of human life: spiritual and corporeal, emotional and intellectual, private and public, individual and social. This was the main concern of Soloviev in his *Lectures*. "All that is essential in what we do, what we know, and what we create," wrote Soloviev, "must be determined by and

12. Odoevsky, "A City without Name." For detailed interpretation of this work, see Mrówczyński-Van Allen, *Between the Icon and the Idol*, 19–26.

13. Solovyov, *Lectures*, 1.

14. Ibid., 1–2.

referred to such [religious] principle . . . If the religious principle is admitted at all, it must certainly possess such all-embracing, central significance."[15]

It seems that on the very first page of his *Lectures* Soloviev challenged the deepest foundation of secular order. The grounding of culture in religion brings about the reintegration of culture itself. Culture is no longer a plethora of unrelated phenomena. If all the elements of human life reflect the divine principle, they also create a special kind of unity. As Soloviev put it: "If we admit the existence of such an absolute center, all the points on the circle of life must be linked to that center with equal radii. Only then can unity, wholeness, and harmony appear in human life and consciousness."[16] This is the true stake in the dispute over religion and culture. The lack of integrity in culture undermines the stability of personal identity. The unity of individual life is possible only in a united culture.

## Russian Thought and Radical Orthodoxy

The history of contemporary Russian thought contains some extraordinary examples for its—greater or lesser—response in the West. Primarily it was writers and poets who were listened to, although some philosophers and theologians may be highlighted as well. Their legacy was undeniably the reason for the establishment and activity of numerous Western research centers studying and popularizing Russian thought. The greatest of them are in France, the United States, and Poland. These centers are universally known for their long traditions and their great numbers of published works; therefore we will not discuss them. Instead, we would like to focus on a recent philosophical phenomenon which is described as Radical Orthodoxy, the creation of which was marked in 1997 by two provocative manifestos, and later by a collection of works entitled *Radical Orthodoxy: A New Theology.*[17]

Radical Orthodoxy has its roots in a specific form of theological realism that was first outlined in the works of John Milbank. The theological realism promoted by Milbank is mainly about the criticism of logic which predominates in philosophy and secular theology, both in its established, modern version and also in the new, postmodern one. This criticism undertakes the quest for theology "on the other side of secular mind" and tries to restore its status as "master discourse," namely of an ultimate and ordering logic that postulates all other disciplines such as philosophy or social

15. Ibid., 1.

16. Ibid.

17. Milbank et al., *Radical Orthodoxy.*

sciences, while itself it is not postulated by them. To Milbank, "This is why it is so important to reassert theology as a master-discourse; theology, alone, remains the discourse of non-mastery."[18] Theological realism, as professed by Radical Orthodoxy, strives to be new in the sense of undertaking once again the attempt to return to historical-pragmatic Christian philosophy (in Maurice Blondel's understanding) and New Theology (in the understanding of Marie Dominique Chenu, Henri de Lubac and Hans Urs von Balthasar). Theological realism plunges into the philosophy of these schools and entirely relinquishes the way of practising natural theology that started from the times of Duns Scotus and William of Ockham. For, in this time, according to Radical Orthodoxy, natural theology capitulated to the secular concept of nature (*physis*) and fell into idolatry of ontotheology, which was unknown in Thomism realism.

By means of renewed philosophical theology, Radical Orthodoxy tries to prove two theses. First, the world we inhabit leads us to some superior "truly existing" reality, which postulates calls for a special theological concept of ontology. Second, this deeper and more intensive existence is given to man by God through the spheres of theory and practice, which require a specific, theological concept of intermediation. These theses of John Milbank, Catherine Pickstock and Phillip Blond, were presented by the authors in a detailed and comprehensive way in the collection *Radical Orthodoxy: A New Theology*. In a scholarly, and also a wider cultural context, Milbank points to the necessity of restoring academic education, and more generally, the intellectual and cultural activity, the three foundations of which shall be theology, philosophy and literature. This project assumes that theology contains biblical criticism and church history, and thus theology relates to all issues of history. Literature should be the third component because both theology and philosophy also exist in poetic and narrative forms, and, starting from Romanticism, it was precisely literature that was frequently the most powerful means of both the defence and advancement of Orthodox doctrine. Since the academic environment mainly studies texts, and while literature combines texts and images, the literary way of artistic expression should prevail in the reformed syllabus, which by no means ousts music and fine arts from the sphere of interest of theology and philosophy.

It is easy to notice some obvious similarities between criticism of secular modernity and the holistic perception of Christian culture represented by Radical Orthodoxy and the basic discourse of Russian Christian thought, which began at least with Gogol and perhaps culminated in Soloviev. For this reason it is hardly surprising that a few years ago a work

18. Milbank, *Theology and Social Theory*, 6.

entitled *Encounter Between Eastern Orthodoxy and Radical Orthodoxy* was published.[19] In this book various philosophers and theologians from Western and Eastern Europe engage in a debate on such issues as: East and West, Theology and Philosophy, Politics and Ecclesiology, Sophiology, Ontology, etc. In the introduction to this collection of essays, the editors point out the common challenges posed by postmodern and neoliberal society, as well as the common heritage that provides an opportunity for an encounter with the honest search for truth.

## Apology of Apology

In Western philosophy the necessity of breaking off the "bizarre dialogue" between East and West, in which the West only spoke and never listened, became evident to all who realized the legacy of Russian Christian thought. However, one has to bear in mind that modernity should not be renounced, for to do so would be to commit the mistake made by its representatives, namely renouncing the previous traditions. Modernity has already become part of our tradition, and its rejection would turn us into proponents of modernity. Emancipation from modernity expresses itself in accepting it as part of our tradition and formulating an answer to it in our own language. If Christ is the center of the universe and of history, philosophy should not be afraid to accept him as its center. Christian philosophy, together with its apologists, is a rational expression of experiencing Christ, an experience arising from the Catholic community.

Hence it is clear that, for a contemporary Western philosopher realising the need for the deep renewal of Western Christian thought, interest in the tradition of Russian Christian thought is something natural. According to Zenkovsky in his *Foundations of Christian Philosophy*, theology was never separated from philosophical thought in the East. "Theology not only was *above* everything, but it also formed the ultimate appeal: not infringing the freedom of thought, it enlightened and justified it, just like all-united truth enlightens and justifies all fragmentary truths."[20]

It is precisely here that the first and foremost apologetic function of philosophy, common to all Christian thinkers, begins: one has to be vigilant against all attempts of isolating and transforming it, in Zenkovsky's words, into "pure philosophy" and leading to a suicidal illusion of self-reliance. The same author, in the introduction to another work, *Apologetics*, aptly

---

19. Pabst and Schneider, *Encounter*.
20. Zen'kovskiy, *Osnovy*, 7.

remarked that "faith is connected with knowledge and culture."[21] This is so because the Christian experience, the encounter of man and Christ, is a "live and indivisible whole"[22] embedded in time, incorporated in history and lived in community, namely the Church. This close relation of faith, knowledge and culture is the most important bastion of the apologetic work of a Christian thinker. This connection allows us to penetrate areas of our interest without fear or complexes, using the vast richness of traditions and cultures that avoided the mistakes of modernity, referring all the time to representatives and continuers of the tradition of Russian thought, which may be helpful to us.

Today the words contained in the intellectual testament of the great forerunner of Russian Christian nineteenth-century philosophy, Peter Chaadayev, and titled *Apologie d'un fou* (*Apology of a Madman*) seem extremely timely and important to us. He courageously proclaims that though "love of country" is a beautiful thing, "there is a [finer thing], namely, love of truth . . . It is not by patriotism but by means of truth that the ascent to Heaven is accomplished."[23] This sentence largely reflects the sense in which we understand "apology" and "culture"—it is a space called to meet with the truth. A truth, which we need especially nowadays to face the emerging dangers of modern nationalisms. Thoughts similar to Chaadayev's insights can be found in the twentieth century in the works of, for example, Ernst Kantorowicz, Alasdair MacIntyre and William Cavanaugh.[24] We hope that the presented book has this special dimension, since it is a result of the meeting of people who adhere to this very beautiful love, the love of the truth. And only the life of faith and culture born in truth may be an expression of apology, of *apo-Logos*.

We have invited selected scholars from Russia, Poland, Spain, Ukraine, Germany and the United Kingdom to investigate in detail how Russian thinkers have combined Christianity with culture, philosophy, literature, social life and finally with their own lives. The contributors to this book analyze the visions of not only philosophers such as Vladimir Soloviev, Nikolai Berdyaev or Ivan Il'in, and theologians such as Pavel Florensky, Georgy Fedotov or Vasily Zenkovsky, but also artists such as Leo Tolstoy, Vyacheslav Ivanov or Maria Yudina and witnesses of faith, such as Mother Maria (Skobtsova). This multi-perspective approach remains faithful to the

---

21. Zen'kovskiy, *Apologetika*, 11.

22. Zen'kovskiy, *Osnovy*, 6.

23. Chaadayev, *Philosophical Letters*, 164.

24. For example: Kantorowicz, "Mystères de l'Etat" and "Mourir pour la patrie"; MacIntyre, *Ethics and Politics*; Cavanaugh, *Migrations of the Holy*.

integrated tradition of Russian Christian religious culture and gives us a great opportunity to analyze our contemporary world under its light.

The book is a sequel to a number of other publications made jointly by the community of scholars interested in Russian philosophy and gathered around the "Krakow Meetings," an annual series of conferences organized, among others, by the Pontifical University of John Paul II in Krakow.[25] We would like to express our gratitude to all those who have helped in publishing this book. Our project was made possible thanks to the support of the Pontifical University of John Paul II, the Copernicus Center for Interdisciplinary Studies in Krakow, Instituto de Filosofía "Edith Stein" in Granada, the International Center for the Study of the Christian Orient in Granada and the Science and Culture Creators Association Episteme in Krakow. We are also grateful to Aeddan Shaw who proofread the whole book.

In Krakow we are proud that Vladimir Soloviev spent a few weeks in our city at the turn of 1888 and 1889. "In Krakow I led a distracted, but virtuous life," he wrote to one of his friends.[26] Perhaps the proposed book is also distracted to some extent, but we hope that it nevertheless remains intellectually virtuous. Besides, it is worth recalling that Soloviev's supposed distraction was only a guise; in fact, in Krakow he worked intensely on a secret memorandum to the Tsar with which he hoped to realize his far-reaching ecumenical projects.[27] Great things begin in Krakow.[28]

## Bibliography

Cavanaugh, William T. *Migrations of the Holy: God, State, and the Political Meaning of the Church*. Grand Rapids: Eerdmans, 2011.

———. *The Myth of Religious Violence: Secular Ideology and the Roots of Modern Conflict*. Oxford: Oxford University Press, 2009.

25. See our earlier books in Polish, Russian and English: Obolevitch and Duda, *Symbol w kulturze rosyjskiej*; Obolevitch and Bremer, *Influence of Jewish Culture*; Obolevitch, *Metafizyka a literature*; Obolevitch and Rojek, *Religion and Culture in Russian Thought*; Obolevitch et al., *Russian Thought in Europe*.

26. Solovyov, *Vladimir Solovyov*, 350.

27. Solovyov's Krakow affair was investigated in detail by Vyacheslav Moiseyev, "Tayna krakovskogo dela."

28. This Introduction is to some extent based on our two previous philosophical manifestos: Mrovchinski-Van Allen, "Russkiye mysliteli i Evropa segodnya," published also in Polish as Mrówczyński-Van Allen, "Rosyjscy myśliciele i Europa dziś," and Rojek, Obolevitch, "Religion, Culture and Post-Secular Reason." Some excerpts from Mrówczyński-Van Allen's paper used in this Introduction were translated into English by Katarzyna Popowicz.

Chaadayev, Peter. *Philosophical Letters and Apology of a Madman.* Translated by Mary-Barbara Zeldin. Knoxville: University of Tennessee Press, 1969.

Dell'Asta, Adriano, ed. *La teologia ortodossa e l'Occidente nel XX secolo: storia di un incontro. Atti del Convegno promosso da Fondazione Russia Cristiana e Commissione Teologica Sinodale del Patriarcato di Mosca*, Seriate 30–31 ottobre 2004, La Casa di Matriona, 2005.

Frank, Semen L. "The Essence and Leading Themes of Russian Philosophy." *Russian Studies in Philosophy* 30 (1992) 28–47.

Hagemeister, Michael. "Wiederverzauberung der Welt: Pavel Florenskijs Neues Mittelalter." In *Pavel Florenskij—Tradition und Moderne*, edited by Norbert Franz and Michael Hagemeister, 21–41. Frankfurt am Main: Peter Lang, 2001.

John Paul II, Pope. Address to the Italian National Congress of the Ecclesial Movement for Cultural Commitment. January 16, 1982.

Kantorowicz, Ernst. "Mourir pour la patrie (Pro Patria Mori) dans la pensé politique médiévale." In *Mourir pour la patrie.* Paris: Presses Universitaires de France, 1984.

———. "Mystères de l'Etat. Un concept absolutiste et ses origines médiévales (bas Moyen Age)." In *Mourir pour la patrie.* Paris: Presses Universitaires de France, 1984.

Kurayev, Andrey. "Kak nauchnyy ateist stal d'yakonom." In *Neamerikanskiy missioner.* Saratov: Izdatel'stvo Saratovskoy Eparkhii, 2005.

MacIntyre, Alasdair. *Ethics and Politics: Selected Essays.* Vol. 2. Cambridge: Cambridge University Press, 2006.

Martínez, Javier. *Beyond Secular Reason. Más allá de la razón secular.* Granada: Editorial Nuevo Inicio, 2008.

Milbank, John. *Theology and Social Theory: Beyond Secular Reason.* Oxford: Blackwell, 1991.

Milbank, John, et al., eds. *Radical Orthodoxy: A New Theology.* London: Routledge, 1999.

Moiseyev, Vyacheslav. "Tayna krakovskogo dela Vladimira Solov'yeva." *Przegląd Rusycystyczny* 1 (2003) 5–21.

Mrówczyński-Van Allen, Artur. *Between the Icon and the Idol. The Human Person and the Modern State in Russian Literature and Thought: Chaadayev, Soloviev, Grossman.* Translated by M. P. Whelan. Eugene, OR: Cascade, 2013.

———. "Rosyjscy myślicielei Europa dziś." Translated by Agata Kędzior. *Pressje* 26–27 (2011) 262–68.

———. "Russkiye mysliteli i Evropa segodnya." In: *XX Ezhegodnaya Bogoslovskaya konferentsiya Pravoslavnogo Svyato-Tikhonovskogo Gumanitarnogo Universiteta: Materialy*, edited by V. N. Vorob'yev, 87–91. Moscow: Izdatel'stvo Pravoslavnogo Svyato-Tikhonovskogo Gumanitarnogo Universiteta, 2010.

Obolevitch, Teresa, ed. *Metafizyka a literatura w kulturze rosyjskiej. Metafizika i literatura v russkoy kul'ture.* Krakow: Uniwersytet Papieski Jana Pawła II w Krakowie Wydawnictwo Naukowe 2012.

Obolevitch, Teresa, and Józef Bremer, eds. *The Influence of Jewish Culture on the Intellectual Heritage of Central and Eastern Europe.* Krakow: Wydawnictwo Ignatianum, Wydawnictwo WAM, 2011.

Obolevitch, Teresa, and Krzysztof Duda, eds. *Symbol w kulturze rosyjskiej.* Krakow: Wydawnictwo Ignatianum, Wydawnictwo WAM, 2010.

Obolevitch, Teresa, and Paweł Rojek, eds. *Religion and Culture in Russian Thought: Philosophical, Theological and Literary Perspectives*. Krakow: The Pontifical University of John Paul II in Krakow, 2014.

———. "Religion, Culture and Post-Secular Reason: The Contemporary Significance of Russian Thought." In *Religion and Culture in Russian Thought: Philosophical, Theological and Literary Perspectives*, edited by Teresa Obolevitch and Paweł Rojek, 5–9. Krakow: The Pontifical University of John Paul II in Krakow, 2014.

Obolevitch, Teresa, et al., eds. *Russian Thought in Europe: Reception, Polemics, Development*. Krakow: Wydawnictwo Ignatianum, Wydawnictwo WAM, 2013.

Odoevsky, Vladimir. "A City without Name." In *Russian Nights*. New York: E. P. Dutton, 1965.

Pabst, Adrian, and Christoph Schneider, eds. *Encounter between Eastern Orthodoxy and Radical Orthodoxy*. Burlington, VT: Ashgate, 2009.

Pickstock, Catherine. *After Writing: On the Liturgical Consummation of Philosophy*. Oxford: Wiley-Blackwell, 1998.

Rojek, Paweł. "Mesjańska teologia polityczna Włodzimierza Sołowjowa." *Pressje* 28 (2012) 160–70.

Solovyov, S. M. *Vladimir Solovyov: His Life and Creative Evolution*. Faifax, VA: Eastern Christian Publications, 2000.

Solovyov, Vladimir. *Lectures on Divine Humanity*. Revised and edited by Boris Jakim. Hudson, NY: Lindisfarne, 1995.

Zen'kovskiy, Vasiliy. *Apologetika*. Riga: Rizhskaya Eparkhiya, 1992.

———. *Osnovy khristianskoy filosofii*. Vol. 1, *Khristianskoye ucheniye o poznanii*. Frankfurt am Main: Possev-Verlag, 1960.

———. *Russkiye mysliteli i Evropa*. Paris: YMCA-Press, 1955.

# PART I

Russian Thought and Secular Reason

# 1

# Man as Spirit and Culture

*Russian Anthropocentrism*

—Marcelo López Cambronero

## Ideocentrism in Russian Thought

The theory of Moscow as the third Rome is paradigmatic for the way in which Christendom can be affected by ideological tensions. It is not a matter of the past, but an ideological stand which, secularized or not, still exerts an influence on power structures in Russia and on the political mentality of the dominant class and people.

It is a concept entertained by some Russian authors and whose origins take us into the past, at the third canon of the Second Ecumenical Council, and the First of Constantinople (381 AD). This canon was adopted at a delicate moment for the occidental part of the Roman Empire, not yet divided (as it would be after the death of Theodosius I) and caused by the pressure of the Visigoth invasion once they crossed the Danube in 376 AD and started heading on to the west, winning and murdering Emperor Valens I at the battle of Adrianople.

Constantinople enjoyed increasing political influence and was in the process of becoming the *de facto* center of Oriental Christianity, in contraposition with the Occident due to the theological argument regarding *filioque*. Finally, as we all know, the Orthodox perspective would end up considering Rome to have fallen into heresy and that the Patriarch of Constantinople was the depositary of the authentic faith.

By the time the Ottomans conquered the city and desecrated the Saint Sofia in 1453, the Russian church was autocephalous, even though it would not have a Patriarch until 1589. From that moment on, the Russians claimed that they were the unique heirs to the Orthodox faith, and began to consider Moscow to be the Third and only genuine and eternal Rome.

When in 1492, at the exact time the Arabs were being expelled from their last Western stronghold in the south of Spain, *The Exposition of the Theory of the Third Rome* emerged, in which the Metropolitan Zosima explained that the Emperor (the Tsar, derived from Caesar), "is the only emperor of the Christianity and ruler of the holy thrones of God, of the Holy Universal Apostolic Church, which, instead of being Roman or Constantinopolitan, is placed in Moscow." It was not merely a matter of displacing the primacy of the Church, but also of moving the capital of the existing empire, in other words, a new imperialist Messianism, impregnated with a tremendous political force:

> In what respect was the conception of Moscow as the Third Rome twofold? The mission of Russia was to be the vehicle of the true Christianity, that is, of Orthodoxy, and the shrine in which it is treasured. This was a religious vocation. "Orthodoxy" is a definition of "the Russians." Russia is the only Orthodox realm, and as such a universal realm like the First Rome and the Second. On this soil there grew up a sharply defined nationalization of the Orthodox Church. Orthodoxy was in this view the religion of the Russians. In religious poetry Russ is the world; the Russian Tsar is a Tsar above all Tsars; Jerusalem is likewise Russ; Russ is where the true belief is. The Russian religious vocation, a particular and distinctive vocation, is linked with the power and transcendent majesty of the Russian State, with a distinctive significance and importance attached to the Russian Tsar. There enters into the messianic consciousness the alluring temptation of imperialism.[1]

The baptism and the Eucharist are sacraments that possess considerable political weight, as they configure a community. By the baptism we are

---

1. Berdyaev, *Russian Idea*, 7–8.

incorporated into the people of God, by the Eucharist we are one in Christ. The political component of the Christian faith is inherent and much stronger than ideological tenets or moral codes, but that is precisely why it can be narrowed down to a set of moral or ideological criteria, contributing thus to mistaking the unity in Christ, which configures the church, with a religious Messianism which is thirsty for power.

In the case of Russia, the maximalism caused by the ideological secularization enclosed by the affirmation of Moscow as the third Rome is expressed in the hegemonic pretension that the Tsar, empire and faith are intermingled to create a monster, one that is difficult to control and that can be taken over by politicians with imperialist aspirations. There is a subtle line between one sphere and the other, illustrated by the fact that, when he came to power, Lenin received numerous letters in which Christians acknowledged him the new Tsar of all the Russias and saluted him as God's envoy to fulfill the destiny of the nation and of the only apostolic Church. No wonder that a linguistic particularity of the Russian language means that words such as "peace" or "justice" (*pravda*) and "government" (*pravitel'stvo*) share a common etymology.

As Orlando Figes has warned, ever since the February Revolution a rearrangement of the language took place to assimilate the new political order with regards religious discourse. Thus, the provisional government was invited "to lead Russia on to the just path of salvation and truth." A group of countrymen and soldiers reminded the Soviet leaders that "you have been blessed by Jesus our Saviour and are leading us to the dawn of a new and holy fraternal life."[2]

If philosophy aims at understanding and transforming reality starting from present information, it implies that a philosopher is willing to change her or his opinion when she or he perceives that it helps in her or his quest for the truth; ideology instead functions on different, largely opposite, mechanisms. Ideological discourse reduces reality to a pre-manufactured scheme about what is truth, good, justice, about who are its enemies, and it will defend such a conceptual net beyond what experience informs, altering, distorting or confounding it, since what it pretends is to have ideology replace reality. When ideology takes a central place in the life of the people, they become easily manipulated and, in the case of rebellion, they are subdued without mercy.[3]

2. Figes and Kolonitskii, *Interpreting the Russian Revolution*, 145–46.

3. On the power of ideology in Russia and its influence on Russian maximalism over the last decades, see Mrówczynski-Van Allen, "La Idea Rusa."

## Christocentrism in Russian Thought

The chief resource that withholds the Russian church from the predominance of ideological stands is what Irénée Hausherr SJ has defined "the primacy of the spiritual,"[4] which translates as the centrality of Christ and the work of God's Grace in the life of the people. The true reality, "the reality of the real," is expressed in the power of the transfiguration by the Grace of God of the people and everything empirical, whose paradigm is to be found in the Eucharist, where the extraordinary character of the ordinary is revealed.

As we have seen, the Russian word for "truth" has the same root as the word for "government;" it is also true that it can be frequently spotted in the company of the word *svet*, meaning "light," suggesting that the way to find the truth is to expose opaque matters to the divine light. In other words, there is something more real than what we perceive, which is not separated from perception, nor is it in a different world, but which overlaps the empirical in order to give it consistency: it is the Light of God, the seal on every creation in so far as it has been created. Capturing this light is essential for an appropriate understanding of the world, which is, given its origin, something more than "natural" (in the sense of pure nature), and it helps to a better—although obscure, always insufficient—knowledge of God. With regards politics, this perspective encouraged the emperor to attend to this source of light when dealing with earthly matters, or, to put it differently, to search for understanding in the closeness to Christ.

Thus, knowing the world and knowing God are two aspirations which can be attained by following one and the same path. There is no division between faith and reason, rather reason must be enlightened by faith to be able to understand the sense of the world and of life, but also that of society, politics or economy. As Vladimir Lossky put it in his classical *Mystical Theology of the Eastern Church*, there is not any disjunctive between mysticism and theology in the Orthodox Church:

> The Eastern tradition has never made a sharp distinction between mysticism and theology; between personal experience of the divine mysteries and the dogma affirmed by the Church. The following words spoken a century ago by a great Orthodox theologian, the Metropolitan Philaret of Moscow, express this attitude perfectly: "none of the mysteries of the most secret wisdom of God ought to appear alien or altogether transcendent to us, but in all humility we must apply our spirit to the

4. Hausherr, "Pour comprendre l'Orient chrétien."

contemplation of divine things." To put it in another way, we must live the dogma expressing a revealed truth, which appears to us as an unfathomable mystery, in such a fashion that instead of assimilating the mystery to our mode of understanding, we should, on the contrary, look for a profound change, an inner transformation of spirit, enabling us to experience it mystically. Far from being mutually opposed, theology and mysticism support and complete each other. One is impossible without the other. If the mystical experience is a personal working out of the content of the common faith, theology is an expression, for the profit of all, of that which can be experienced by everyone.[5]

Symeon the New Theologian (949–1022), whom the Eastern church places alongside John the Baptist and Gregory of Nazianzus, has a central place in this theological vision. For Symeon, the encounter with Christ fills man with divine light, thus lifting up reason, which alone, is not capable of the knowledge of God, not even of the "factic."[6] Symeon introduced into Russian thought the rejection of certain dualisms that, over the time, had become fixed in some Christian sectors, hindering the understanding of the life of faith and, at the same time, of the place of man in creation.

## Natural, Supernatural, and State-Centralism

In contraposition to this theological conception present in Orthodox Christianity, and threatened by the ideological pressure of "Russian maximalism," the Occidental Christianity, both Catholic and Protestant, has evolved into a specific form of secularization, also under the pressure of a specific ideology. The dispute between the Emperor and the Pope, culminating, among others, with the "Investiture Controversy," but generally carried on throughout the Middle Ages, left a dualist print in Western culture, described by the great theologian Henry de Lubac as one between the *natural* and the *supernatural*.[7]

The assertion that man has two finalities, a natural and a supernatural one, was defended by different theologians at different courts, and left its mark in classical texts like Dante Alighieri's *De Monarchia*, who writes,

Ineffable Providence has thus designed two ends to be contemplated of man: first, the happiness of this life, which consists in the activity of his natural powers, and is prefigured by the

5. Lossky, *Mystical Theology*, 8.
6. See Symeon the New Theologian, *Hymnen*.
7. Lubac, *Surnaturel*.

> terrestrial Paradise; and then the blessedness of life everlasting,
> which consists in the enjoyment of the countenance of God,
> to which man's natural powers may not attain unless aided
> by divine light, and which may be symbolized by the celestial
> Paradise.[8]

Later on he points out,

> To the former we come by the teachings of philosophy, obeying
> them by acting in conformity with the moral and intellectual
> virtues; to the latter through spiritual teachings which transcend
> human reason, and which we obey by acting in conformity with
> the theological virtues, Faith, Hope, and Charity.[9]

We must recall that the aim of this text is to reduce the tension between the Emperor and the Pope, *güelfi* and *ghibellini*, and thus bring peace, which is for Dante the ultimate aim of social life, whether in the city or throughout their reign.[10] The same dualism flourished after the seventeenth century conflicts in Central Europe through the works of the Jesuit Father Francisco Suárez, and spread across the Jesuit institutions of education.

The distinction of aims was also a distinction of orders, as previously presented, and ended up determining the way in which practical life and Christian morality were conceived. Accordingly, man lives simultaneously in two spheres, each having their particular aims. On the one hand, there is everyday life, conducive to "natural" aims, which are specific to mundane activities, such as politics (power), economy (possession), etc., and whose finality is welfare. The only influence of Christ in this sphere is the endowing of life with a certain moral sense—which results in a dry moralism and cuts it away with grace—since it is rooted in the human effort to reach virtues and in the response to specific impermeable normative systems. As a result of this perspective, one can affirm that monogamous and indissoluble matrimony is "natural," whereas the Christian tradition has always affirmed that the said reality can be experienced only by the grace of God. In fact, the Church affirms that only matrimony contracted between two baptized persons is valid. On the other hand, we would deal with another sphere of life, in which other goods, "supernatural" and spiritual are to be pursued. Christ is confined to this aspect of life, of pious practices which seem to be disconnected from life. This is the main cause of secularization, as it

---

8. Dante Alighieri, *De Monarchia*, III, XVI, 7.
9. Ibid.
10. Ibid., I, V, 7–8.

provokes an immediate moralization and ideologization of Christians, and renders Christ irrelevant for our lives.

We should not be surprised that Russian authors such as Vladimir Soloviev, Nikolai Berdyaev, and before them Gregory Skovoroda, and writers like Fyodor Dostoevsky, Boris Pasternak or Vasily Grossman saw in western civilization the displacement of the person from the central interests of philosophy, as it grew to be a part of the social machinery, citizens whose vital sense is no more given by their belonging to Christ, by their freedom or individual originality, but by their dependence on the state. Now it is the state which is called, as the political arm of (economical) capitalism, to fulfill, that is, to satisfy, our "natural" desires.

## The Direction of the Conscience and the Rebirth of Man

Russian Christian thinkers, following in the steps of the Church Fathers, have not displayed this type of dualism, which suffocates and destroys Christian experience. For them there are not two different aims and orders in human life, rather the human being, as an incarnated spirit, is at the crossroads of the two worlds, the material and the spiritual, and it is called to elevate the flesh, or, on the contrary, it is deemed to fall prey to its own passions. There is a two way aperture for the conscience and the person has to make its own choice freely. We could say that it is a freedom that chooses assisted by grace, but it would be an incomplete formulation: freedom opens itself to the grace and received God to the extent to which its finiteness and aperture allows it to.

Nikolai Berdyaev expresses this idea very vividly in his "bourgeois metaphysics" in many of his works.[11] Berdyaev's stand will help us illustrate the criteria of Russian culture with regard to this aspect.

As introduced earlier, Man stands at the crossing point between two worlds, namely the spiritual world and what we could call the "objectified" world. The later does not relate to "reality," nor with the "natural," but with the external dynamics of the human being, whether the laws of nature, social laws, or, markedly, in the ideological frames he encounters, all of which try to define who he is and how it is reasonable for him to live his life. We are not dealing with two distinct realities or worlds, but with the effect on the human being of that "direction" which man takes as primordial in his conscience. Thus, the human being can be diluted by objectivizing, and live

---

11. See Berdyaev, *Bourgeois Mind; Solitude and Society; Slavery and Freedom*; and *The Divine and the Human*.

subdued by his passions and social and ideological structures, or he can overcome them by embracing reality in its totality, that is, attending primarily to the light that illuminates and gives a sense to the human being, and whose origin is undoubtedly divine. It is not an ontological, but an anthropological dualism, one which exercises such a force in human existence that it ends up presenting man with two different manners of living, and two different structures of being, among which he has to choose, in a first, decisive act of freedom.

In this sense the spiritual sphere is not overruled or opposed to the material sphere, but uplifts it and restores it to its real being, accommodating the emotional and the rational in a major sphere which is also more real. This is how the radical dichotomy between the natural and the supernatural is overcome, just as it is overcome the net distinction between idealism and realism. The last two theories of knowledge are equally false to the extent to which they do not grasp the true nature of the problem: knowledge needs to be active, but it is not a mere projection of the subject, but the encounter between a spiritual being and a world whose real sense it needs to unveil and develop from his own being and provided it remains open to God's grace.

The characters of Pasternak's and Grossman's short stories find themselves in the same situation when Anna Akhmatova's poetry is debated, who, after a lifetime of suffering, acknowledges in "A Land not Mine" that "the secret of secrets is inside me again." It is the same perception that we identify in Dostoevsky's novels, wrongly decoded in the West as "psychological novels." When Velchaninov, the protagonist of the minor but splendid work *The Eternal Husband* (1870), is confronted in the first chapter with the contrast between his moral conceptions and his remorse, we need not deepen into his "unconsciousness," "subconscious" or "psychological problems," but into the profundity of his heart, where this division of conscience takes place, this struggle between the spirit and the objectivizing process.

Similarly in Russian culture, there are no clear-cut separations between "public life" and "private life," between faith and reason, although this tendency is changing under the influence of western thought. There is no analytical decomposition, but rather the synthetic integration of every human experience, through a perspective that goes beyond the external manifestations. This is what Raskolnikov finds out when, once the old pawnbroker in *Crime and Punishment* (1866) is murdered, he does not interpret his action as psychologically problematic, but as a decision about his place in the world, which would make Sonia's character fall apart.

Even though this line of thought contains irrefutable positive elements, it would be a mistake to overlook the fact that Orthodoxy has embraced, on many occasions, the division of conscience which took it to a dualism that is unacceptable. Practices such as the prohibition on women from entering the church during her menstrual period, the obligation to submit herself to a ritual of purification the first Sunday after her wedding and forty days after she has given birth, the prohibition of sexual intercourse during Lent and Advent, on the eve of all religious feasts, the prohibition of the spousal kiss during a day in which one has taken Holy Communion, all these are denigrating and contrast with our new life in Christ.

To sum up, in Russian culture, let alone similar deviations, we find some modes that are for us, in the Western world, of paramount importance if we want our conscience to stand firm against the ideological forces to which we are constantly exposed. The certainty that we are God's children, and that our destiny is not determined by the state apparatus or the mainstream culture allows us to face the possibility of a renewed culture with more freedom to embrace man in its plenitude without the constraint to give in to the processes of objectivizing enforced on us by society. The intimacy with Christ, our vital axis, is therefore essential in our attempt to overcome the dualism so deeply embedded in secularization and the loss of direction in Christian life; we refer to this bias, of the earlier discussed "double direction in conscience" which presents itself under the guise of dichotomy between the natural and the supernatural, between the "natural" and "supernatural" finalities of man.

## Bibliography

Berdyaev, Nicolas. *The Bourgeois Mind and Other Essays*. London: Sheed & Ward, 1934.
———. *The Divine and the Human*. London: Geoffrey Bles, 1949.
———. *The Russian Idea*. New York: Macmillan, 1948.
———. *Slavery and Freedom*. London: Geoffrey Bles, 1939.
———. *Solitude and Society*. London: Geoffrey Bles, 1938.
Dante Alighieri. *De Monarchia*. Translated by Aurelia Henry. Boston: Houghton, Mifflin, 1904.
Figes, Orlando, and Boris Kolonitskii. *Interpreting the Russian Revolution: The Language and Symbols of 1917*. New Haven: Yale University Press, 1999.
Hausherr, Irénée. "Pour comprendre l'Orient chrétien: La primauté du spirituel." *Orientalia Christiana Periodica* 33 (1967) 351–69.
Lossky, Vladimir. *The Mystical Theology of the Eastern Church*. Crestwood, NY: St. Vladimir's Seminary Press, 1976.
Lubac, Henri de. *Surnaturel. Études historiques*. Paris: Aubier-Montaigne, 1946.
Mrówczyński-Van Allen, Artur. "La Idea Rusa y su interpretación." In *La Idea Rusa*, edited by Marcelo López Cambronero and Artur Mrówczynski-Van Allen, 225–300. Granada: Nuevo Inicio, 2009.
Symeon the New Theologian. *Hymnen*. Edited by Athanasios Kambylis. Berlin: de Gruyter, 1976.

2

# The Trinity in History and Society

*The Russian Idea, Polish Messianism, and the Post-Secular Reason*

—PAWEŁ ROJEK

VLADIMIR SOLOVIEV STAYED IN Krakow for a few weeks at the turn of 1888 and 1889. He was returning from Paris, where he had formulated his great theocratic and ecumenical program, to Saint Petersburg, where he hoped to realize it; Krakow was at that time the last city before the Russian border. He stopped here to finish a secret memorandum for Tsar Alexander III, by which he believed he would be able to convert him to his own ideas.[1] Soloviev met a few friends in Krakow and discussed with them his philosophy and perhaps his secret plans. Apparently, one of Soloviev's Krakow friends was Professor Stanisław Tarnowski (1837–1917), the great Polish historian, literary critic and conservative politician.[2] Shortly after the visit, Tarnowski published a detailed review of Soloviev's *L'idée Russe* in his journal *Przegląd Polski* to which Soloviev replied soon after in the "Lettre á la Rédaction."[3] A

1. For details of Soloviev's "Krakow affair" see Solovyov, *Vladimir Solovyov*, 350 and Moiseyev, "Tayna krakovskogo dela."

2. Soloviev and Tarnowski met probably on the customary Thursday parties arranged by Count Paweł Popiel (1807–1892) in his house on św. Jana street 20 in Krakow, see Popiel, *Rodzina Popielów*, 66, 73.

3. Tarnowski, "Głos sumienia z Rosyi;" Soloviev, "Lettre á la Rédaction," see also brief Tarnowski's rejoinder "Odpowiedź." The first Russian translation of Soloviev's letter was published in émigré journal *Novyy Zhurnal* by the Krakow scholar Grzegorz Przebinda, see his *Włodzimierz Sołowjow*, 222.

few months later Tarnowski published extensive commentary on Soloviev's new book, *La Russie et l'Église universelle*,[4] which was unfortunately left without answer. Tarnowski's papers was the first serious Polish, and perhaps also first European, reaction to Soloviev's great theocratic writings.

I am not going to analyze here the discussion between Tarnowski and Soloviev, which undoubtedly deserves careful examination. In this paper I would like to develop one quite obvious observation made by Tarnowski. He noticed that Soloviev's ideas were very close to the doctrine of Polish Messianists, particularly Zygmunt Krasiński (1812–59) and August Ciesz-kowski (1814–94). Tarnowski wrote,

> Though it is unfortunately very probable that Mr. Soloviev has never read them, and therefore he found his way of thought without their help, nevertheless these authors have at least priority in order of time; I do not want to discuss whether they have also priority in the depth and the power of thinking.[5]

Afterwards, many other Polish and Russian scholars indicated similarities between the Russian Idea and Polish Messianism. For instances, Marian Zdziechowski compared Soloviev and Andrzej Towiański,[6] Nikolai Berdyaev found similarities between Soloviev and August Cieszkowski[7] and Andrzej Walicki indicated a closeness between Soloviev and Adam Mickiewicz.[8]

I would like to develop Tarnowski's thesis by comparing two works by Krasiński and Soloviev. Krasiński in the unpublished treatise *On the Position of Poland form the Divine and Human Perspective* (1841–1847) tried to reveal the destiny of Poland in the divine plan of Providence. Exactly the same attempt in regard to Russian history was made forty years later by Soloviev in his famous lecture *The Russian Idea* (1888). Soloviev wanted to reveal "not that what nation thinks about itself in time, but that what God thinks about it in eternity,"[9] that is, in Krasiński words, the position of Russia from the Divine perspective. I would like to focus on their insights on

---

4. Tarnowski, "Wykład idei."

5. Ibid., 34; Tarnowski suggested that some of the common elements in Polish and Russian thought stem from the common inspiration of German Idealism; I would rather point to a shared Christian tradition and the recent influences of French post-revolutionary religious thought, see Walicki, "Philosophie de l'Histoire," 189, "Mickie-wicz's Paris Lectures," 75, and *Philosophy and Romantic Nationalism*, 239–77.

6. Zdziechowski, *Pesymizm, romantyzm a podstawy chrześcijaństwa*, 414.

7. Berdyaev, *Russian Idea*, 228.

8. Walicki, "Mickiewicz's Paris Lectures," "Solovëv's Theocratic Utopia," and *Russia, Poland, and Universal Regeneration*. For an attempt to analyze the possible influences of Polish Messianism on Soloviev see Strémooukhoff, *Vladimir Soloviev*, 196, 363–4.

9. Solov'yev, "Russkaya ideya," 220.

human nature, universal history and social order. It is amazing how close they were to each other in these fundamental issues. Nevertheless they differed gravely in the details of their visions: Krasiński believed that Poland was the only country able to realize Christian principles in social and political life, whereas Soloviev granted that great mission to Russia.

I believe that both the Russian Idea and Polish Messianism have not only historical, but also great contemporary importance. It seems that these two intellectual movements in the same vein undermined the secular dualism so characteristic for modernity, and placed God at the center of human life, history and society. In this, Russian and Polish Christian thinkers anticipated the crucial ideas of Nouvelle Théologie, Second Vatican Council, Radical Orthodoxy, the School of Granada and other recent fashionable currents in Christian post-secular thought.[10] Apparently, they simply went beyond secular reason before it was cool.

## Christ and Human Nature

Christianity offers a straightforward answer to the question of human nature. When Pilate pointed at Jesus and said "Ecce homo" (John 19:5), he actually made the most proper, although merely ostensive definition of man. Indeed, Jesus Christ is the paradigm of man. To be a true man is to imitate Christ. Now, if being a true man involves uniting with God, then religious life is not something external for man, but rather something which realizes human nature. If Divine humanity is the true humanity, then divinization is the true humanization. This is the fundamental principle of Christian anthropology, which overcomes the modern dualism between self-sufficient nature on the one hand and optional supernature on the other, and calls for the positive reintegration of all human reality in Christ.

It seems that this fundamental intuition might be found both in Krasiński and Soloviev. Krasiński starts his treatise by declaring that man is called to "complete its own creation" and to "grow" towards God.[11] The end of this growing is given in Christ, since His life was "the archmastery of life."[12] More particular, Christ "revealed clearly, convincingly and vividly, by words, but most of all by acts, that the human nature is called to divinization, if only it agrees and freely fits his will to will of God."[13] Krasiński

10. In the interpretation of the dialectics of secular reason I rely most of all on the brilliant essay by Msgr. Javier Martínez in *Beyond Secular Reason*.

11. Krasiński, "O stanowisku Polski," 5.

12. Ibid., 8.

13. Ibid.

consequently developed that idea. The fulfillment of that calling is the same as the realization of the human nature. Therefore there is no worry about the supposed loss of humanity in divinity. "The more you unite with God, the more you become yourself; since if the result of this uniting was different, you would be not driven toward life, but toward death, and God finally would be your eternal death."[14] It is so because grace does not destroy, but rather perfects nature. Krasiński went on and claimed that divinization is in fact a natural objective of man. In some sense, there is nothing miraculous about it. "Our hitherto mundane nature is a *miracle* of our refractoriness and embroilment, and that what is usually called *miracle* is rather our inner, ultimate and true nature."[15]

The same anthropological principle might be found in Soloviev, although not exactly in the relatively short *Russian idea*, but rather in *Lectures on Divine humanity*, where he gave a more profound anthropological basis for his historiosophical and political constructions. Soloviev, in the same vein as Krasiński, believed that the divinization is the proper object of man and the personal life of each individual men and the history of universal mankind should be a processes of achieving that great goal. Soloviev expressed the fundamental principle of Christocentric anthropology perhaps even in more provocative way: "The human person can unite with the divine principle freely, from within, only because the person is in a certain sense divine, or more precisely, participates in Divinity."[16] In a subsequent passage Soloviev explained in what sense man might be called divine. The human person is divine since it has the capacity to be divinized. "Divinity belongs to human beings and to God, but with one difference: God possess Divinity in eternal actuality, whereas human beings can only attain it, can only have it granted to them, and in the present state there is only possibility, only striving."[17] This possibility is essential for man and its realization is in fact a self-realization. Becoming God does not exclude but rather presupposes and reinforces being a man. Religion is therefore a fulfillment, not an exclusion of human nature.

> Religion is the reunification of humanity and the world with the absolute, integral principle. That principle is integral or all-embracing, excluding nothing. Therefore, true reunification with it, true religion, cannot exclude, suppress, or forcibly subject to

14. Ibid., 25
15. Ibid., 28.
16. Solovyov, *Lectures on Divine Humanity*, 17, translation improved.
17. Ibid., 23

itself any element whatever, any living force in humanity or in
its world.[18]

We should not therefore be afraid of religious life in temporality and divinization in eternality. We would not lose anything, but would rather win
everything.

## Messianism and Missionism

Jesus Christ revealed the true human nature. This revelation is important
not only for individual human life, but also for human communities. We are
all called to imitate the life of Christ, both in our personal and social lives. In
the case of individual men it leads to personal salvation, while in the case of
communities it involves the building of the Kingdom of God on Earth. Both
Krasiński and Soloviev were particularly interested in that second historical
process. They believed that people are supposed to realize Christian doctrine not only in their private life, but also in public spheres of economics,
politics and international affairs. In this they were both genuine Messianists.

The term "Messianism" was originally introduced by Józef Hoene-
Wroński, a Polish eccentric mathematician, philosopher and inventor writing in French, who published in 1831 a treatise entitled *Messianisme*.[19] The
term was then adopted by Adam Mickiewicz and popularized in his famous
Paris lectures in Collège de France (1840–44); Wroński never forgave him
for this supposed intellectual theft. The term "Messianism" subsequently
started to stand for many quite different views and attitudes, some of which
are perhaps expressed more properly by the term "millenarism" (a belief
that the world needs universal religious reintegration), others by "Missionism" (a belief on the special mission of some or all nations), and finally by
"passionism" (a belief on the special value of collective suffering).[20] "Messianism" eventually became a label for almost all Polish philosophy in the
mid-nineteenth century. Jerzy Braun, a Polish writer and scholar, explained
the proper meaning of this term in the following way:

> Hebrew *Mashiah* is the same as Greek *Christos*, hence "Messian-
> ism" means the same as "christianism." Wroński used that term
> in the meaning: completed, integral Christianity, penetrating all

18. Ibid., 10

19. Hoene-Wronski, *Messianisme*; Wroński was apparently a prototype of a mysterious Polish master in Balzac's novel *The Quest of the Absolute* (1834).

20. I proposed an integral theory of Messianism in my "Mesjanizm integralny;"
notice that these three components of Polish Messianism correspond roughly to the
three offices of Christ, distinguished in Patristic and recalled in contemporary theology.

domains of public life, beginning from philosophy and culture, and ending with state organization, economic order, and international affairs.[21]

Messianism is therefore a tendency towards the full realization of the principles of Christianity in social life. In other words, to the building of the Kingdom of God on Earth. This mundane Kingdom should not, however, be confused with the ultimate salvation. Messianists believed in human progress, but nevertheless realized that its final fulfillment implies a New Earth. To use Eric Voegelin's popular terminology, they certainly immanentized the eschaton, but not so much.[22]

Krasiński, though he did not called himself a Messianist, stated perfectly clear the fundamental principles of that doctrine. The meaning of history was the gradual transformation of all reality according to revealed principles. He wrote for instance:

> The ultimate goal of our earthly history is . . . the universal sacred Kingdom of God on Earth, powered not by our arbitrary will but the human will united with the Divine one; that is, Christian order actualized and realized, concerning not only individual souls, but also all humankind, all rules, laws and institutions, transforming the Earth into one great sanctuary of the Holy Spirit.[23]

The sense of history was therefore the process of divinization, that is—according to the anthropological principle—humanization of all spheres of human life. Krasiński spoke about "religionization,"[24] "Christization,"[25] or even "kingdomization"[26] of private, social, state and international life.

Soloviev manifested the same active attitude of a Christian engaged in transforming the whole world. He wrote: "To take part in the life of the universal Church, in developing the great Christian civilization, to take part in this task according to its own power and capacities—this is the true aim, the only true mission of every nation."[27] The ideal is already given in Christianity; now is the time for its realization in the world.[28] Using the terminology

21. Braun, *Kultura jutra*, 348.

22. Voegelin, *New Science of Politics*.

23. Krasiński, "O stanowisku Polski," 29

24. Ibid., 36.

25. Ibid., 17.

26. Ibid., 12–13.

27. Solov'yev, "Russkaya ideya," 228.

28. Ibid., 239.

of the later *Lectures on Divine Humanity*, the task of each nation and whole humankind is a participation in the divine and human process of realization of Christian ideals on Earth.

The unanimity of Krasiński and Soloviev is strikingly manifested in their interpretation of Matthew 22:21. Soloviev noticed in 1889, in his *Russia and the Universal Church*, that

> the precept "Render to Caesar the things that are Caesar's, and to God the things that are God's" is constantly quoted to sanction an order of things which gives Caesar all and God nothing. The saying "My Kingdom is not of this world" is always being used to justify and confirm the paganism of our social life, as though Christian society were destined to belong to this world and not to the Kingdom of Christ. On the other hand, the saying 'All power is given Me in Heaven and Earth' is never quoted."[29]

In the same spirit Krasiński proposed in the foreword to his great poem *Predawn*, published in 1843, a surprising interpretation of Christ's dictum:

> These words contain all the future movement of humankind. Since everything belongs to God, therefore the division between God's and Caesar's domains is only temporary and must gradually decrease. Things that yesterday was counted as Caesar's, today must be counted as God's, until the City of Caesar would be nothing, and Kingdom of God would be everything.[30]

I distinguish, following Nikolai Berdyaev and Andrzej Walicki, Messianism and Missionism. Messianism says about the great task of the universal religious regeneration of the world, whereas Missionism simply states that at least some nations have specific missions in the universal history. This mission might be a part of a great messianic task, but not necessary.[31] Russian Slavophiles, for instance, were Missionists, but not Messianists, whereas Hoene-Wroński was Messianist, but not Missionist.

Both Krasiński and Soloviev were at once Messianists and Missionists. They believed that nations are not contingent cultural constructions, but organic spiritual communities and both defined nations as "organs"

29. Solovyev, *Russia and the Universal Church*, 8.

30. Krasiński, *Pisma literackie*, 148–9; for a religious interpretation of this poem see Sokulski "*Przedświt* jako tekst profetyczny."

31. Berdyaev, "Aleksey Stepanovich Khomyakov," 171; Walicki, *Slavophile Controversy*, 81.

of humankind.[32] The national missions were therefore thought by them as parts of the great messianic task of all humankind. Ultimately every nation was called to serve every other one. However, they differed in many aspects of their visions. First of all, Krasiński believed that Poles would play a crucial role in the messianic process, whereas Soloviev hoped it would be Russia. Secondly, Krasiński had the tendency to recognize Poles as the chosen nation, whereas Soloviev thought about the mission of Russia in a much more pragmatic way. "God can handle without Russia," he wrote.[33] Some Polish late Messianists even suggested that after the revolution, the abandoned Russian mission had returned to Poland.[34] Thirdly, they held opposing views on the relationships between Jews and Christians; Krasiński was convinced that the Jews were no longer the chosen nation, whereas Soloviev was much more faithful to the idea. Finally, Krasiński denied any positive role of Russia in history, whereas Soloviev was generous enough to admit the great spiritual achievements of Poland. To be honest, Krasiński was one of the fiercest Polish Russophobes. He even wrote secret memoranda to Pope Pius IX and Napoleon III in which he warned them and encourage them to take action against Russia. Unfortunately, his most horrifying vision of the alliance between Russian Empire and Communism turned out to be not a prejudice, but a prophecy.[35]

## The Trinity in History and Society

The founding act of modernity was the separation of religion on the one hand and the world on the other. In effect, the religion became an isolated sphere with no real consequences in other spheres of life. The result of this separation was probably best expressed by Immanuel Kant in the famous dictum: "The doctrine of the Trinity, taken literally—he wrote—has no practical relevance at all."[36] It seems significant that both Krasiński and Soloviev, on the contrary, considered the Trinity as the model of quite practical issues. Their treatises are based on the analogy between the Trinity and

32. Krasiński, "O stanowisku Polski," 12–3; Solov'yev, "Russkaya ideya," 220.

33. Soloviev, "Lettre á la Rédaction," 182.

34. Jankowski, *Idea Rosyjska Sołowjewa*, 24–9.

35. For the details of Krasiński's hard-shell vision of Russia see Nowak, "Rosja i rewolucja," and Fiećko, *Rosja Krasińskiego* and *Krasiński przeciw Mickiewiczowi*. It is worth noting that the differences between Krasiński and Soloviev largely coincide with the differences between Krasiński and Mickiewicz, see Fiećko, *Krasiński przeciw Mickiewiczowi*. It proves that some types of Polish Messianism other than Krasiński's were even closer to the Russian Idea.

36. Kant, *Religion and Rational Theology*, 264.

the human reality, though the first saw the Trinity mostly as a pattern of historical development, whereas the latter made it primarily a paradigm of political relationships.

Krasiński's treatise, finally titled *On the Position of Poland from the Divine and Human Perspective*, had two alternative working titles: *On the Trinity* and *On the Trinity in God and the Trinity in Man.*[37] That last title reveals the underlying idea of the whole work. The Holy Trinity is the unity of the three fundamental principles of Being, Thinking and Acting or Living, corresponding to the Father, the Son and the Holy Spirit respectively. According to Krasiński, these three principles manifest also themselves in human reality. Being is reflected in Thought, and the Act is a unity of these two principles. These three elements roughly correspond to the human Body, Soul and Spirit. Krasiński was most interested in applications of these modes in the historical life of nations. Firstly, he believed that nations, as well as persons, have their own Body, that is what they have (historical heritage), Soul, which is what they think (present ideas), and Spirit or what they do (creative activity related to future). Secondly, he maintained that the principles of Being, Thinking and Acting reveal themselves throughout history in the order of time.

> As every created whole, the history of humankind must consist on three parts, corresponding firstly to Being, secondly to Thought and its struggle with Being, and thirdly to the reconciliation and unification of the struggling parties into the one Spirit. Only after such dissolution of the Trinity in the time and space humankind will tune up to it and the collective history of the human spirit will be fulfilled.[38]

Accordingly, Krasiński believed that the Antiquity realized the principle of Being, the Middle Ages was the embodiment of the principle of Thought, then we witnessed the struggle between these two principles, and now we are on the threshold of new era of Spirit. One can see this dialectics in the example of the relations between the State and Church: the Romans built the foundations of the State, medieval Christians formulated the ideal of the Church, and now we are supposed to reconcile State with the Church in a higher unity.

Moreover, for Krasiński, historical functions are distributed not only between different ages, but also between different nations. Nowadays, in his view, the Italians, Spaniards and French are still attached to the political principle of Being, the Germanic nations realized the philosophical

37. Krasiński, "O stanowisku Polski," 295–96.
38. Ibid., 32.

principle of Thought, whereas the Slavic peoples are supposed to open a new era of religious Act. The Slavic New Age will "not allow the separation between the law of God in Haven and the human law on Earth, but will instead reconcile in one justice and in one order the Real and the Ideal, the temporal and the spiritual, the state and the church, politics and Christian love, that what is and that what ought to be."[39] In would be therefore a final age of human history, the realization of the Kingdom of God on Earth.

Krasiński was mainly concerned in looking for traces of the Trinity in history. He believed that the harmonious heavenly pattern realized itself on Earth through dialectics of struggles and reconciliations. Besides this, he also briefly sketched in an extensive note an original political interpretation of the Trinity, investigating the consequences of the schismatic Trinitarian theology for Russian political form. He accused the Orthodox Church of not developing the Trinitarian dogma in its fullness. The lack of the *Filioque* was supposed to be responsible for the most crude features of the Russian regime. What is the meaning of such an undeveloped Trinity?

> Eternal Jehovah, the mere omnipotence, causes and makes everything. He generates the Son, which however cannot give anything to his Father. The Son cannot commune with Him as equal . . . Incredible autocracy, boundless *auctoritas paterna*. The government is everything, on earth as it is in Heaven. Government generated everything; he provides everything . . . Such image of the world and the history is inevitable among schismatics, since on earth is as it is in Heaven . . . This is all antichristian. The yoke, loaded on that nation, is contained in the false concept of divine Trinity, which is divine in so far as its persons are perfectly equal and harmonious.[40]

In short, the Orthodox Church, according to Krasiński, due to the lack of Filioque, remained too monotheistic and not Trinitarian enough, and mere monotheism, as he suggested long before Peterson's "Monotheism as a Political Problem," unavoidably leads to autocracy. The form of theological thinking therefore shapes the form of political institution. The parallel between Krasiński and Peterson is striking.[41]

The political and institutional dimensions of Trinitarian dogma was further developed by Soloviev. He firmly stated that the task of Russia, but also that of every other nation, as well all as the whole humankind, is to

39. Ibid., 54.
40. Ibid., 61.
41. Peterson, "Monotheism."

"restore on earth a faithful image of divine Trinity."[42] He explained that the imitation of the Trinity consists of the projection of the relations between divine persons of the Trinity into relations between social institutions on earth. The "realization of social trinity" means that "each of the three organic principles, namely Church, State and Society, remains in absolute freedom and power, neither separating from others, nor devouring or destroying them, but instead accepting its own absolute internal relations with them."[43] More precisely, Russia and other Christian nations should "subordinate the power of the State (the royal authority of the Son) to authority of universal Church (Father's priesthood) and provide a proper space for social freedom (acts of the Spirit)."[44]

Soloviev presupposed that the institutions of Church, State and Society in human communities corresponded to the persons of Father, Son and Holy Spirit in the divine Trinity. The Trinity makes the perfect unity, which however does not exclude distinctions of persons and differences in relations between them. It also does not exclude the central position of the Father, who generates the Son and emanates the Spirit. The image of this unity in differences is Jesus Christ, who besides being the Second Person of the Holy Spirit, also united the three messianic offices of King, Priest and Prophet, corresponding to the Father, Son and Holy Spirit. Christology is therefore a mediating element between Trinitarian and political theology. Humankind inherited messianic offices, which are embodied in three distinct institutions of spiritual authority, political government and free social activity, that is Church, State and Society. Using a little bit contemporary terminology, one may say about three spheres of religion, politics and civil society. Since these institutions are, as Soloviev said,[45] instruments of each persons of Holy Trinity, their relations should mirror relations between Father, Son and Spirit.[46]

What are the recommended relations between human institutions? Since Religion corresponds to the Father, it should have a distinguished place in social order and the two other spheres, corresponding to the two

42. Solov'yev, "Russkaya ideya," 246.

43. Ibid.

44. Ibid., 245.

45. Ibid., 243.

46. A close intuition was developed by Wolfgang Grassl, who adopted the principles of Trinitarian theology for economy. He does not speak, however, about the trinity of Church, State and Society, but rather the spheres of Society, State and Market, which differ in the adopted principles of exchange, see Grassl, "Ekonomia obywatelska," and Kędzierski, "Ekonomia trynitarna," Rojek, "Program ekonomii trynitarej," "Ekonomia, wzajemność i Trójca Święta."

other divine persons, should be subordinated to it. The power of the Father does not, however, overwhelm the Son, for he is not Cronos devouring his own children, so the power of the Church should not suppress State and Society. And, conversely, the Son willingly accepts the power of the Father, since he is not Zeus looking for the opportunity to devour Cronos, so the State should accept the authority of the Church. Soloviev was painfully aware that the current state of the political order is a caricature of the life of the Holy Trinity. The Father renounces of his son, the son rebels against his father, brothers come together to kill their father and finally murder themselves: the Church gives up its influence on State, the State wants to dominate religion, and social reformers rise up against both Church and the State. Moreover, Soloviev in *A Short Story of the Anti-Christ* described the alliance between Church and State without which elements of free prophecy turn into a caricature of theocracy.[47] The relationships between these three institutions demands urgent hierarchical arrangement, and the pattern of this should be the Holy Trinity. Interestingly enough, it seems that Soloviev's Trinitarian model of theocracy presupposes the principle of Filioque. The prophets, that is "free movers of progressive social movements,"[48] should respect both Church and State. The direct link between the Second and the Third institutions makes the construction more balanced and harmonious. Krasiński and Peterson would perhaps have approved of it.

Krasiński's and Soloviev's provocative reference to the Holy Trinity as a model of historical and social order is perhaps the most conspicuous common feature of their treatises. Tarnowski highlighted precisely that point in his commentary to Soloviev's work. "Triplicity mirroring the Divine Trinity in creation and human history—he wrote—is not a new idea . . . we Poles has seen it in works of Krasiński and Cieszkowski."[49] The Trinitarian analogy is also the most subversive for the dominating modern and secular way of thinking. Though Krasiński's historical visions and Soloviev's political speculations might seems to be too arbitrary, too artificial and too fabulous to be defended in details, nevertheless their general insight that "on earth is as it is in Heaven" is the central idea of pre- and post-secular Christian thought.[50] God is not, as Ludwig Feuerbach thought, a projection of hu-

47. Solovyov, *War, Progress, and the End of History*, 159–94; I owe this interpretation to Janusz Dobieszewski, *Włodzimierz Sołowjow*, 426; for an alternative account see Mrówczyński-Van Allen, *Between the Icon and the Idol*, 97–101.

48. Solov'yev, "Russkaya ideya," 243.

49. Tarnowski, "Wykład idei," 34; for Cieszkowski's Triniatran interpretation of the history see his "Prolegomena to historiosophy;" Cieszkowski and Krasiński were close friends and deeply influenced each other.

50. For more on social implications of Trinitarian dogma see: Volf, "The Trinity Is Our Social Program" and Rojek, "Program ekonomii trynitarnej."

mankind, but on the contrary, humankind is a projection of God. The mission of the Church and the whole of humankind is to make this resemblance in the world more explicit.

## Beyond Secular Reason

In the introduction to this paper I indicated that the glorious revolt against secular reason in the twentieth century started with the *Nouvelle Théologie*, a circle of Catholic theologian with Henri de Lubac, Hans Urs von Balthasar, Jean Daniélou, Yves Congar and other great figures. This informal group prepared the great event of the Second Vatican Council both intellectually and spiritually. I agree with Monsignor Javier Martínez, archbishop of Granada, that

> it would be possible, and perhaps necessary, to show that the deep meaning of the teaching of the Second Vatican Council, and in fact the very key to understand its teaching, is exactly its attempt to recuperate the Holy Tradition from the marshlands in which the semi-conscious acceptance of liberalism and secular reason has thrown it. The same could be said of the teaching of the post-conciliar popes, especially John Paul II.[51]

I believe that the documents of the Council might be read as a kind of constitution of the new post-secular order. For this reason I would like to briefly recall some its crucial ideas relevant for Polish Messianism and the Russian Idea.

The principle of Christocentric anthropology is explicitly expressed in the famous Paragraph 22 of *Gaudium et Spes*. "Christ . . . in the very revelation of the mystery of the Father and his love, fully reveals man to himself and brings to light his most high calling."[52] The Modern order rests on the separation of the domains of the natural and the supernatural, which yields the separation of culture, politics, economy on the one hand, and religion on the other. This separation, as it is well known, leads inevitably to the disappearance of religion.[53] However, if the true human nature is revealed in Christ, then this modern dualism cannot be maintained anymore. Religion is seen now as the completion of man, not as an additional option. As Msgr. Martínez noticed, "this quotation, when taken seriously, makes

---

51. Martínez, *Beyond Secular Reason*, 96.
52. Second Vatican Council, *Gaudium et Spes*, no. 22.
53. See Martínez, *Beyond Secular Reason*, 73–85.

it impossible for a Catholic to maintain a liberal position, and goes beyond any secular dualism or fragmentation."[54]

Next, some crucial ideas of Messianism (in contrast to Missionism) might be easily found in the Constitution *Lumen Gentium* in the paragraphs concerning the tasks of lay people. For it is precisely the laity, not the ecclesial hierarchy, who is primary called to transform the world according to Christian principles. "The laity, by their very vocation, seek the kingdom of God by engaging in temporal affairs and by ordering them according to the plan of God."[55] As a result of this effort "all types of temporal affairs" should "continually increase according to Christ."[56] "The world may be permeated by the spirit of Christ and it may more effectively fulfill its purpose in justice, charity and peace . . . Through the members of the Church, will Christ progressively illumine the whole of human society with His saving light."[57] What is specifically significant is that the Fathers of the Council recalled the traditional teaching on the three offices of Christ, which was constantly presented in the works of Polish and Russian Messianists. We read that every Christian continues the priestly, the prophetic and the royal functions of Jesus Christ.[58] So, the people of God is the true messianic nation. The lacking element in Council vision is the theology of nation, which could serve as a base for national Missionism.

Finally, one can find in the council constitutions the most radical and subversive idea of the Holy Trinity as a social program, so characteristic for Polish and Russian religious philosophy. "The Lord Jesus, when He prayed to the Father, 'that all may be one. . . as we are one' (John 17:21–22) opened up vistas closed to human reason, for He implied a certain likeness between the union of the divine Persons, and the unity of God's sons in truth and charity. This likeness reveals that man . . . cannot fully find himself except through a sincere gift of himself."[59] The line of reasoning is clear. If Christ is the model of man, then His relations with the Father and Spirit should be the pattern for all human relationships. Anthropological Christocentrism therefore leads to social Trinitarianism.

The teaching of the Second Vatican Council has been developed and deepened by John Paul II, the true Slavic Pope, who fulfilled the prophecies of the Polish poets and went beyond the dreams of Russian philosophers.

54. Ibid., 95–96.

55. Second Vatican Council, *Lumen Gentium*, no. 31.

56. Ibid.

57. Ibid., no. 36.

58. Ibid., nos. 34–36.

59. Second Vatican Council, *Gaudium et Spes*, no. 24.

The two above quoted paragraphs of *Gaudium et spes* were his most beloved citations. There are even evidences that the "Trinitarian" no. 24 "probably owes its shape to Wojtyła."[60] I would like only to recall that the first Encyclical Letter of John Paul II starts with a splendid affirmation that "the Redeemer of man, Jesus Christ, is the centre of the universe and of history."[61] This statement summarizes all the post-secular teaching of the Second Vatican Council and perfectly agrees with both Polish and Russian religious thought. "Again, it is text that, if it is received in an intellectual honest way and is taken seriously, goes 'beyond secular reason,' and makes cleat the deep incompatibility of the Catholic faith with liberal modes of thinking."[62]

The remaining great task is the detailed investigation of the possible influences of Polish Messianism and the Russian Idea on contemporary Catholic post-secular teaching. Some authors argued that Henri de Lubac, the founding father of the theological revival in the twentieth century, might be directly influenced by Russian thought.[63] It is worth noting that he was also acquainted with the messianic works of Mickiewicz. Moreover, there is a considerable amount of exciting evidence for direct messianic inspiration in the thought of John Paul II.[64] As far as we know, he was also interested in Russian religious philosophy. The history of the post-secular revolution still awaits its explorers.

Finally, I think that the heritage of Polish Messianism and the Russian Idea should not only be recognized as a surprisingly early expression of post-secular intuition, but also as a source of some inspiration for contemporary post-secular thought. Two points seem to me especially important: Polish and Russian Messianists were much more courageous in thinking about the state than most contemporary Christian thinkers,[65] and they formulated a specific philosophy and a theology of nation, which could be an impulse for a more faithful approach to that issue for contemporary theologians.[66] In

---

60. Skrzypczak, *Karol Wojtyła na Soborze Watykańskim II*, 109; see also Waldstein, *Three Kinds of Personalism*, 8.

61. John Paul II, *Redemptor hominis*, no. 1.

62. Martínez, *Beyond Secular Reason*, 96, n. 35.

63. Dell'Asta, *La teologia ortodossa e l'Occidente*; I owe this reference to Artur Mrówczyński-Van Allen.

64. For instance, during World War II, a young Karol Wojtyła was a member of the secret organization Unia, led by declared Messianist Jerzy Braun. For some historical evidences see: Mazur, "Jerzy Braun i mesjanizm Jana Pawła II," for a more systematic study: Rojek, "Pokolenie;" I am currently working on a detailed Messianistic interpretation of John Paul II's thought.

65. See for instance Mrówczyński-Van Allen, *Between the Icon and the Idol*.

66. See for instance Pabst and Schneider, "Transfiguring the World," 16; for an example of positive Polish theology of nation see Bartnik, *Formen der politischen Theologie in Polen*, "Problematyka teologii narodu," and *Teologia narodu*.

short, I believe that the works of Mickiewicz, Krasiński, and Cieszkowski on the one hand, and Dostoevsky, Soloviev and Florensky on the other, should not be considered as a mere historical curiosity, but as a challenge for contemporary Christian thought.

When Stanisław Tarnowski in 1889 noticed the similarities between the Russian Idea and Polish Messianism, Soloviev had a rather obscure and quite a negative opinion on Polish philosophy. Ten years before meeting in Krakow he wrote to one of his friends: "I have come to know the Polish philosophers to some extent. Their general tone and aspirations are very sympathetic, but, like our Slavophiles, they have no positive content."[67] It seems that the discussion with Tarnowski and others changed his mind, although during the very debate he maintained his critical attitude.[68] Ten years after the Krakow meeting, Soloviev gave a speech in Moscow at a ceremony to the memory of Adam Mickiewicz. He not only praised his poetry, but also declared his acceptance of some of the fundamental principles of Polish Messianism.

> As far as I know, along with of some minor errors (like, for instance, the cult of Napoleon), this movement proclaimed some truths of paramount importance, truths which have a legitimate right to recognition in the Christian world—above all, the truth about the continuous growth of Christianity. If the world still exists so many centuries after Christ, it means that something is being prepared in it for our salvation; and taking part in this is our duty, if Christianity is really a religion of divine humanity.[69]

In these words, as Walicki put it, "the greatest religious philosopher of nineteenth-century Russia paid homage to Mickiewicz's religious Messianism."[70] I believe that Soloviev could have repeated these words for Krasiński, if only he had known him. I also believe that contemporary Christian post-secular thinkers could pay similar homage to both Polish Messianism and the Russian Idea. If only they knew them.

67. Letter to countess S. A. Tolstoy, April 27, 1877, quoted in Florensky, *Pillar and Ground of the Truth*, 240.
68. Soloviev, "Lettre á la Rédaction," 182–83.
69. Solov'yev, "Mitskevich," 211.
70. Walicki, "Mickiewicz's Paris Lectures," 64.

# Bibliography

Bartnik, Czesław S. *Formen der politischen Theologie in Polen*. Regensburg: F. Pustet, 1986.

———. "Problematyka teologii narodu." In *Polska teologia narodu*, edited by Czesław S. Bartnik, 9–42. Lublin: Towarzystwo Naukowe KUL, 1986.

———. *Teologia narodu*. Częstochowa: Kuria Metropolitalna w Częstochowie, Tygodnik Katolicki Niedziela, 1999.

Berdyaev, Nikolai. *The Russian Idea*. Translated by R. M. French. Hudson, NY: Lindisfarne, 1999.

Berdyayev, Nikolay. "Aleksey Stepanovich Khomyakov." In *Sobraniye sochineniy*. Vol. 5, *Aleksey Stepanovich Khomyakov. Mirosozertsaniye Dostoyevskogo. Konstantin Leont'yev*. Paris: YMCA-Press.

Braun, Jerzy. *Kultura jutra, czyli nowe oświecenie*. Warsaw: Fronda, 2001.

Cieszkowski, August. "Prolegomena to historiosophy." In *Selected Writings*, edited and translated by André Liebich, 49–81. Cambridge: Cambridge University Press, 1979.

Dell'Asta, Adriano, ed. *La teologia ortodossa e l'Occidente nel XX secolo: storia di un incontro. Atti del Convegno promosso da Fondazione Russia Cristiana e Commissione Teologica Sinodale del Patriarcato di Mosca*, Seriate 30–31 ottobre 2004. La Casa di Matriona, 2005.

Dobieszewski, Janusz. *Włodzimierz Sołowjow. Studium osobowości filozoficznej*. Warsaw: Scholar, 2002.

Fiećko, Jerzy. *Krasiński przeciw Mickiewiczowi. Najważniejszy spór romantyków*. Poznań: Wydawnictwo Poznańskie, 2011.

———. *Rosja Krasińskiego. Rzecz o nieprzejednaniu*. Poznań: Wydawnictwo Naukowe UAM, 2005.

Florensky, Pavel. *The Pillar and Ground of the Truth: An Essay in Orthodox Theodicy in Twelve Letters*. Translated by Boris Jakim. Princeton: Princeton University Press, 2004.

Grassl, Wolfgang. "Ekonomia obywatelska. Trynitarny klucz do odczytania ekonomii papieskiej." Translated by Marek Przychodzeń. *Pressje* 29 (2012) 58–82 (English original version has not been published yet).

Hoene-Wroński, Józef Maria. *Messianisme. Union finale de la philosophie et de la religion, constituant de la philosophie absolute*. Paris: G. Doyen, 1831.

Jankowski, Józef. *Idea Rosyjska Sołowjewa a posłannictwo polskie. Karta z dziejów mesjanizmu rosyjskiego*. Warsaw: Instytut Mesjaniczny, 1926.

John Paul II, Pope. *Redemptor hominis*. March 4, 1979.

Kant, Immanuel. *Religion and Rational Theology*. Translated by A. W. Wood and G. di Giovanni. Cambridge: Cambridge University Press, 1996.

Kędzierski, Marcin. "Ekonomia trynitarna." *Pressje* 29 (2012) 26–39.

Krasiński, Zygmunt. *Dzieła literackie*. Vol. 1. Warsaw: PIW, 1973.

———. "O stanowisku Polski z Bożych i ludzkich względów." In *Pisma filozoficzne i polityczne*, 5–65. Warsaw: Czytelnik, 1999.

Martínez, Javier. *Beyond Secular Reason. Más allá de la razón secular*. Granada: Editorial Nuevo Inicio, 2008.

Mazur, Krzysztof. "Jerzy Braun i mesjanizm Jana Pawła II. Zapomniane inspiracje myśli papieża." *Pressje* 28 (2012) 149–57.

Moiseyev, Vyacheslav. "Tayna krakovskogo dela Vladimira Solov'yeva." *Przegląd Rusycystyczny* 1 (2003) 5–21.

Mrówczyński-Van Allen, Artur. *Between the Icon and the Idol. The Human Person and the Modern State in Russian Literature and Thought: Chaadayev, Soloviev, Grossman.* Translated by M. P. Whelan. Eugene, OR: Cascade, 2013.

Mrówczyński-Van Allen, Artur, and Aaron Riches. "Jeśli nie w Polsce, to nigdzie. Jan Paweł II przeciwko entropii sekularnego rozumu i liberalnej polis." Translated by Jędrzej Grodniewicz, Karol Kleczka and Paweł Rojek. *Pressje* 29 (2012) 86–111 (English original version has not been published yet).

Nowak, Andrzej. "Rosja i rewolucja—Zygmunt Krasiński." In *Strachy i Lachy. Przemiany polskiej pamięci, 1982–2012*, 65–141. Krakow: Biały Kruk, 2012.

Pabst, Adrian, and Christoph Schneider. "Transfiguring the World through the Word." In *Encounter between Eastern Orthodoxy and Radical Orthodoxy*, edited by Adrian Pabst and Christoph Schneider, 1–25. Burlington, VT: Ashgate, 2009.

Peterson, Erik. "Monotheism as a Political Problem." In *Theological Tractates*, 68–105. Stanford: Stanford University Press, 2011.

Popiel, Paweł. *Rodzina Popielów herbu Sulima z przydomkiem Chrościak. Rys historyczny.* Krakow, 1936.

Przebinda, Grzegorz. *Włodzimierz Sołowjow wobec historii.* Krakow: Arka, 1992.

Rojek, Paweł. "Ekonomia, wzajemność i Trójca Święta. W obronie ekonomii trynitarnej." *Pressje* 32–33 (2013) 260–68.

———. "Mesjanizm integralny." *Pressje* 28 (2012) 20–49.

———. "Mesjańska teologia polityczna Włodzimierza Sołowjowa." *Pressje* 28 (2012) 160–70.

———. "Pokolenie kapłanów, proroków i królów? Mesjańska antropologia Jana Pawła II." *Pressje* 24 (2011) 28–38.

———. "Program ekonomii trynitarnej." *Pressje* 29 (2012) 10–14.

Second Vatican Council. *Gaudium et Spes.* December 7, 1965.

———. *Lumen Gentium.* November 21, 1964.

Skrzypczak, Robert. *Karol Wojtyła na Soborze Watykańskim II.* Warsaw: Centrum Myśli Jana Pawła II, 2011.

Sokulski, Michał. "*Przedświt* jako tekst profetyczny." *Dyskurs* 1 (2005) 105–32.

Solov'yev, Vladimir. "Mitskevich. Rech' na obede v pamyat' Mitskevicha 27 dekabrya 1898 g." In *Literaturnaya kritika*, 205–12. Moscow: Sovremennik, 1990.

———. "Russkaya ideya." In *Sochineniya v dvukh tomakh*, 2:218–46. Moscow: Pravda, 1989.

Soloviev, Vladimir. "Lettre á la Rédaction du *Przegląd Polski*." *Przegląd Polski* 92 (1889) 179–187.

Solovyev, Vladimir. *Russia and the Universal Church.* Translated by Herbert Rees. London: Centenary Press, 1948.

Solovyov, Vladimir. *Lectures on Divine Humanity.* Revised and edited by Boris Jakim. Hudson, NY: Lindisfarne, 1995.

———. *War, Progress, and the End of History: Three Conversations, Including a Short Story of the Anti-Christ.* Hudson, NY: Lindisfarne, 1990.

Solovyov, S. M. *Vladimir Solovyov: His Life and Creative Evolution.* Faifax, VA: Eastern Christian Publications, 2000.

Strémooukhoff, Dimitri. *Vladimir Soloviev and His Messianic Work.* Translated by Elizabeth Meyendorff. Belmont, MA: Nordland, 1980.

Tarnowski, Stanisław. "Głos sumienia z Rosyi." *Przegląd Polski* 91 (1889) 32–58.

———. "Odpowiedź na list Włodzimierza Sołowjowa do redakcji *Przeglądu Polskiego*." *Przegląd Polski* 92 (1889) 187–89.

———. "Wykład idei i powołania Rosyi." *Przegląd Polski* 94 (1889) 1–45.

Voegelin, Eric. *The New Science of Politics*. Chicago: University of Chicago Press, 1952.

Volf, Miroslav. "The Trinity Is Our Social Program: The Doctrine of the Trinity and the Shape of Social Engagement." *Modern Theology* 14 (1998) 403–23.

Waldstein, Michael. "Three Kinds of Personalism: Kant, Scheler and John Paul II." *Forum Filozoficzne* 10 (2009) 1–21.

Walicki, Andrzej. "Adam Mickiewicz's Paris Lectures and the Russian Thinkers." *Dialogue and Universalism* 17 (2007) 63–78.

———. "La Philosophie de l'Histoire d'Adam Mickiewicz." In *Le verbe et l'histoire: Mickiewicz, la France et l'Europe*, edited by François-Xavier Coquin and Michel Masłowski, 188–94. Paris: Institut d'études slaves, 2002.

———. *Philosophy and Romantic Nationalism: The Case of Poland*. Notre Dame: University of Notre Dame Press, 1994.

———. *Russia, Poland, and Universal Regeneration: Studies on Russian and Polish Thought of the Romantic Epoch*. Notre Dame: University of Notre Dame Press, 1991.

———. *The Slavophile Controversy: History of a Conservative Utopia in Nineteenth-Century Russian Thought*. Notre Dame: University of Notre Dame Press, 1975.

———. "Solovëv's Theocratic Utopia and Two Romantic Poets: Fëdor Tjutčev and Adam Mickiewicz." In *Vladimir Solovëv: Reconciler and Polemicist*, edited by Wil van der Bercken et al., 473–84. Louven: Uitgeverij Peters, 2000.

Zdziechowski, Marian. *Pesymizm, romantyzm a podstawy chrześcijaństwa*. Vol. 2. Warsaw: IFiS PAN, 1993.

# 3

## Georgy Fedotov's *Carmen Saeculare*

*A Reflection on Culture as a Judgment of Modernity from the Philosophy and Theology of Some Nineteenth- and Twentieth-Century Russian Thinkers*

—Artur Mrówczyński-Van Allen

Usually, every era has the culture that it deserves and perhaps that it is why we should be attentive to the signs it sends us. They can help us recognize the direction that the times in which we live are leading us.

"The future is always around us—just like the past. Events leave a long shadow. The past leaves its footprints: the future speaks through signs. Only it is very difficult to understand its language," wrote Georgy Fedotov in his article entitled *Carmen Saeculare* published in the journal *Put'* in 1928.[1]

This article begins with a mention of the festive public celebrations, the so-called *Laudi Saeculares* (Secular Games), organized by Emperor Augustus in May of the year 17 BC in order to announce the beginning of a new era, a new *saeculum*.[2] These celebrations were usually held approximately every one hundred and ten years, and they had a clearly political-religious, and what today we would call cultural, character. The great poet Horace was commissioned to compose the hymn *Carmen Saeculare*, sung

1. Fedotov, "Carmen Saeculare," 101.
2. Ibid., 101–15.

43

by the choir during the main act of worship, the sacrifice of a white bull in honor of the gods Diana and Apollo.[3] The poetry that was recited or sung in these public celebrations suggested the cyclic passage of time, while above all reaffirming the identity of Rome, an identity that was based on its cults. Horace's *Carmen Saeculare* was sung on the Palatine and Capitoline hills at the end of the festival's most important day, one of prayer and sacrifices.[4] Naturally, behind these proclamations, celebrations, and cults, as Fedotov continued in his article, there is always an idea that is found at the root, in the beginning of a culture.

With modernity it is no different, and in the course of the aforementioned article Georgy Fedotov, known as a "philosopher" or "theologian of culture," as he was called, for example, by Father Alexander Men.[5] He analyzed several aspects of modern Western European culture, such as the cult of sports and technology, as well as the changing relationship between what is spiritual and what is of the body. In this he tries to read the footprints of the past and the signs of what is to come in order to better understand the world around us and to understand ourselves. In the light of his interpretation, this singular cultural event, the *Laudi Saeculares*, takes on a specific value, emblematic for its era, and which we can try to understand by attentively listening to what the *Carmen Saeculare* tells or sings to us. In keeping with Fedotov's inspiration, or we could even say his methodology, we will therefore try to consider modernity as reflected in the culture thereof, relying on some representatives of Russian philosophy and theology for support.

Fedotov very clearly realized that the twentieth century had brought with it the destruction of the foundations of the preceding centuries' culture, and he asked himself "but what does it give us in return?"[6] In order to be able to answer this question with Fedotov, we will not herein analyze the contents of the *Put'* article that serves as a reference, although of course it would be very interesting to do so. Rather, we will use the article as a tool, an instrument, given to us by this philosopher of culture, so that by following his example we can, as he himself wrote, "look into the chaos of new forms, in order to see its ideas."[7]

With this aim, and given the limitations inherent to this essay format, instead of addressing various aspects of modernity as Fedotov does in his

---

3. Horace, "Carmen Saeculare," 413.

4. Putnam, *Horace's Carmen Saeculare*, 49.

5. Men, "Vozvrashchenie."

6. Fedotov, "Carmen Saeculare," 103.

7. Ibid.

article, we will mention only one example of European cultural life at the beginning of the twentieth century. In my opinion, this example is particularly significant when reflecting upon and perhaps defining the very character of modernity, and I am convinced that it could be identified as the *Carmen Saeculare* of modernity, for at the beginning of the twenty first century, we too can find our very own *Carmen Saeculare*. And at the same time, I also hope that with this exercise we can demonstrate that Russian thought is not just an exciting field of research in the history of philosophy which is considered rather "exotic" by many, but is also an exceptionally apt instrument for interpreting the contemporary world. Therefore, by establishing Georgy Fedotov's article *Carmen Saeculare*, not as a text to be analyzed, but rather as a methodological tool, we can, in a practical way, try to establish the outline of a reflection on contemporary culture, a reflection that will take on the character of a specific judgment of modernity, from the perspective of the chosen authors, who in our case will be Vladimir Soloviev, Father Pavel Florensky, and Paul Evdokimov.

That said, in order to pursue our objective, we must first dedicate some time to addressing the concept of culture itself. Pavel Gurevich, in the introduction to his work *Philosophy of Culture*,[8] indicates that the phenomenon of culture can be interpreted as a search for meaning. Or better put, as a consequence, as a sign of the search for the meaning of life, of the question of man. A search that is ever more complex and confusing as modernity advances, for which reason Gurevich recalls Soloviev's words: "Here we have Voltaire, Bossuet, the Madonna, the Pope, Alfred Myusse, and Filaret." And he continues with the words of Florensky, who also wondered what culture was, "if the Gospel of John, together with the Luciferian gospel of Pike, together with the church and the tavern, with the penitential canon of Saint Andrew of Crete and the works of the Marquis de Sade? How can we differentiate what is culture from what is not?"[9]

Father Pavel Florensky tries to find the answer to this question by analyzing the relationship between culture and cult (in the sense of worship or a system or community of religious worship and ritual, rather than in the colloquial sense of an extremist religious sect). Cult is the essence of religion, Father Florensky shows us: a set of rituals, prayers, and sacraments, through which the believers honor, adore, and praise God. Supported by the diverse historical forms of human activity, cult is the core of culture.

Father Pavel precisely defined the location of the center of culture as a phenomenon of the search for the meaning of life and of the world. In

---

8. Gurevich, *Filosofiya kul'tury*.

9. Ibid., 8; Florenskiy, *Filosofiya kul'ta*, 110.

his well-known work *Philosophy of Cult*, to which Gurevich makes reference, in the second lesson, entitled, "Cult, religion, and culture,"[10] Florensky explains that culture, arising from cult, is "the activity through which and in which man first makes himself man,"[11] but under the condition of the truth of the cult, which is the center of the culture.[12] And it is within the cult that "the primary activity" ("*pervodeyatelnost'*") appears and takes place; this primary activity is the result of the encounter with the Word made Flesh,[13] due to which man, in an anthropological sense, is *homo liturgus*,[14] because the heart of all human activity is in the liturgy, which is the center. It is there where the *pervodeyatelnost*,' that "primary activity," takes place.[15] The rite of the cult is what brings the community together, and is the source of culture and myth, adds Florensky. Because when the myth tries to orally interpret and explain the cult in a retroactive way, we take the first step towards the secularization of the liturgy and, consequently, so too the first step towards the secularization of the culture, to in the end reject the cult itself.[16] Florensky was also aware that man could reject the cult, and that this decision appeared at the core of modern culture. The decisive figure in the genesis of the thought that gave rise to this culture was Kant. "Kant did not want to know anything about cult. The only significant reality for him was himself and his placement at the absolute center of the universe, and that was the essence of the spirit of the new times in Western Europe."[17]

If we agree with Florensky's affirmation that cult prefigures culture, it would seem legitimate to affirm that behind every culture there is some type of cult. Therefore, the Kantian rejection of cult, which Florensky himself points out, left an "empty space" in which "the Western European spirit" of modernity established a cult specifically of its own that was fundamental to its culture. In my opinion, the character of this culture and the nature of the cult characteristic of Western modernity, a cult that this modernity does not want to recognize and tries to hide, appears paradigmatically in a specific cultural event, in what we could call the *Carmen Saeculare* of modernity, also sung one day in the month of May, nineteen hundred twenty-three years after the imperial celebrations in Rome.

10. Florenskiy, *Filosofiya kul'ta*, 51.

11. Ibid., 55.

12. Ibid., 58.

13. Ibid., 55.

14. Ibid., 59.

15. Ibid., 60.

16. Ibid., 76–77.

17. Ibid., 104.

I am referring to the opera by Richard Strauss whose libretto was taken directly from the text of Hedwig Lachmann's German translation of Oscar Wilde's tragedy *Salomé*. The debut in Dresden at the end of 1905 caused such a stir, or even such a scandal, that the next performance could not be held in the Hofoper Imperial in Vienna, but rather had to be transferred to the elegant, though provincial, city of Graz. There, it was presented to the world—and made history—on May 16, 1906.

The audience, which included such authentic celebrities of European cultural life at the beginning of the twentieth century as Gustav Mahler, Giacomo Puccini, Arnold Schönberg and his brother-in-law Alexander Zemlinsky, filled the seats without hiding their excitement. They all knew that they had the privilege to be taking part in an historic event. They were surrounded by many young people who had traveled to Graz from far and wide, many of whom had paid for the trip by borrowing money from friends or family members, like the young painter from Linz, Adolf Hitler.[18]

Even before the opera began, the atmosphere was full of excitement. The first sounds, however, threw most of the audience off guard. Strauss, known for his mastery in building the first chords of his works (everyone had in mind the beginning of his *Thus Spoke Zarathustra*), this time opted for an unsettling beginning, introducing a half step into the first few notes that created a particularly uncomfortable sound interval for the ear, a sound that musicians call *diabolus in musica*. It was a beginning that was perhaps a warning of the story of disconcerting love to follow, that perhaps also revealed the prophetic character of the work which would start a new era for art, ushering in the twentieth century. Because art, as Fedotov noted, can always proclaim in advance what still remains to come.[19]

The libretto's action takes place on a night with a full moon, in the palace of King Herod Antipas, and, through Wilde's interpretation, tells the well-known Gospel story of Salomé and John the Baptist (Jochanaan). As we will remember, Herod asks Salomé to dance for him, *Danz für mich, Salome*, promising to reward her with her heart's desire, even if it were half of his kingdom. Salomé makes him swear that he will keep his word, and prepares herself for the *Dance of the Seven Veils*. In this dance, very oriental in orchestration, the princess Salomé removes her veils one by one, until she is lying naked at Herod's feet. She then demands her desire: the head of the prophet on a silver platter. Herod desperately tries to dissuade her with other offerings, including jewels and even the sacred veil of the Temple. But she is resolute: the only thing she desires is the head of the man who did not

---

18. Ross, *El ruido eterno*, 20.
19. Fedotov, "Carmen Saeculare," 103.

accept her love, who rejected her advances. She remains firm in her demand for Jochanaan's head. Finally, even though it terrifies him, Herod concedes.

John the Baptist's execution precedes the climax of the work. It is not seen on stage, but rather is registered by the orchestra. After a desperate monologue by Salomé, a guard presents her with the head on a platter. Salomé declares her love to the severed head, finally passionately kissing the lips of the dead prophet, to the horror of the audience (*Ich habe deinem Mund geküsst*—"I have kissed your mouth"). When the princess kisses John's bloody head, a horrified Herod, leaving the stage, orders the soldiers to kill her. The final chords echo Salomé's theme of love.

This short description of the work should help us remember that its main subject is love, a combination of *eros* and *thanatos*, Salomé's love for John. We could affirm that the cult revealed in this work and, through its medium, in the culture that it represents, is the cult of love. But what love? In this context it may surprise us to remember how Father Florensky begins his work *Philosophy of Cult*, but even more than surprising, this beginning is revealing. The first words of the first conference are "Love, love, love and once again love. . ." And he continues:

> Repeated innumerable times by innumerable people who have never approached the threshold of religion, this mysterious word has lost all of its meaning. But, like a type of unifying fabric, it has grown; it has filled the entire space dedicated to the religious conscience of our contemporaries and in so doing has pushed the entire religious content out of it. The true content of this sacred word has now become: *no religion*, and the secret meaning of the discourse on love is always (now), more or less conscious or unconsciously, a hostile stroke against religion. The reasonable transformation of the religious fabric has now turned it into an account on love.[20]

We find what Florensky was able to understand as "love" in Vladimir Soloviev's text *The Meaning of Love*:

> The truth, as a living force, taking possession of the inward essence of man, and effectively rescuing him from false self-assertion, is termed Love. Love, as the effectual abrogation of egoism, is the real justification and salvation of individuality. Love is greater than intellectual knowledge, yet without the latter it could not take effect as an inward delivering force, enhancing, and not annulling the individuality. Only thanks to a rational consciousness, (or, what is the same thing, a consciousness of

20. Florenskiy, *Filosofiya kul'ta*, 27.

the truth), can a man discriminate his very self, i.e., his true individuality, from his egoism, and therefore sacrificing this egoism, and surrendering himself to love, he finds in it not merely
living, but also life-giving power, and does not, together with
his egoism, forfeit his individuality, but on the contrary makes
it eternal.[21]

Further down he continues,

The meaning of human love, speaking generally, is *the justification and deliverance of individuality through the sacrifice of egoism*. On this general foundation we can also solve our particular
problems to explain the meaning of sex-love. Not in vain is it
that sexual relations are not merely termed love, but that, by
general acknowledgment, also they represent love *par excellence*, exhibiting the type and ideal of all other kinds of love (cf.
the *Song of Songs* and the *Apocalypse*).[22]

Therefore, writes Soloviev,

The fundamental falsehood and evil of egoism lies not in this
absolute self-assertion and self-estimation of the subject, but
in the fact that, rating himself in accordance with what is due
to unconditional significance, he unjustly refuses to others this
same significance. Recognizing himself as a center of existence,
which as a matter of fact he is, he relegates others to the circum-
ference of his own being and leaves them only an external and
relative value.[23]

Therefore, the Russian philosopher concludes,

Asserting himself apart from all that is other, a man by that very
act divests his own authentic being of meaning, deprives himself
of the true content of existence, and reduces his individuality
to an empty form. In this way egoism is by no means the self-
recognition and self-affirmation of individuality, but on the
contrary is self-negation and death [*gibel'*].[24]

What Soloviev describes here has, more than a century later, been called
the "necrophilia of modernity" by the contemporary thinker Catherine
Pickstock, and has been described as the principal characteristic of modern

---

21. Solovyev, *Meaning of Love*, 22.
22. Ibid.
23. Ibid., 23.
24. Ibid., 24.

times.[25] Therefore, if culture, as we indicated at the beginning, is the search for meaning, there is only one meaning that can give meaning to this search, to culture, to the life of man. Love. A love that is stronger than death. And Salomé, in her last words, appears to recognize this truth: "The mystery of love is greater than the mystery of death."

But is this love that wins out over egoism and over death possible? Soloviev gives a clear answer to this question, and his response appears in the evident context of culture. We find it in his "lost" letter to Leo Tolstoy. The process of the occupation of the "religious fabric" by a false concept of love, as Florensky expressed it, clearly appears in what Soloviev defined as "*lzhekhristianstvo*," referring to Tolstoy's social thought. And for that reason Soloviev can unequivocally address Tolstoy, writing the following: "Our entire dispute can be reduced to one specific point: the resurrection of Christ."[26] It is love that wins out over death. A specific love. Nuptial love, between a man and a woman, made possible thanks to the concrete love of Jesus Christ.

It is no coincidence that what this *Carmen Saeculare* of modernity dramatized in Graz in 1906, already appears today as the source of the totalitarian ideology of our time, the so-called "gender ideology," and that its main weapon is an attack on women, the falsification of the feminine spirit. Its most dramatic and unmistakable result is death, the death of millions of innocent beings assassinated in the wombs of their mothers. It is an ideology that is no more than another expression (perhaps the definitive expression) of *libido dominandi*, of its own ambition to dominate, of which it is itself slave and victim—as Saint Augustine described it,[27] that which was not foreign to our history even at the beginning of Christianity;[28] the force that Eric Voegelin[29] called a characteristic trait of modernity or, essentially, the foundation of the final phase of the evolution of the pagan cultures that Vladimir Soloviev defined as the *phallic era*.[30]

The way we understand love is inextricably tied to the way we understand what men and women are, to the way we understand the relationship between masculine and feminine, that relationship that in the most profound way determines our relationship with life and, simultaneously, with

25. Pickstock, *After Writing*, 105–6.

26. Solov'yev, "Pismo k L. Tolstomu," 97.

27. Augustine, *De Civitate Dei. Contra paganos*, I, Praefatio: "Unde etiam de terrena civitate, quae cum dominari appetit, etsi populi serviant, ipsa ei dominandi libido dominatur."

28. Camastra, *Libido Dominandi*.

29. Voegelin, *Anamnesis*, 106.

30. Solov'yev, "Mitologicheskiy process," 26.

death—and this determines, in the deepest part, the cult and culture that can create this cult.

Allow me, therefore, in conclusion, to assume that the fact that the protagonists of Horace's hymn were Diana and Apollo, and that the protagonists of Oscar Wilde's story put on stage by Strauss were a man and a woman, Saint John the Baptist and a Jewish princess, has a more than symbolic dimension. This will perhaps help us find an image that can show us where to find the source of the answers to the challenge presented to us by the dominant contemporary culture (which is perhaps not so different from that of Antiquity). When Paul Evdokimov, aware of the falsity of the anthropology that hides behind modernity, describes the masculine and feminine archetypes in his work *Woman and the Salvation of the World*,[31] he refers to a (paradigmatic) example of the intimate union of cult and culture, to an icon, to the icon called *Deisis*, in which we find "the archetypes of the masculine and feminine: Saint John the Baptist and the *Theotokos*"[32] seated to the left and right of the Lord holding the Gospel. The pair, writes Evdokimov, man—woman, arises from the archetypal Mary—John the Baptist pair, in which all fragmentation (caused by egoism, Soloviev would add, or by falsified love, Florensky would say) is overcome by the presence of Jesus Christ, by the work of Love and Truth that is Jesus Christ.

This icon also teaches us something more with regard to our position in the face of the dominant culture of modernity, as *Deisis* means supplication, prayer. Because the vocation of the Church, of the culture that grows from it, is not merely to judge the world around it, but rather to justify it, to pray for it. In what way? In keeping with the inspiration given to us by Georgy Fedotov in his text, we could respond that in the face of the *Carmen Saeculare* of modernity, the vocation of Christian culture is to find itself once again as a participant in the *Deisis*, in this *Laudatio Saecularis et Aeterna*, always new and restorative. Because, as Georgy Fedotov wrote, Horace in the final analysis did not err in writing a hymn to announce the beginning of a new era, because at that time, "truly a new era was being born."[33]

---

31. Evdokimov, *Woman and the Salvation.*

32. Ibid., 231.

33. Fedotov, "Carmen Saeculare," 101.

# Bibliography

Augustine, Saint. *The City of God against the Pagans*. Edited by R. W. Dyson. Cambridge: Cambridge University Press, 1998.

Camastra, Francesco, ed. *Libido Dominandi. La teoría política da Gregorio Magno a Gregorio VII*. Milan: Edizioni Unicopli, 1997.

Evdokimov, Paul. *Woman and the Salvation of the World*. Translated by Anthony P. Gythiel. Crestwood, NY: St. Vladimir's Seminary Press, 1994.

Fedotov, Georgiy. "Carmen Saeculare." *Put'* 12 (1928) 101–15.

Florenskiy, Pavel. *Filosofiya kul'ta*. Moscow: Mysl', 2004.

Gurevich, Pavel. *Filosofiya kul'tury*. Moscow: Mysl', 2001.

Horace. "Carmen Saeculare." In *Odes and Carmen Saeculare*. Translated by Guy Lee. Leeds: Francis Cairns, 1998.

Men', Aleksandr. "Vozvrashcheniye k istokam." Introduction to Georgiy Fedotov, *Svyatye drevney Rusi*. Moscow: Moskovskiy rabochiy, 1990.

Pickstock, Catherine. *After Writing: On the Liturgical Consummation of Philosophy*. Oxford: Wiley-Blackwell, 1998.

Putnam, M. C. J. *Horace's Carmen Saeculare: Ritual Magic and the Poet's Art*. New Haven: Yale University Press, 2000.

Ross, Alex. *El ruido eterno. Escuchar al siglo XX a través de su música*. Barcelona: Seix Barral, 2009.

Solov'yev, Vladimir. "Mitologicheskiy proces v' drevniem' yazychestvie." In *Sobranyie sochinieniya*. Vol. 1. Brussels: Zhizn' z Bogom, 1966.

———. "Pismo k L. Tolstomu o voskriesenii Khrista." *Put'* 5 (1926) 97–99.

Solovyev, Vladimir. *The Meaning of Love*. Translated by Jane Marshall. London: Geoffrey Bles, The Centenary Press, 1945.

Voegelin, Eric. *Anamnesis*. Notre Dame: University of Notre Dame Press, 1978.

# 4

# The Polyphonic Conception of Culture as Counterculture in the Context of Modernity

*Fr. Pavel Florensky, Mikhail Bakhtin, and Maria Yudina*

—Olga Tabatadze

IN 1924, METROPOLITAN ANTHONY (Khrapovitsky, 1863–1936) in an article on Orthodox culture, wrote that the concept of any culture, in the first place, "includes religion or philosophical system to replace it (Utilitarianism, moral autonomy, Marxism, etc.)."[1] Indeed, since the beginning of the so-called "modernity"—with the establishment and prevalence of anthropocentrism and ethnocentrism, the rationalization of human activity, the decomposition of a holistic, organic understanding of the world in the areas of knowledge and objects, the increasing importance of politics, law and market, the transformation of the person into a mere individual, the appearance of all modern philosophical systems, our understanding too of culture was changing, indeed it was shedding its heretofore religious or spiritual aspect. In the words of Metropolitan Anthony (Bloom, 1914–2003), the entire Western world, including Russia, "went up by leaps and bounds of

---

1. Antoniy (Khrapovitskiy), *Izbrannyye trudy*, 535.

53

the Christian faith,"[2] where the main value was God and all types of culture expressed this fundamental principle of Theocentrism.

> Architecture, painting and sculpture of the Middle Ages were "Bible in stone and paint," literature was permeated through with religious themes and Christian faith, music were almost exclusively religious character, philosophy was almost identical to theology, ethics and daily culture was based on biblical precepts. Sensual world was considered only as a temporary "refuge of man," in which only the Christian is just a pilgrim, who seeks to attain the eternal abode of God and looking for a way to make yourself worthy to enter there.[3]

Nevertheless, since the end of the twelfth century, a new understanding of the world has come into being. According to this new worldview, in terms of what objective reality and its meaning consists of came to be understood now more in abstraction from the wonder that there is something rather than nothing, reality became more of a presumption devoid of mystery and so giving way, in the sixteenth century, to a new culture and art which was thoroughly secular and utilitarian. This art, undoubtedly great but secular, helped people to understand the visible world and themselves better, but its objective value was nothing more than informative, entertaining and moralizing. Humanism, which owes its origins to Christian culture, but divided the culture on religious culture and out-of-religious, contributed to the creation of the kingdom of culture, autonomous in relation to the Christian virtues and claims the Magisterium instead of the Church. So Christian culture, deprived of its sacral and sacred values, and cut off from its religious roots, lost its general meaning and turned into a subculture or, one might even say, the counterculture, of a community of believers within the framework of the common national culture.

Following the words of Father Pavel Florensky—that "the culture is always produced from cult," we will analyze what thing we render a "cult" to, what is a "heart" not only of the cultural, but all human activity?

The Orthodox Archbishop of San Francisco John (Shakhovskoy, 1902–89) in the article "What Is Culture?" wrote,

> Culture is the work of man, moved by love. Not a forced labor, which is a curse, but a free labor, which is a blessing. Meaningless and fruitless are the attempts to build a life only on the materialistic ideas and interests . . . Gray, stifling, poor is in the

---

2. Yakovlev, *Ocherki istorii*, 20.

3. Sorokin, *Chelovek*, 430.

world, where there is only a game of human material interests, but there is no culture of spirit and culture of love.[4]

Father Florensky wrote in his *Note on Christianity and Culture* that

the building of the culture is defined by the spiritual law, announced by the Lord Himself: "Where is your treasure, there will be your heart." Treasure is a spiritual value, a thing that we recognize like an objective meaning and a justification of our life. The heart, in biblical terms, means the center of all our spiritual powers and abilities, the node, which knotting our personality. The Savior says that our personality, and, consequently, all of its manifestations, is entirely determined by our treasure; so, our cognition is determined by what is approved by us as the Truth . . . Cultures of modern times by their proclamation of human autonomy have established as a "treasure" a non-discussed subject of faith—ourselves. Instead of God they have put an idol, a person who is not god, in his place and thus, the necessary aftermath was the further deployment of a culture whose aim was to justify human self-deification.[5]

Prince Evgeniy Trubetskoy, speaking about culture, believed that

the idea of Christ, Who came in the flesh, for a Christian expresses itself as the main task of culture, the principle, which the idea was called to incarnate in life; and the recognition behind culture its positive task is thereby its justification. Inasmuch as the beginning of the religious life of human society is the incarnation of the divine in the human, the human mind and the human will are encouraged to the creative participation in the work of God. Christian ideal . . . requires from us the selfless devotion to God with the greatest energy of human creativity. Man is called to be on the ground a collaborator in the construction of the house of God; and to this task should serve the whole human culture, science, art and social activities.[6]

We cannot disagree that every cultural manifestation is an expression of a certain understanding of the world and that the center or the "treasure" of our worldview motivates our actions and creativity. If we do not serve God, then we serve "mammon," i.e. money, power, sensual pleasures, etc. However, if the treasure of our heart is Christ and His Saving Love, then it

4. Ioann (Shakhovskoy), *Izbrannoye*, 423–24.
5. Florenskiy, "Zapiska."
6. Vasilenko, *Vvedeniye*, 167.

will certainly find the expression not only in cultural, but also anthropological and ontological order.

So, the concept of *sobornost,'* put forward for the first time by the
Slavophile Alexei Khomiakov (1804–1860), is defined by the thinker as a
unity of all members of the Church, based on freedom and unanimous love
of Christians to God and their mutual love in Jesus Christ. The author wrote
that the love towards a neighbor expresses in deeds, to God—in prayer, to
a man—in a spiritual brotherhood. Khomiakov identified the principles
of *sobornost'* and of community and affirmed that the Russian people for
whom love is a metaphysical, not sensual, manifestation, is predisposed to
live in community. In this sense, it is a rural community which is a typically
Russian phenomenon, where life is carried out throughout all the world,
and which does not know the individualistic and fragmented West. By Khomiakov the *sobornost'* i.e. unanimity, unity in voices, "unity in multiplicity"
or community, that has grown up in the spiritual unity of its members and
has tied by love and freedom, is the ideal form of common live of persons
who loves mutually and helps spiritually to each other.[7]

Konstantin Aksakov (1817–60) also sees in the *sobornost'* the "choral
beginning," where a personality is not suppressed, but only deprived of egoism. The thinker wrote:

> The community is a formation of people who have refused
> their egoism, their personality, and have manifested their gen-
> eral agreement. This is the act of love, Christian high action,
> which is expressing more or less vaguely in various (other) its
> manifestations. The community is, thus, a moral choir, and as
> in a choir the voice is not lost, but, obeying the general order,
> is heard in concord with all of the voices. So, also in the com-
> munity, personality is not lost, but abandoning its exclusivity
> for the consent of the common, it finds herself in the supreme,
> purified form, in agreement of evenly selfless personalities. As
> in consent of voices each voice gives its own sound, so in moral
> common sounding of personalities each person is heard, but not
> alone, indeed in accordance. And appears high phenomenon of
> friendly united being of reasonable creature (consciousness);
> appears the brotherhood, the community, triumph of the hu-
> man spirit.[8]

The principle of all-unity of Vladimir Soloviev (1853–1900)—not a
new theme in the history of philosophy, but proposed as a purification of

---

7. See Emel'yanov et al., *Istoriya russkoy filosofii*, 77–78.

8. Ibid., 53–54.

creative thought from abstraction and as a answer to the disunity of the modern world—is described as "the body of ideas" covered by love.[9]

> I call true or positive all-unity, something, in which The All exists not at the expense of all or to their detriment, but in benefit of all. False negative unity suppresses or absorbs incoming into it elements and itself turn out, thus, *emptiness*; true unity preserves and strengthens its elements, implementing in them like *fullness* of being.[10]

With the principle of all-unity Soloviev connected the concept of Godmanhood. He proceeded from the fact that Christ is the Head of all creatures, the Head of the Church and the example of the life according to the Gospel, of the life with full self-dedication in the service of God and of neighbor. "There cannot be Godmanhood without God-man, the Word made flesh. It covers everyone who is going around Christ and Gospel, who responds to God's call to enter in his Church and serve to sublime truth."[11]

The Church, the all-united divine-human community, "is this environment, where a person learns to distinguish between good and evil according to the precepts of God"[12] and perceives "the love, facing away from the Absolute to the multiplicity of entity and causing reciprocal love of man."[13] Man, according to Soloviev, is called to be a conductor of all-unity, the bearer of spirit. He must enter with his love into the love that exists in the depths of all-unity. To do this, he needs to overcome his egoism. It is impossible to do this with the power of the mind—because theoretical thinking can be motivated by the ego. Only love abolishes egoism. The general meaning of love, according to Soloviev, is "the justification and salvation of individuality through the sacrifice of egoism"[14] and "affirming" of the other "in God."[15]

The Prince-brothers Trubetskoy also saw divine Love at the root of all-unity. Prince Evgeniy Trubetskoy, following Soloviev, considered in his works the theme of all-unity and Godmanhood—which is the beginning of the common life of the Church, the content and the purpose of world history—but the idea of Trubetskoy was more ecclesial, and retains only some continuity with his mentor.[16] As Evgeniy Trubetskoy put it, "The world-cov-

9. Ibid., 105.
10. Ibid., 101.
11. Ibid., 96.
12. Ibid., 126.
13. Ibid., 103.
14. Solovyov, *Meaning of Love*, 42.
15. Ibid., 88.
16. See Vasilenko, *Vvedeniye*, 156.

ering temple of God with its icons, understood as a source of appeasement of creature in the spirit of love, as a place of the community of all creation, as the preimage of the coming transfigured humanity and cosmos."[17] Russian iconography

> often depicts a temple, which unites around itself all under-heaven creation. In icons . . . we find the Our Lady on the background of the temple and around the temple—"angelic assembly," "human race," paradisiacal vegetation, and in other icons—animals and birds—in a word, as like community of all creatures around the Mother of God as a Loving Heart of the universe. In icons . . . we see again the universe, the human race, Angels, animals, birds, paradise vegetation and hosts of heaven, and in the center—Christ, surrounded by celestial spheres. This is the coming cosmos, gathered in Christ, the world warmed by maternal love of the Virgin and resurrected in God, Who in Christianity opposes to the chaos, which is reigning on earth today.[18]

This theme is common to other Russian thinkers as well which we have not cited here, but who also wrote about *sobornost'* and all-unity as about the community of people directed to Christ and united by His Love, or, in other words, to the unity in multiplicity, loving God and one another in God.

This one-entity of loving God, for Father Pavel Florensky (1882–1937) was the *agape*, fraternal love, along with which he distinguished the irreducible to it and inseparable from it *philia*, friendly love. So, he believed that the limit of fragmentation of the agapic community (common unity) of Christians "is not the human atom that from itself relates to the community, but a community molecule, a pair of friends, which is the principle of actions"[19] and represents a new antinomy personality-dyad. Uniting by the love "by their essence, and forming a rationally unknowable dual-unity, friends enter into a unity of feeling, will, and thought that completely excludes divergence of feeling, will, and thiought."[20] This friendly one-thinking "comes from the Trinity, since, by nature, the main characteristic of the Trinity is unity and internal peace."[21] Relying on the Holy Fathers, the thinker emphasized the need for "common-lives," being together, being external, corporeal, empirical and of everyday. Florensky notes that such unity is not "a mediumistic

17. Ibid., 159.

18. Ibid., 163.

19. Florensky, *Pillar and Ground of the Truth*, 301.

20. Ibid., 312.

21. Ibid., 310.

mutual-possession of persons, not their immersion in and impersonal and indifferent (and therefore unfree) element of the two," not "the dissolution of individuality, not its depreciation, but its raising, consolidating, fortifying, and deepening."[22] "In friendship, the irreplaceable and incomparable value and originality of each person is revealed in all its beauty. In the other I, a person discovers his own actualized potential, made spiritually fruitful by the other I.[23]

Florensky compares friendship with consonance:

> Life is a continuous series of dissonances. But through friendship they are resolved. In friendship, social life acquires its meaning and conciliation . . . In the concept of consonance we . . . have an antinomy, for the consonant tones must somehow equal but, at the same time, different. But whatever the metaphysical nature of friendship, friendship is an essential condition of life.[24]

Thus, we see how in Florensky's thought, grace, divine love, lives in the life of the Church not only as *agape*, but as *philia*, uniting the Christian community by fraternity and friendship, promotes to the symphony of two on the earth[25] and to the consonance of common life,[26] in which each one sounds fully, in the complete realization of his life.

Mikhail Bakhtin in his book the *Problems of Dostoevsky's Poetics*, analyzing the sound of voices of the author and of the heroes in the structure of the works of Fyodor Dostoevsky, spoke about the unity of the polyphonic novel, using a musical term as a figurative analogy. The literary critic believed that the creation of polyphonic novel promoted "Dostoevsky's particular gift for hearing and understanding all voices immediately and simultaneously," "organizing and shaping this diversity in the cross-section of a given moment."[27] In Bakhtin's opinion, the world of Dostoevsky is "the artistically organized coexistence and interaction of spiritual diversity."[28] "If we were to seek an image toward which this whole world gravitates, an image in the spirit of Dostoevsky's own worldview, then it would be the church as a communion of unmerged souls, where sinners and righteous men come together."[29] The unity of Dostoevsky's works is created not by the author's

22. Ibid., 312.

23. Ibid.

24. Ibid., 315.

25. See ibid., 303.

26. See ibid., 311.

27. Bakhtin, *Problems*, 30.

28. Ibid., 31.

29. Ibid., 26–27.

idea, not by the unity of consciousness, but by the unity of life, the coexistence of the multiplicity of the full-weighty words, of clear voices, which
have its own consciousness and freedom. In "a world of yoked-together se-
mantic human orientations"—says Bakhtin—"Dostoevski seeks the highest
and most authoritative orientation, and he perceives it not as his own true
thought, but as another authentic human being and his discourse. The image of the ideal human being or the image of Christ represents for him the
resolution of ideological quests. This image or this highest voice must crown
the world of voices, must organize and subdue it."[30] According to Bakhtin's
words, the method of the continuous test of faithfulness of his convictions
for Dostoevsky was Christ and following of Him.[31]

Thus, according to Bakhtin, polyphonic unity, unity in multiplicity,
the center of which is Christ, is also at the base of Dostoevsky's polyphonic
novel. However, despite the fact that the literary critic and thinker used this
term only metaphorically, we would like to remind the reader that polyphony—"simultaneous singing in several voices"[32]—originated in the East as a
technique of liturgical music, and existed in the early Christian communities and in ninth to the thirteenth centuries was used in the West in the
monasteries and abbeys to adorn the liturgy.[33] So, we cannot ignore the fact
that the early polyphony was a singing technique made for the prayer of
the Church, i.e. for the common prayer of the church community, which
consisted in communion, the common unity of the personal prayers of each
of Christians.[34]

This understanding of unity in multiplicity, directed to Christ and
permeated by His love, is realized in the polyphonic community and coexistence of self-sounding, free voices, and it strongly differs from the
monological, monophonic sounding of one-conscious collectivism and
fragmented, disunited individualism, which found its incarnation in history, philosophy, culture, etc. of Europe (and America) and Russia since the
nineteenth century until today. In this sense, culture, understood as polyphony, radically differs (and even opposes) the culture of modernity, borne
from collectivism, individualism or any other anthropocentric worldview.

At the beginning of the twentieth century, in Soviet Russia, which was
attempting to build the socialist ideal and where the spiritual *sobornost'* was
replaced by faceless collectivism (Nikolai Berdyaev) and the great Russian

30. Ibid., 97.

31. See ibid., 72.

32. Gallo, *Historia de la Música*, 319.

33. See ibid., 101–3.

34. See ibid., 310.

culture was squeezed into the framework of Soviet realism, there were a lot of different personalities of culture—theologians, philosophers, writers, artists, musicians and others—who, despite all the difficulties, remained faithful to the tradition of the Church and to their religious experience and were able to create a "polyphonic" culture based on love to God and to each other in God. Among these persons we would like to distinguish the pianist Maria Yudina (1899–1970), theologian Father Pavel Florensky (1882–1937) and the theorist of culture Mikhail Bakhtin (1895–1975).

The life and work of Maria Yudina, the famous Russian pianist, a talented musician and thinker, was held in close relation and friendship with many Russian cultural figures, such as Mikhail Gnessin, Boris Pasternak, Fr. Vsevolod Shpiller, Sergey Prokofiev, Ivan Kanaev, Mikhail Prishvin, Dmitry Shostakovich, Vladimir Favorsky, Fr. Nikolai Golubtsov, Igor Stravinsky, Korney Chukovsky and others, but the names of Fr. Pavel Florensky and Mikhail Bakhtin were especially dear to her. For Yudina, brought up both spiritually and philosophically on the works of Vladimir Soloviev, Pavel Florensky, prince Sergey Trubetskoy, Vyacheslav Ivanov, Lev Karsavin and others, because of whom she converted to Orthodoxy in 1919, the friendship was "faithfulness to the grave and exchange of the spiritual gifts."[35] In fact, the friendship of Maria Yudina with Fr. Pavel, whom she met in 1927 in Saint Petersburg in the house of her spiritual father, Fyodor Andreev (1887–1929), and with Mikhail Bakhtin, the first meeting with which took place in 1918 in Nevel's philosophical circle, passed through her life and included their families also, whom she tirelessly helped, visited, maintained, corresponded with in the difficult years of the Stalinist period and throughout her life. Professor Yudina, "whose life to God—as she approved herself—was lying through art," was expelled from Conservatories of Saint Petersburg and of Moscow in 1929 and 1951, respectively, for unconcealed religiosity and in 1960, under the pretext of her transition to retirement, forcibly dismissed from the Gnessin Institute. Nevertheless, the great pianist, whose force and talent of playing, as whose personality, indeed, did not leave anyone indifferent (even Stalin), who loved the polyphony of Bach, the music of which she understood like a sounding Gospel, as well as the polyphonic music of other masters like Sergey Taneev, Mikhail Glinka, Alexander Glazunov, Nikolai Miaskovsky, Rodion Shchedrin, etc. She played their music many times, lived entirely for others, for friends, leaving nothing for herself, not having even her own piano and dispensing only the most necessary, but giving herself in love and living exclusively the precept of the love of God and thy neighbor.

---

35. Nazarov, *Portret.*

The lifelong friendship of Yudina with Bakhtin and with Florensky, this *philia* love, that existed in Yudina in parallel with agape love, which she exercised to those around here, is a vivid illustration of how the love of God and for each other in God, becomes a "treasure" of the human heart. Furthermore, that it is able to give rise to the unity of lives in the multiplicity of consciousness, freedoms, talents, creativities. This is the authentic source of true humanity, a "polyphonic" culture, which can offer an answer to the fragmented, rationalistic and materialistic culture of modernity.

# Bibliography

Bakhtin, Mikhail. *Problems of Dostoevsky's Poetics*. Translated by Caryl Emerson. Minneapolis: University of Minnesota Press, 1984.

Antoniy (Khrapovitskiy), mitropolit. *Izbrannyye trudy. Pis'ma. Materialy*. Moscow: Izdatel'stvo Pravoslavnogo Svyato-Tikhonovskogo Gumanitarnogo Universiteta, 2007.

Emel'yanov, Boris V., et al. *Istoriya russkoy filosofii*. Moscow: Akademicheskiy Proyekt, 2005.

Florenskiy, Pavel. "Zapiska o khristianstve i kul'ture." In *Sochineniya v chetyrekh tomakh*, 2:547–59. Moscow: Mysl', 1996.

Florensky, Pavel. *The Pillar and Ground of the Truth: An Essay in Orthodox Theodicy in Twelve Letters*. Translated by Boris Jakim. Princeton: Princeton University Press, 2004.

Gallo, F. Alberto. *Historia de la Música*. Vol. 1, *El Mundo Medieval. El Renacimiento*. Madrid: Akal, 2003.

Ioann (Shakhovskoy), arkhiyepiskop. *Izbrannoye*. Petrozavodsk: Svyatoy ostrov, 1992.

Nazarov, Yakov S. *Portret legendarnoy pianistki. Mariya Veniaminovna Yudina*. Documentary film. 2000.

Solovyov, Vladimir. *The Meaning of Love*. Translated by Jane Marshall, revised by Thomas R. Beier. Hudson, NY: Lindisfarne, 1985.

Sorokin, Pitirim A. *Chelovek. Tsivilizatsiya. Obshchestvo*. Moscow: Politizdat, 1992.

Vasilenko, Leonid I. *Vvedeniye v russkuyu religioznuyu filosofiyu*. Moscow: Izdatel'stvo Pravoslavnogo Svyato-Tikhonovskogo Gumanitarnogo Universiteta, 2009.

Yakovlev, Aleksandr I. *Ocherki istorii russkoy kul'tury XIX veka*. Moscow: Izdatel'stvo Pravoslavnogo Svyato-Tikhonovskogo Gumanitarnogo Universiteta, 2010.

# 5

# Pavel Florensky on Christ as the Basis of Orthodox Culture and Christian Unity

—Nikolai Pavluchenkov

Pavel Florensky was destined to live in a very difficult and ambiguous period of world history. He was born in 1882, when Russia and Europe seemed to be quite stable from the outside but internally the first disasters were ripening. These disasters, namely the First World War and the Russian Revolution of 1917, emphasized the relevance of how to attain an authentic Christian culture and unity. During the entire twentieth century, people kept searching for these ways alongside with the growing secularization of the society, making it worldlier, both in the "free" West and in Soviet Russia, where aggressive atheism had won. Florensky died after four years (1933–37) of imprisonment in Russian jails and cages, but before that, like many others, he had to witness the full-scale attempt of the new government to destroy the very basis of Christian religion and build a totally new godless culture, in which even the name of Christ would have been erased from people's minds forever.

The Russian Church in that period shed the blood of new martyrs in Christ's name, but still, every now and then, propagandists would appear who had voluntarily defrocked themselves to preach the so-called "scientific" atheism. It is no wonder that among Russian religious philosophers of the twentieth century it was most relevant to find the reasons for the ongoing refusal of Christians to believe in Christ the Savior. If the Christian culture of a great country can tumble down so quickly and to such a great extent (it is essential to remember that those were Russian Orthodox Christians who destroyed their own temples and took part in the destruction of the Christian heritage of their ancestors), there must be some concrete mechanisms that had been undermining this culture for ages. Denial of Christ must have been a latent process of which the Christians themselves were unaware. The events after 1917 only exposed the spiritual wounds of Russian society.

Florensky was one of the Russian philosophers who noticed and understood it. His estimation of what was happening surpassed the limits of any particularities, no matter how important they might seem. According to Florensky, any destructive process begins with some seemingly trifling situation when something other than Christ starts playing the most important role in the life of a Christian. It is this Christ-centric concept that Florensky considers to be the essential one for the formation of Christian culture and unity.

In general, Pavel Florensky's concept of culture is quite well known. During different periods of his religious and philosophical studies, he examined a number of culture-related topics. Already in one of his first lectures, "The First Steps of Philosophy" (1909), he maintained that in the history of the humankind "medieval" and "Renaissance" cultures alternated. In his *Pillar and Ground of the Truth*, Father Pavel described the Renaissance culture as non-organic, divided, subjective, distracted and superficial. He criticized severely the world's recognized masterpiece, the Mona Lisa by Leonardo Da Vinci. According to Florensky, all the mystery in her smile is no more than just a "smile of sin, seductiveness, and spiritual waywardness, a lecherous and corrupt expressing nothing positive . . . except some sort of inner confusion . . . without repentance."[1] All of this is said in the context of indicating the ontology of sin as "disharmony, decay, and decomposition of spiritual life" when the soul "loses its substantial unity" and gets lost itself "in a chaotic vortex of its own states."[2] For Florensky, it was common for the entire culture of Modern Age, which has lost its direct relation to the religious cult, reflecting directly the chaos in the human soul that strives to confirm its autonomy and independence from God.

In his later works (including *The Iconostasis*, 1922) and other lectures and articles of the 1920s) Florensky never gives up his quite radical position. At the same time, developing the philosophical concept of a symbol allowed him to clarify a number of important peculiarities of his perception

---

1  Florensky, *Pillar and Ground of the Truth*, 129–30.

2.  Ibid., 129.

of culture in general, and of a culture that positions itself based only on worldly, non-religious concepts that are beyond any cults. Many of the ideas of this prominent Russian philosopher are just as relevant nowadays as well.

In the late 1920s, two years before his first arrest and short-time exile,[3] Florensky, in his autobiographical article for *The Granat Encyclopedia* (1927), emphasized his role as a "medieval scholar." Obviously, he meant the medieval culture according to his classification, declaring his inclination to implement its main features. Those are, according to Father Pavel, first of all, a deep organicity and, as he wrote, "religious stability" of mindset. "Any culture," he wrote in his *Autobiography*, "is a targeted and intertwined system of means of substantializing a certain value perceived as a main and unconditional one, i.e. it serves to a certain object of belief."[4] This means that if we talk about Christian culture, such value must be nothing other than Christ Himself, but as this was a Soviet edition, there was no way Florensky could have declared that openly.

According to Florensky, "the belief defines the cult, and the cult defines the worldview, which is the base of culture."[5] If we go into more detail of this culture genesis plan, it reflects, first of all, *myth* going out of the cult as a synergy of formulas and concepts to *explain* the cult. Then the myth becomes the base of philosophy, literature and science, which are thus related with each other and with the cult base. However, striving for independence, they divide gradually, acquiring a more worldly character.

In the "symbolic ontology" created by Florensky (mostly in his later works) all this process, to some extent, is perceived as a totally normal direction of development. The spirit must reflect in a substance at different levels. At the same time, at each level it must be an *apparition of spirit* or, as Florensky puts it, a phenomenon that is inextricably intertwined with its noumenon. According to Florensky, this is the ontological nature of a symbol, where supreme existence shows through its lower level. It is this pivotal concept Father Pavel was referring to in the now well-known letter to Vladimir Vernadsky of September 21, 1929, where he gave the name of "pneumatosphere" to the material substances most "elaborated" by the spirit.[6] Among other things, certainly, it includes manifestations of culture, which makes them impossible to equal neither to the general circulation of

---

3. Florensky was arrested in 1929 and spent three months of his exile in Nizhny Novgorod.

4. Florenskiy, "Avtoreferat," 39.

5. Ibid.

6. Florenskiy, "Pis'mo Vernadskomu."

life in the biosphere, nor to what Vernadsky, following Teilhard de Chardin, called *the noosphere*.

Thus, in Florensky's "symbolic world concept," the activities of a person that are related to culture occupy *a special* place in the existence hierarchy and must not be identified with the cult itself. Florensky's concept "all the culture comes from a cult" does not want to limit the culture by a temple as it was before. The culture must be outside the temple, keeping its living inextricable connection with the cult. Otherwise it can become extinct, for in this case it is a phenomenon without a noumenon, which is, in Florensky's ontology, an empty "case" with no objective content which, like a mirage, does not exist in the world created by God.

If a cult is a direct involvement of a human into contacts with "other worlds" (as Florensky puts it, into connection with noumenal bases of existence), culture is the continuation of the cult in the realities of "earthly" life, in the world of phenomena, i.e. organization of life according to the impetuses given by the cult practice. Each lifestyle is defined by a corresponding culture, while cultural attitudes and values are "cult derivatives." The relation between cults and cultures has its own subtle consistent patterns, the violation of which is equally negative for both the cult and the culture: the cult (the essence of a religion) degenerates, being replaced by a system of rite beliefs, or by a speculative dogmatic scheme, not related to real religious experience, while culture decays, losing its objective reality.

For Florensky, to lose the objective reality means to go from the ontological level to a sheer *psychological one*, which is accompanied by losing real unity and, as a result, collapse of the self-conscious personality that belongs to the given culture. The same (i.e. a gap between the cult and the culture) explains the tragic replacement of spiritual values by the "nice" ones. Living in a completely worldly culture, one stops understanding the difference between those values, ending up having no idea of what is spiritual, considering just the subtle esthetical delight to be spiritual.

Florensky maintains that the supreme goal of a human being is to be "a liturgical person," i.e. do sacred things with themselves and with the world. It is the religious cult that is the center of the whole of existence, which has several other levels.[7] The problem is not some levels being closer to the center than others. Distortion, degradation and the eventual collapse of a phenomenon begin when the periphery loses contact with the center. In this case, the esthetic that must reveal the Divine Beauty is now "on its own,"

7. In the ontology of Florensky, these levels are characterized by different extent of the spirit reflecting in substance, and, respectively, by energetic tension. Each next level, according to Florensky, is called a phenomenon related to a noumenon (a level that is closer to the center). See Pavlyuchenkov, *Religiozno-filosofskoye naslediye*, 117–25.

and the person who does not feel the replacement begins praising spiritual "ugliness" as though it was "beautiful" and (like in the case of the *Mona Lisa*) admiring a sin that can bring nothing but destruction and death.

As for the concepts of sin and salvation, Florensky defines them mostly in ontological categories, which can make you believe that the issues of the religion as personal relationship and communication with God are for him one of the least important ones. Looking closer at his concept of culture shows us that this conclusion does not embrace his Christian vision to a full extent.

In late 1920s, in the Soviet publication of *The Granat Encyclopedia* Florensky managed to indicate clearly that Christ is a global factor that prevents the world from collapse. According to him, the law of chaos is the major law of the world, which does not only destroy everything but also unifies everything by erasing all beauty and harmony of the world's diversity. The only thing that can resist it is the Logos, which also must be the base of any culture, which is conscious struggle against world equalization.[8] Thus you can see two ideas here: firstly, culture possesses the necessary ontological function only if it is based on Christ; secondly, the culture that is being created in the Soviet Russia on the equalization paradigm is doomed to decay, for its goal is to be implemented without Christ.

In the early 1920s, Florensky spoke about the issues of Christian culture due to the revival of ways to unite Christians in Europe. It is well known that in that period a great ecumenical conference was prepared (it took place in Stockholm in 1925). Christians felt they needed to unite to face the growing threat of European secularization and the aggressive atheism in the newly formed Soviet Russia. In 1923, two articles by Florensky about this aspect were sent abroad, translated into English, and one of them (*Note on the Christianity and Culture*) was published in *The Pilgrim* in 1924. There, Father Pavel indicated that the Christian world is actually united internally, but only by one criterion—the decline of the Christian religion. It also launches a process of the formal union of Christian confessions "just for the sake of it," without Christians living in the truth and charity,[9] without the conscience of all Christians being aimed at Christ.[10] The Christians dispute on dogmas, canons, rites, but they approach both their own religion and that of the others "from outside, like archaeologists." One extremity is to consider traditions to be dogmas, the other is to prevaricate and, striving to seem united, call someone's creed errors the truth. The reason for all of

8. Florenskiy, "Avtoreferat," 39.

9. Florenskiy, "Zapiska o khristianstve i kul'ture," 643.

10. Ibid., 641.

this is lack of a "sincere attitude to Christ,"[11] which is the only one that can allow you to know the main from the secondary, and which makes all errors temporary in due time.

So what Florensky suggests is that all Christians stop their "defending apologetics towards each other" to analyze what place Christ occupies in their aspirations. "We must confess," he insists,

> that the real reason for the Christian world being split is not the differences in rites, beliefs or church organization, but deep mutual distrust in belief in Christ as the Son of God in flesh. We must confess that such suspicions are not vain, for the deepest spiritual base of the faith has really weakened, which shows the fruit of the lack of faith—the anti-Christian Culture.[12]

According to Florensky,

> What humankind needs today is Christian culture, a genuine culture genuinely related to Christ. Everyone must understand if they want and believe in one. If not, they should stop talking about Christianity, confusing themselves and the others with vague hopes for an unreal dream.

"In this case," adds Father Pavel, "Bolshevism is right in demanding efforts to organize life in some other way. In this case, the powerless protests against the Bolsheviks' giving up on Christian virtue ideals are naïve."[13]

This idea can be found in several works and notes by Pavel Florensky: the reason for something negative can be found, first of all, not in similar situations, not in external influences, not in someone sabotaging on purpose. The reason is to be found among the internal processes that bring it about. If the anti-Christian culture was brought about by the Christians themselves going away from God, you need to struggle with corresponding means against it: not by meetings, reunions and ecumenical conferences, not by endless resolutions disapproving of European secularization and the Bolshevik terror in Russia. It should be done by getting Christ back to the top of the hierarchy of values, both individually and socially.

In fact, Florensky emphasized a very important idea about Christian culture not being something homogenous and monotonous; it is an image of human art that cannot be limited by some strict rules. Dividing real errors (distortion of the creed) from local spiritual traditions, Father Pavel wrote that his appeal to the repentance of the Christian world "makes no

11. Ibid., 646–47.
12. Ibid., 642.
13. Ibid., 641.

one give up on the forms that they have acquired along with their faith, it only suggests that everyone plunge deeper into their own faith. The only thing it imposes is spiritual activity."[14]

In other words, if the Christian culture were a building, it could have a lot of possible architectural solutions. The essential thing is for them to have one basis, which is Christ. Father Pavel believed that sincere aspiration to Christ and, imposition of all expectations on Christ, without seeming unification and while conserving all the rich diversity of different Christian traditions would help to gradually overcome all of the errors which had accumulated in the past.

We can show that all those ideas have a solid ontological basis in different works by Florensky. For example, in his *Contemplations*, the Eucharist is the ontological basis of the world; the "entire circle of existence is around" a part of the holy sacraments.[15] In the end, his wish to pave the way to churching all of the aspects of the life of a human means the idea of putting the Eucharist back into the center of life. It hallows the whole world and the life of a person. In particular, a dinner table is the continuation of a mass or better, its end."[16] Understanding this, our ancestors tried not to lean on the table, not to knock on it, not to put their hats on it etc. Defining the values of one's earthly life, one coordinated with the Eucharist, i.e. with Christ. This idea is a major one in all the works of Father Pavel concerning the interaction between Church and culture. According to him, you must begin with the main basis of the Church—with Christ, or better, with defining one's attitude towards Christ. "If in the cultural aspects we are not with Christ, we are inevitably against Christ, because there can be no neutrality towards God."[17] And then we must bear in mind that "the God that we only concede a corner in our lives, leaving other things to other people, is not perceived as God."[18]

In spite of his conviction that the modern Christian Church had managed to preserve all of the purity of early Christianity,[19] despite the positive impression of orthodox, sacred service as the highest manifestation of any religious cult, Florensky had no illusions concerning the spiritual state which the Russian church was in at the moment of the disaster of 1917. Already in 1909, he was very concerned about the Russian "folk's" faith on

14. Ibid., 647.

15. Florenskiy, *Filosofiya kul'ta*, 468–79.

16. Ibid., 416.

17. Florenskiy, "Zapiska o khristianstve i kul'ture," 640.

18. Ibid., 638.

19. El'chaninov et al., *Istoriya religii*, 161–63.

what he referred to as "the lifestyle,"[20] i.e. the lifestyle customs that can be called the folk culture that formed beyond direct contact with sacred service and the Eucharist as its center. As soon as those customs were slightly undermined by the growth of industrialization in Russia in the 1900s, by the reforms of 1905 etc., such a culture in Russia collapsed, and its ruins served as the basis for the same Russian people to build a surrogate culture aimed at the new "social class," that had no lifestyle at all, which allowed them to acquire newly created conditions of life.

"The present condition of Russia, wrote Florensky in 1923, is not a random disease or lack of funds, it is a deep destruction of the state that had been weakened by many generations."[21] Even today, in these words we can hear the appeal not to repeat previous errors: the reviving Orthodox culture in Russia must be aimed not at some "Russian traditions" just for the sake of it, which would be, according to Florensky, "replacing religion by ethnicity"[22]), but at the universal church-ism, the head and the heart of which would be Christ. And in general, the only thing religious activists need is complete and eternal "redemption" as a change of way of thinking, so that Christ would be their major treasure. Then, the folk culture hallowed by Christ, with all its peculiarities and local uniqueness, will really make humans organize their entire lives around the Eucharist, which is the genuine center of existence. The simplest way of expressing his idea of reviving Christian culture is that first things come first. Then everything else will "automatically" fall into place in the values hierarchy for both each individual and for the society in general.

## Bibliography

El'chaninov, Aleksandr V. et al. *Istoriya religii*. Moscow: Pol'za, 1909.

Florenskiy, Pavel A. "Avtoreferat." In *Sochineniya*, 1:37–43. Moscow: Mysl', 1994.

———. *Filosofiya kul'ta*. Moscow: Mysl', 2004.

———. "Pis'mo Vernadskomu V. I." *Nyne i prisno* 1 (2004) 31–32.

———. "Zapiska o khristianstve i kul'ture." In *Khristianstvo i kul'tura*, 637–648. Moscow: Folio, 2001.

———. "Zapiska o pravoslavii." In *Khristianstvo i kul'tura*, 627–36. Moscow: Folio, 2001.

Florensky, Pavel. *The Pillar and Ground of the Truth: An Essay in Orthodox Theodicy in Twelve Letters*. Translated by Boris Jakim. Princeton: Princeton University Press, 2004.

20. Ibid., 187–88.

21. Florenskiy, "Zapiska o pravoslavii," 635.

22. Ibid.

Pavlyuchenkov, Nikolay N. *Religiozno-filosofskoye naslediye svyashchennika Pavla Florenskogo. Antropologicheskiy aspekt.* Moscow: Izdatel'stvo Pravoslavnogo Svyato-Tikhonovskogo Gumanitarnogo Universiteta, 2012.

# 6

# The Problem of Christian Culture in the Philosophy of Vasily Zenkovsky

—OLEG ERMISHIN

THE IDEA OF CHRISTIAN culture was the leading one in the work of Vasily Zenkovsky during his emigrant period (1920–62). In 1923 Zenkovsky published the article "The Idea of Orthodox Culture" in which he represented the religious and philosophical ideal.[1] The reason which induced Zenkovsky to address the justification of the idea of Orthodox culture was his understanding of the deep European spiritual crisis which had achieved its most vivid manifestation in the form of World War I. According to Zenkovsky, the European people had reached a deadlock and the creative origins of European civilization were unsettled yet the external material and technical aspects of culture prevented the realization of the process of internal disintegration.

Zenkovsky was of the opinion that any culture is religious in its foundations. In his opinion, the crisis of European civilization is primarily the crisis of Catholic ideas and the tragedy of a Christian culture which had lost its unity. The Catholic Church began to look for ways of directly affecting historical reality through external power and hierarchy. Russian culture, despite its close interrelation with Western Europe, represents another type of culture based on the Orthodox idea of inner personal transformation.

1. Zen'kovskiy, "Ideya pravoslavnoy kul'tury."

Zenkovsky was convinced that the true conversion of the person to Christ arises not by means of external authority, but only at "the peak of freedom."

Zenkovsky claimed that it was necessary to look not just for "indirect external submission of a historical material, but the transformation of human soul and culture within."[2] The transformation of the human soul is to be concurrent with the creation of Orthodox cultural system which is inextricably connected with the comprehensive religious ideal. Zenkovsky considered that the concept of freedom was to be found in the origin of the Orthodox ethos and therefore he claimed that "the system of Orthodox culture cannot be anything other but the system of free creativity, free activity—but in Christ and with Christ."[3]

Zenkovsky developed the concept of Christian freedom in the article *Freedom and Conciliarity* (1927) and the brochure *Gift of Freedom* (1932). He distinguished between natural freedom and Christian freedom. In spite of a formal resemblance, Christian freedom is a special graceful order in which natural freedom changes and unfolds. However, Christian freedom had different ways of developing in history. According to Zenkovsky, the outward universalism in the Catholic Church distorted the idea of Christian freedom like the individualism and rationalism of the Protestant Churches did it in its turn. Zenkovsky wrote, "Freedom in Christ reveals in the personality, but not the personality is the subject of freedom but Church as a whole."[4] The world in its ideal foundations mystically abides in Church, and this mystical concentration can become real only through freedom.

Zenkovsky considered that the concept of the Christian gift of freedom turned into "law" and the formal principle in the twentieth century. The finding of freedom is said not to a spiritual transformation, and there is enough declaration of "natural freedom." Zenkovsky, on the contrary, understood freedom as a choice between good and evil. In his opinion, original freedom is a life in Truth, in the Church. Freedom and creativity are the basis for the creation of the Christian culture.

In the first half of the 1920's Zenkovsky wrote the work which he called in the preface *Introduction to the system of Orthodox philosophy*, but in fact the manuscript could equally be titled *Introduction to the system of Orthodox culture* (a move left undone when it was first published in 2011). In the work mentioned, Zenkovsky analyzed European culture and civilization to understand the reasons for the crisis of modern European society. In his opinion, the creation of the entire integral religious culture might offer

2. Ibid., 77.
3. Ibid., 83.
4. Zen'kovskiy, "Svoboda i sobornost,'" 173.

a way out of the growing crisis. Christianity is the foundation of European civilization, and after a stage of disintegration, it should seek the creation of new unity.

One of the signs of a deep European crisis for Zenkovsky was the surging and development of the strength of the spiritual quest and mental distemper, the reason being, according to him, the imperfection of social and political relations. Zenkovsky noticed: "Under the cover of refined forms and accomplishments made long beforehand—day by day, among the daily routine and the little nothings of life—in-depth contradictions in the external and internal life of Europeans became constant."[5] Zenkovsky's main task was to realize this historical experience and to make it the basis for cultural creativity. If there was a disintegration of spiritual life in the autonomous spheres, a system which is capable of accomplishing the synthesis of cultural processes is necessary.

Zenkovsky decomposed the material aspects of life which reflect the spiritual essence of culture, he analyzed the policy. In his opinion, political institutions are an example of the legal creativity of social groups, and the essence of legal creativity itself is the development of a sense of justice. The formation of the nation states and their emergence at a time of special cultural national types was one of the results of the political processes during the Modern Age of European history. The communication of nationalities leads to intensive cultural development and the prosperity of cultural types. At the same time, cultural synthesis in no way weakens the social unity of nationalities. According to Zenkovsky, the nationality is the collective personality which forms a metaphysically steady social and spiritual unity.

Zenkovsky believed that Christianity assumes the political ideal is understood as the transformation of the inorganic international relations in organic and harmonious relations. Zenkovsky wrote penetratingly about contemporary life: "Political balance was not and could not be: there can be age of historical calm, of marshalling forces and preparations for future war, but there are no conditions for political balance."[6] The contradiction between an instinct of national self-preservation and the idea of imperialism is the reason for such political instability. National creativity conducts the self-affirmation of each particular nation, while in the idea of imperialism there lives an aspiration beyond this definition, to a broader sense of mankind. As a result of the similar development of ideas, the European people had come to a historical standstill when it was impossible to resolve the antagonism of two historical factors. According to Zenkovsky, imperialistic plans are in

5. Zen'kovskiy, "Vvedeniye v sistemu filosofii pravoslaviya," 8.
6. Ibid., 45.

many respects based on the distorted interpretation of Christianity, when the creation of God's Kingdom was not understood as the transformation of human soul, but something built up by means of external political association. Zenkovsky saw the resolution of the deadlock in the Christianization of national development when there would be a veritable spiritual association of mankind when there was no oppression of nationality, and each nation found the right of free development. The political and economic life of Europe for Zenkovsky was closely interconnected. Zenkovsky found a contradiction in the economic relations between economic individualism and an economic unitary system. At the heart of economic individualism lies the property instinct, a thirst of enrichment destroys the spiritual foundations of society. However, the intensive development of economic relations leads to the creation of close international relations, to interaction between national economies. The contradictions between individualism and the international economic system cannot be overcome and, therefore, Zenkovsky claimed that "the way of internally overcoming economic individualism opens only on a way of religious transformation of public relations."[7]

According to Zenkovsky, the problems of policy and economy must be considered in a cultural context. Only by analyzing the spirit of modern culture is it possible to understand the essence of political and economic processes. Zenkovsky considered the basic fact of culture to be "interaction between the personality and the social environment."[8] People in history are the real carriers of the creative act, but they are implanted in a tradition, impregnated with the spirit of the times and included in some social structures. Therefore, the fundamental duality is already rooted in culture and history: the historical process assumes individual creativity, but the subject of this process appears to be the social whole that is the whole of mankind. Based on a similar duality, conflict inevitably arises when imperialistic tendencies, having a central underlining idea of the world state, encounter the resistance of certain nations.

The dialectics of Zenkovsky's reflections leads to the argument that the appeal to the concept of the personality is inevitable for an understanding of culture. Zenkovsky considered personality to be the special beginning of identity which has metaphysical roots. The metaphysical kernel of identity defines the life of the personality, the aspiration to justice and good. According to Zenkovsky, the good appears for the person in the form of three ideals: individual, social and religious (ideals of advantage, social truth and sanctity). However, the moral consciousness of modern times tended to

7. Ibid., 86.
8. Ibid., 91.

understand the good as something impersonal and transpersonal. The general and theoretical conception of good leads to its depersonalization and thus will result in a culture's depersonalization. Zenkovsky notices: "The impersonal good, like Moloch, swallows up hide and hair all personal, individual, and as a result we receive that system of an ethical impersonalism, system of suppression and the abolition of the personality."[9] Such a process of depersonalization in culture means the creation of general and abstract ideals and all concrete reality with living people are made a sacrifice to them.

In Zenkovsky's opinion, it is necessary to understand the two roots of personality. On the one hand, personality is connected with the metaphysical realm, while on the other it is related to the social sphere. Bond-breaking with one of these spheres necessitates the decline of personality. Relying upon this idea, Zenkovsky considered personal enhancement to need to happen in view of individual and social aspects of life. The internal, spiritual transformation of the personality assumes the creation of a just social order.

How can the social ideal be carried out, and what prevents one from doing it? Western Europe inherited the developed private, individual law from the Roman Empire. Over the course of history, Roman law led to the formation of a specific legal culture, to a steady tradition that favored the external regulation of social relations. Certainly, the development of a sense of justice had a number of positive results and in many respects promoted a culture blossoming, but at a certain stage it led to juridical rationalism and a desk-top approach to the person as subject of law. Then, according to Zenkovsky, Christianity with its teaching about love began to resist legal formalism. Zenkovsky considered juridical rationalism to create unnatural social relations while Christianity creates an organic social culture. Only by harmoniously combining the two types of social relations is it possible to avoid the framework of juridical rationalism entering Christianity, resulting in the intermixture of different foundations.

Zenkovsky noted a substantial difference in their understandings of personality: juridical equality of personality means only the external attitude to the person who is the carrier of rights, just as Christianity approves of the metaphysical exclusiveness of personality, the uniqueness of her internal, spiritual life. Furthermore, legal relations are imposed during modern times on impersonal economic relations which have an exclusively external, material character. In Zenkovsky's opinion, the juridical culture and economic system has its limits in the creation of a social order and shall be added with the new organic social relations which are based on freedom and love.

9. Ibid., 121.

Essentially, Zenkovsky tried to prove a new type of Christian culture. The Christianization of culture is necessary for harmony to exist between the personality and the social environment. The unity of mankind is not possible on the basis of political or economic structures but through the creation of general cultural values. The reconstruction of Christian culture has to lead to fraternal relations between the people.

The idea of a Christian culture became the basis for the subsequent system of Christian philosophy (*The Foundations of Christian Philosophy*, 2 volumes, 1961–64). In the aforementioned Zenkovsky's archival text from the 1920s, two chapters are missing. They were probably published in the form of articles or included in the first edition of *The Foundations of Christian Philosophy*. The most probable evidence for such a hypothesis is that the chapter "Two ways of world cognition (The problem of cultural dualism)" from the first volume of *The Foundations of Christian Philosophy*. Zenkovsky saw the contradiction between two types of knowledge in the culture of the nineteenth and twentieth centuries—an understanding by means of autonomous reason and Christian knowledge. Thomas Aquinas separated Revelation and the natural light of reason (*lumen naturale rationis*) in the thirteenth century and thus formed a model of scientific knowledge independent of the Church. The gap between Christian theology and science led to the creation of two cultures—religious and secular cultures. The contradictions between two cultures assume two different doctrines about the world and the personality. The fact that modern science has ancient sources (for example, Aristotle's rationalism and monism of Plotinus) won minds in Europe as well due to the fact that Christianity had seldom and inadequately researched the problems of the world and personality. Science seeks to understand the world without God, by means of autonomous reason. The knowledge in science is based on universal (impersonal) reason that, in combination with an understanding of the person as the subject of law and the economic relations, lead to the further depersonalization of culture. In Zenkovsky's opinion, Christian philosophy should be appended to traditional theology. When this occurs, Christian philosophy will include the doctrines about the world and personality and could demonstrate the foundation of religious culture. Zenkovsky did not supply a comprehensive answer to the question about the possible revival of Christian culture. He considered that the essential condition for overcoming of cultural dualism was not only the freedom of the secular (scientific) world-view but also the religious. The conception of cultural dualism is the conclusion of Zenkovsky's reflections about the essence and future of Christian culture.

## Bibliography

Zen'kovskiy, Vasiliy V. "Ideya pravoslavnoy kul'tury." In *Sobraniye sochineniy*, 2:65–86. Moscow: Russkiy put', 2008.

———. "Svoboda i sobornost.'" In *Sobraniye sochineniy*, 2:161–83. Moscow: Russkiy put', 2008.

———. "Vvedeniye v sistemu filosofii pravoslaviya." In *Sobraniye sochineniy*, 4:7–210. Moscow: Russkiy put', 2011.

# 7

# Overcoming the Gap between Religion and Culture

*The Life and Works of Mother Maria (Skobtsova)*

—Natalia Likvintseva

The life of Saint Mary of Paris (Mother Maria Skobtsova, 1891–1945), canonized in the Eastern Orthodox Church in 2004, strikes us by combining things that seem to have an indisposition to combine. On the one hand, it is a life journey of Christian endeavor, of true self-dedication and devotion to all who need help. After becoming a nun she has founded a society "Pravoslavnoe delo" in Paris that extended active aid to needy Russian emigrants, opened some cheap dormitories, especially a famous House on Lourmel Street where the poor could receive board and lodging. She also served those social groups that were completely forgotten and helpless, including those suffering from tuberculosis and mentally diseases before laying down her life for her friends—as a member of French Resistance she was arrested by the Gestapo and died in Ravensbrück concentration camp. On the other hand, it is a cultural creative process, of the various and full realization of creativity. Before emigration she was a poet close to the Acmeist Movement, published two volumes of poems and produced paintings. After emigrating, she wrote short stories and memoirs, continued to write poems which reflected her spiritual life, wrote philosophical and theological articles, painted icons and made embroidery. From a young age until the end of her life, her name ranked with those of the most famous cultural figures of the twentieth century: among her friends there were poets like Alexander Blok and Nikolai Gumilev, philosophers Nikolai Berdyaev, Georgy Fedotov, church leaders and theologians like Metropolitan Eulogius (Georgievsky) of Paris and Rev. Sergey (Bulgakov).

The problem of creativity was at the center of cultural pursuits in the Silver Age, the Renaissance of Russian culture and religious philosophy. The future Mother Maria, who at the time was known as the poet Elizaveta Kuzmina-Karavayeva, actively participated in cultural pursuits: she visited Gumilev's "Guild of Poets" and Vyacheslav Ivanov's "Wednesdays" in his famous "Tower" and at the same time she became ever more moved towards Christianity, studied theology and did part-time theological studies at the Saint Petersburg Theological Academy. In the center of attention for many artists of that era was the problem of life and creativity, the fusion of art and life: the gap between them looked dangerous and threatening. After the catastrophe of the Russian Revolution and Civil War, many thinkers found that the facts previously considered by them as discoveries and a new stages of cultural development appeared to be defeat and deprivation. In 1924, Elizaveta Skobtsova (it was her family name after marrying Daniil Skobtsov) published her memoires about the Silver Age titled *Latest Romans*. She described the creative ascent of the cultural Renaissance as the reverse side of another gap—namely the gap between the intelligentsia and the common people, the isolation of the intellectual elite from the masses, the parallel existence of two worlds with different languages so that their clash in the Revolution was inevitable. Already at that time she understood the disastrous consequences of this division and tried to overcome it by coming back "to the earth" returning to her family mansion near Anapa, by getting into politics (she was a member of the Socialist-Revolutionary Party, and was the mayor of Anapa during the revolutionary years) and making efforts to influence social and public life directly.

Later, when pondering the problem of creativity and the questions linked with it—already not only in cultural and philosophical but also in the theological perspective—she saw the reasons for and the roots of this division more deeply and clearly. She realized that they are all derived from the gap between formally belonging to the Church and true creativity, from the dividing culture into the "church" and secular parts, from the distance between creative people and the Church. Like a true Church person, Mother Maria conceived of this problem (together with the catastrophes suffered by Russia in the twentieth century resulting in millions of victims) from inside the Church itself, which means in the light of her own responsibility, and the guilt of all us as Christians and Church members who were incapable of avoiding all these divisions. Such a viewpoint helps to overcome the impasse of the old question on the gap between culture and life, intellectuals and the common people, between true creativity and Church culture, because it is the Church who would be able to make the links between such completely separate parts and bring true creativity back "into the Church gates." In the article entitled *In the Search for Synthesis* (1929) Mother Maria considers the cultural development of mankind and the problem of creativity from the point of view of Godmanhood (*Bogochelovechestvo*, the term of Vladimir Soloviev), as a perfect, God-inspired realization of the Divine plan about man.

> We should struggle now not for a divine principle and not for an anthropological principle—not for the Church without man and not for Humanism, but for the Godmanhood. We have to realize fully a Church dome above us, we have to receive the mystery of the Revelation to the full extent. And at the same time we need to emphasize through and through and to bless not only the right, but the duty of humanity to make human deeds.[1]

Only such synthesis of true church conscience with true creativity and attention to culture can be a proper foundation for the future. It ensures against the depletion of culture and gives the show that Christianity is not a dying religion in a secular world, not just a formal belief in rituals, but a living entity.

Mother Maria reflects theologically not only on the destiny of creativity in the modern world but also on the sources of all creativity rooted in Creator. In her article "The Sources of Creativity" she analyses in detail all of the patterns of creativity and creative actions in the Bible. The author concentrates most attention on the evangelical idea of creativity as it is presented in the fourth Gospel, trying to follow Saint John's usage of the verb "to create" and discovering "several parallel lines that define the creative act as a relationship between God-Creator and man-creator."[2] Contemplating the gospel image of Christ, Mother Maria comes to the understanding that "out of all men-creators Jesus Christ, being the perfect man, was also a perfect creator, He was the most creative person—the absolute Creator. It is true even when we talk of him as a man. And even more so when we

---

1. Mat' Mariya (Skobtsova), *Vospominaniya*, 2:134.
2. Ibid., 140.

speak about him as a divine being. The Divine Man is the ultimate creative incarnation."[3]

Then the example for the human creativity can be founded in the creative behavior of Christ and creative principles proclaimed by Himself: "My food is to do the will of him who sent me, and to complete his work" (John 4:34); "the Son can do nothing on his own, but only what he sees the Father doing; for whatever the Father does, the Son does likewise" (John 5:19). Peering into this example of perfect creativity totally free from either self-expression or self-realization, but merely trying to become an obedient instrument in the hand of the creating Father, Mother Maria discovers in this mystery of the creative obedience, a feature rarely associated with creative activity, but in fact forming the core of Divine creation. The name of that quality is Love. "What is a possibility of such creative experience and of the transformation of this mission done by the Father?—she writes—And yet I am not alone, because the Father is with me." "And all mine are thine, and thine are mine. . ." This last text, with its absolute turn to the Father—there is not only a unilateral penetration of the Son by the will of the Father—there is an interpenetration, there is a law of the interpenetrating love. The Son is not a "tool" of the Father, but He is at one with Him, the creative will of the Son through the action of creative love is identified with the creative will of the Father. And the moment of creativity originates even earlier—from the moment of voluntary obedience of the Son based on His Divine love—to the will of the Father. It would be wrong to say: "The Father creates by His Son" or "The Son is an instrument of the creating Father." We have to say: "In Christ's deeds and creativity these two are creating, the Father and the Son—the Father, sending His Son, and the Son, accepting his mission from the Father. They create in the undivided unity of creative love."[4]

Therefore, the love that is at the heart of true creativity does not separate the man-creator from God and the world, but becomes a new way of approaching them, a new link that unites man with God as the source of love and with the world as its object, with all these afflicted, hungry and miserable persons whom Mother Maria's served up to the end of her life. She writes,

> So the force behind any creativity on earth is the Spirit of Truth which teaches, proclaims and enables one to communicate with the primary source of all creativity in the world. This makes it impossible for creativity to be isolated—by its nature, creativity would be the act of a sort of *sobornost*,' of a sort of absolute

3. Ibid., 142-43.
4. Ibid., 143-44.

communication, not only with God, but through God with the whole world, because all the world in its possibilities defined as if one with God.[5]

In this gospel-based concept of creativity there is one more aspect which is essential for the understanding of the fruitful and gradual process of overcoming the division between religion and creative culture that happened in Mother Maria's life: it is the unusually wide range of meanings of the term "creativity" in her texts. The reasons for this breadth can be found in the same Gospel according to John, in the spectrum of meanings for the word "to create," in the list of creative actions performed by the most creative person—the Divine Man Jesus Christ, thereby demonstrating "the creative character of all the Son's actions on earth,"[6] i.e. of any true act of man, any contribution to the reservoir of "common actions."

In her article announcing the foundation of the society Orthodox Action (*Pravoslavnoe Delo*, 1935) she calls for grand words to be left behind in favor of "little acts."[7] In this regard, her work in the kitchen where she spent the most of her day cooking for a soup kitchen in the house at Lourmel is no less a creative act than her poems or embroideries. Thus, such a wide interpretation of creativity that unites it with simple human deeds for our neighbors returns creativity to its divine origins, and opening it for love and "the communication not only with God but through God with the whole world,"[8] becomes a step towards the "synthesized" "whole culture." The necessity of it is proved in Mother Maria's article "In the Search for Synthesis."[9] Let us look at a model of such culture, more precisely at a model of something greater than culture itself and at the same time includes it, namely, the wholeness of life. A sort of laboratory for creating this wholeness became the favorite "offspring" of Mother Maria—the famous House at Lourmel Street, opened in 1934. It was an incarnation of the principle of an open Church: a hospitable house where all are welcomed. First of all it was a dormitory where cheap rooms were available for rent: cheap lodging was the first need for emigrants, because in order to find a job (there were the years of economic crisis and unemployment) they had to have a permanent place of residence. In the house there was also a soup kitchen that fed many more people than the residents. There was a Church, but attending services was not obligatory for the inhabitants. In the evenings, various encounters

5. Ibid., 147.

6. Ibid., 141.

7. Kuz'mina-Karavayeva, *Izbrannoye*, 362.

8. Mat' Mariya (Skobtsova), *Vospominaniya*, 2:147.

9. Ibid., 134.

and meetings took place in the refectory: missionary and other courses, Berdyaev's Academy of philosophy, literature and theological disputes, Sunday cultural center. Through them, a lot of people were encouraged to think, to create, to communicate with each other. The payment for board and lodging, although very low, often symbolic, nevertheless transferred the idea behind this house from the domain of charity as an impersonal donation into the domain of respectful attention to every person who paying his franc for dinner or helping in the kitchen could participate in the common activity of the housekeeping. In this realization of the idea of communal life, two moments are of the special importance. First, this was life in its everyday reality, and the second, this life was shared, all the residents and guests were included into the "oneness of acting."[10] This life becomes alive indeed through its connection to the Life Giver, to One who is Life himself; only this way it can be a gift for all who need, for all who are near. The House at Lourmel Street was designed as such place of shared and gifted life.

We can share our life only in our joint activity; life can flow through it like through our capillaries. The importance of the idea of "activity" organizing the commonality of life and the "synthetic culture" created through it, is reflected in the founding in 1935 the society named the Orthodox Action with the main office in the same House at Lourmel Street. Mother Maria became the president of this society, her close friend Feodor Pyanov was its secretary, among its members there were a famous philosopher Nikolai Berdyaev, a historian and a religious thinker Georgy Fedotov, a historian of literature and critic Konstantin Mochulsky. Among the founders there was the famous theologian Father Sergey Bulgakov. The Metropolitan Evlogy (Georgievsky) of Paris blessed this new initiative. The uniqueness of the Orthodox Action and of its tasks is quite important for our reflection over the process of bridging the gap between religion and culture. This society was purely a religious organization (its title clearly reflects it), it was founded for specific and practical purposes of charity and Christian love. At the same time, among its members there were prominent thinkers, the authors of famous books and articles, professionals in their domains that had realized fully their rich creative talents. They understood the unusual and new task which they were given well: not only producing simple acts of charity but creating the space for the communal life where a place could be found for all those who need it, and it would be impossible to give a beggar a piece of bread, without seeing him as a personality, for this piece of bread would really become the bread of life. The new character of this task encouraged them not only to think and be aware of the methodology of this "deed"

---

10.  Mat' Mariya (Skobtsova), *Vospominaniya*, 1:151.

but to draw theological conclusions from their experience. The real act of Christian help to a neighbor and the writing of a theological text, the text of culture (in the wide sense of the word) appeared here as two intertwined tasks. This commonality of life that was born in the process of this joint activity also influenced the character of the text of culture that was created as a result of common reflection: in 1939 the group published their collection of articles (the authors thought to do the first number of a periodical but it turned out to be the first and the last number). Apart from the articles by all of the authors mentioned above, the book also included the text by Rev. Lev Gillet who was close to the Orthodox Action. It is significant that each author was ready to put his/her name under each of the articles in this collection, to such an extent that they realized their "oneness of mind."[11]

Right from the beginning it was clear for the participants of the Orthodox Action that they were trying to represent and articulate something that was not yet evident and in existence, something unknown and required, that they wanted to find and approach: "It is not something that has already got some experience and tradition in the world, but something that is just sought-after."[12] This way the theological thought turned out to be a prophesy, a prediction of something that had to appear in the future. In the same article, Mother Maria wrote:

> In a hundred years there will be an order or a Fraternity, a real living organism, a true *sobornost,*' an ecclesiastical body, the Body of Christ. Christ will be the Head of this Body, in this sense it will be a true little ecclesia, the real part of the whole Universal Orthodox Church. This organism will contain an alive, loving, rejoicing and suffering Heart—an inner group of people that are united ideologically, spiritually and fraternally. They, with their united and intense life, with their love, with their ideological oneness and with their desire to be active, will nourish and unite the whole organism staying with it in a real and unseparated connection. This organism will not be some public charity institution, but the *sobornost*' itself, the idea of the union of personalities projected on all kinds of human activity. Whereas there may be an infinite variety of practical activities. If there will be schools, then all the pupils of such schools would be not only well-educated young people but also an inseparable

11. Mother Maria in the introduction to the second volume of this book (that was not be published), remembering the first one, wrote: "In the strict sense, in the domain of intellectual life of the 'Orthodox Action' our published book realizes such degree of our oneness that each its article could be signed by each of the authors of other articles." Ibid., 253.

12. Ibid., 256.

part of the whole organism together with their teachers and the creators of the whole action. The same could be said about dormitories, refectories, about groups involved in any activity. It will be a real actualization of the common action, because in some depth the Orthodox Action can exist only as a Common Action, as Liturgy coming from the Church into the world.[13]

Thus, one can see that the work to overcome the gap between religion and culture turns out to be fruitful in both cultural and religious sense when neither one nor another part of this dichotomy is accentuated, but they both integrate and develop into embracing them entirely. That entirety turns out to be the alive life, the alive and creative common action in which each person can realize his own potential and through this realization already can deny himself and come out to meet the needs of other people, one's neighbors, anyone who needs our help here and now.

## Bibliography

Kuz'mina-Karavayeva, Elizaveta Yu. *Izbrannoye*. Moscow: Sovetskaya Rossiya, 1991.
Mat' Mariya (Skobtsova). *Vospominaniya. Stat'i. Ocherki.* 2 vols. Paris: YMCA-Press, 1992.

13. Ibid., 262–63.

# 8

# Apology of Culture in *The Journals* of Father Alexander Schmemann

—Svetlana Panich

Russia needs Pushkin much more than Typikon. It is impossible to kill for the love of Pushkin, to murder or to imprison in his name. For the love of Typikon all these things are quite possible . . .

—Rev. Alexander Schmemann, *Journals*[1]

In the address to the Memorial Conference on the theological heritage of Rev. Alexander Schmemann that took place in Paris in December of 2008, the Russian poet Olga Sedakova thanked Father Alexander for "justification and blessing of poetry," for his ability to discern in it a message "of salvation that is more powerful than death."[2] A reading of the *Journals*, first published in Russian in 2005[3] allows us to extend this observation to his approach to culture as whole. A great number of names and cultural allusions leave no doubts about the place of culture in Schmemann's theology—it was a source

1. Shmeman, *Dnevniki*, 81.

2. Sedakova, "Poeziya kak vesti," 20.

3. For English edition see Schmemann, *Journals*; the entries absent in the English version are quoted from the Russian edition.

and a "sustenance," nourishing his vision, creating the very "air" for the development of his theological thought, determining and explaining the ways and process of the Church history,[4] defining the sense and flow of time, in which the timeless sacrament of Kingdom is celebrated. Such a perception of culture as a "home of being," as Heidegger would say, explains a plenty of literary and philosophical quotations, not only serving as an authoritative confirmation or didactic illustration, or pointing to the broadness of the author's intellectual horizons, but "shaping" his thought, completing it, bearing even more significant message than the author's narrative itself:

What, who should one be in this world? What is the meaning of life here of this earth? Understandable, true are the words:

> but then the words—a child, an animal, a flower. We must feed, cultivate, "educate" a child, an animal, a flower. We are a part of history, "in the sweat of our brow," in creativity. What remains, what is sure is a *simple sense of duty* (cf. the last words of a simple sailor in one of Bunin's short stories: "I think that I was a rather good sailor"). Simplicity, clarity, ontological modesty of Christianity.[5]

It would be right to say that Alexander Schmemann does his theology "from inside culture" taken in a huge range between "his constant friend,"[6] "terrifically dear infidel, debaucher and blotter"[7] Paul Léautaud, the paradoxical, tragically honest Julien Green and T. S. Eliott, Paul Claudel, Alexander Pushkin, Leo Tolstoy, Georgy Adamovich, Andrey Platonov and Alexander Solzhenitsyn. As his critics sarcastically noticed, "he prefers secular literature many times more than writings of the Church Fathers." It is true. As he has confessed himself,

> if someone would learn the sources of my theology (!) he would scarcely guess that, for instance, Nicolas Kasbasilas, Dyonisius the Areopagite and others like them made me really depressed. What did really play the strange, but doubtless role in *cheminement obscur* of my worldview, thoughts and convictions these are ministering in the church, Russian and French poetry, André Gide, the diaries of Julien Green and of Paul Léautaud, and infinitely many of various biographies."[8]

4. Such an approach to culture defines, for instance, the methodology and style of Schmemann's key historical writing, *Historical Road.*

5. Schmemann, *Journals*, 269–70.

6. Shmeman, *Dnevniki*, 602.

7. Ibid., 36.

8. Ibid., 236.

*The Journals* reveal a very attentive, thankful and passionate reader. His judgments about certain figures can be quite short ("The child in Tolstoy's personality is genius, while the adult in him is infinitely stupid"[9]), but such harshness is explained not so much by petulancy of literary tastes, as by his belief in the highest responsibility of culture, seen as a "space of Revelation." For keeping faith, he wrote, it is better to read good philosophers and writers, even agnostics, than theologians,[10] and his "reader's lists," which come across *The Journals*, clearly show the sources of his theological inspirations. Schmemann's confidence to culture as a "treasurer" of the God-given meanings, inaccessible for theologians just because "they have connected their fate with erudition, with learning, whereas they would be better off following poetry, poets and arts,"[11] allows to suggest that he does not merely try to balance the ideological "cultureclasm" with the affirmation of the positive meaning and usefulness of culture, but shifts the discussion about the issue to another higher level where the contradictions between sacred and secular, human history and God's kingdom, creativity and humility are eliminated just because "ultimately the whole novelty of Christianity consisted (consists) in destroying . . . this polarization."[12] Culture in his theology is not opposed to faith like an "earthly" to "heavenly," or like "emotional" to "spiritual" (Schmemann radically denied such oppositions), but co-exists with it in the living, dynamic and challenging connection. Such vision of the relations, traditionally seen as conflicting, allows us to suggest that Rev. Alexander Schmemann has elaborated a whole new, especially for the Eastern Orthodox context, apology of culture. This paper presents an attempt to describe some of the basic features of it.

Why have we chosen *The Journals* as a source text? Indeed, they are shot through with reflections about culture, in connection with cultural phenomena and events. The author stays in constant dialogue with culture, it appears to be a standard of trustworthiness, including the theological one, however, it is not only Alexander Schmemann's text which permits us to affirm the prominent role of culture in his theological thought. It is another matter that a journal narrative, being private and confessionary, allows the expression of the views, even most controversial, with maximal openness, without a backward glance to the "uncomprehending" or critical reader, as well as without clarifications and reservations required by every public

9. Ibid., 26.

10. It is worth to mention that Rev. Alexander Schmemann is one of the very few Orthodox theologians who dared to speak openly about the "emptiness" and "tiredness" of the conventional religious and theological language.

11. Schmemann, *Journals*, 16.

12. Ibid., 233–34.

statement. Being utterly personal, "between God and me only" journal entry, especially when it is not a part of the literary game with a reader, provides a total freedom of the "direct word." Although it is still discussed whether Alexander Schmemann intended them for publication,[13] it is clear that for him it was a "private space," where he could express his views and feelings most openly.

It may seem that in his polemics with "cultureclasts" Schmemann tends to another extreme: he idealizes culture, endows it with such excessive "capabilities," which it is not supposed to have. However, the value and novelty of his apology become clear only on the background of the centuries-old controversies between "Athens and Jerusalem." The key issues, as well as radicalism of these disputes, were defined by the famous statement of Tertullian: "What indeed has Athens to do with Jerusalem? What concord is there between the Academy and the Church?"[14] At the risk of the excessive schematizing and simplification, we would dare to say that during many centuries the tension, described by Tertullian, eased by the justification of culture through its obedience to faith or "usefulness" for transmitting of the revealed truth and Church doctrine. "Worldly intellectual culture"[15] was of value only if it could bear, on the word of Saint Justin Martyr, "the seed" of the Christian message.

> The followers of Stoic teaching, because they were praiseworthy at least in their ethics, as were also the poets in some respects, because of the seed of reason implanted in all mankind—he wrote.—For each one of them, seeing, through his participation in the seminal Divine Word, what was related to it, spoke very well. . . The truth which all men in all lands have rightly spoken, belong to us Christians.[16]

The same attitude to the "worldly culture" can be traced in almost all early patristic writings. Thus Saint Basil the Great, in his famous Homily

---

13. Thus, Daniil Struve, a son of Nikita Struve, who was very close to Rev. Schmemann and actively participated in the preparation of the Russian edition of *Journals*, insisted in oral discussion that they were intended by the author for publication after his death, or at least he wouldn't have been against it. However the difficulties in choosing the entries for the publication (many of them, as the editor of the Russian version Elena Dorman has pointed, are controversial and subjective) prove that he wrote "for himself" without any appealing to the "remote reader." Speaking publicly, whatever it could be, lecture, article or talk, he was many times more accurate.

14. Quintius Tertullian, "Prescription," VII.

15. Averintsev, *Ad Fontes*.

16. Saint Justin Martyr, "Second Apology," VIII, 13.

XXII said that the writings of the "heathen authors" being only "the shadows of the truth," can nevertheless teach basic moral lessons:

> Into the life eternal the Holy Scriptures lead us . . . But so long as our immaturity forbids our understanding their deep thought, we exercise our spiritual perceptions upon profane writings, which are not altogether different, and in which we perceive the truth as it were in shadows and in mirrors. . . The greatest of all battles lies before us, in preparation for which we must do and suffer all things to gain power. Consequently we must be conversant with poets, with historians, with orators, indeed with all men who may further our soul's salvation.[17]

In the Modern age, secular culture tried to settle this controversy "from secular side." In our context it would be worth to mention how it was solved by Pushkin, who was for Schmemann poet *per excellence*: "Beauty in Pushkin's writings, being always praise and thanksgiving is inseparable from truth. . . and kindness. His creative world is filled with compassion, mercy and sympathy, and at last, above all this world of truth, goodness and beauty there is lightful, good and loving God."[18]

As Irina Surat has noticed, quite early Pushkin has realized his poetical vocation as a whole-life ministry of the joyful "obedience to "God's command," which overcomes gap between creativity and faith making poet the messenger of the Kingdom.[19] Hot discussions as well as impossibility of dialogue between clergy and "intelligentsia," between "faith" and "arts" during nineteenth and in the beginning of the twentieth century reveal how problematic was such harmony for the "post-Pushkin" Russian culture. The same time, evident failure of the conventional religious language to express the novel religious experience and quests arose in the twentieth century made both theologians and artists search for a new language of witness. The hope of finding it, not for the last time, was addressed to poetry and, more widely, to culture.

In Russian émigré circles, the discussion of faith and culture continued mainly in the context of witness and role of the Church in a totally new situation of losing all traditional "moorings." Two positions typical for the milieu where Rev. Alexander Schmemann was formed will be of the special interest here. The first is the idea of the "churching of culture," presented at the founding convention of the Russian Students' Christian Movement (Přerov, 1924). In 1930 this idea inspired the foundation of the Orthodox

17. Saint Basil the Great, "Address to Young Men."

18. Shmeman, "O Pushkine," 410.

19. See Surat, "Pushkin kak religioznaya problema."

Culture League: among the members of it there were Nikolai Berdyaev, Vasily Zenkovsky, Ilya Fondaminsky and Elizaveta Skobtsova (the future Mother Maria). In September 1930, at the VIII Annual convention of Russian Students' Christian Movement she gave a talk "The Orthodox Culture and the Future of Russia." As one of the participants recalled, she particularly emphasized the necessity of "uniting all Orthodox intellectual forces for the elaborating of the different issues of culture in the light of the Orthodox teaching and praxis."[20] A year later, Vasily Zenkovsky in his article *Ways of the Movement and Russia* described the idea of the "church culture" as "a task of sanctification and transformation of all our life according to the Church spirit. It is not a move to Church only, but a move out of Church as a new, grand task."[21]

Thus, the "churching of culture" was seen as an attempt to feel with "Christian intension" all spheres of personal and collective creativity, as Mother Maria has put in her article "The Sources of Creativity," to reveal and affirm the link between human creativity and God's creative acts, to rethink culture as a "liturgy after liturgy," in which every creative action can be both offering and thanksgiving.

The second position was presented by Rev. Georges Florovsky in the article "Faith and Culture" (1955). In Florovsky's opinion, the "crisis of culture," shaking "Post-Christian world—whatever the exact meaning of this pretentious phrase may actually be"[22] once again fuels the eternal question: "Does one need 'culture,' and should one be interested in it, when he encounters the Living God, Him Who alone is to be worshipped and glorified? Does 'culture' after all possess any intrinsic value of its own? Is it *service* or *play*, obedience or distraction, vanity, luxury and pride, i.e. ultimately a trap for souls?"[23]

He recognizes that culture itself "is not, and by its very nature cannot be an ultimate value, and should not be regarded as an ultimate human goal or destiny, or even as an indispensable component of true humanity."[24] It is ambiguous, not only "in predicament," but "a predicament itself" that can be solved only theologically. In this way, the conflict between faith and culture, expressed either in the resistance of Christians to culture or in the indifference to it, can be resolved by creating such a theology of culture which, taking into consideration all the doubts about its existence, would

20. Nikitin, "VII godichnyy s"yezd," 29.

21. Zen'kovskiy, "Puti Dvizheniya," 14.

22. Florovsky, "Faith and Culture," 10.

23. Ibid., 14.

24. Ibid.

be able to justify it in the connection of biblical teaching on creation and human's vocation to co-work with Creator:

> Man was created by God for a creative purpose and was to act in the world as its king, priest, and prophet. The fall or failure of man did not abolish this purpose or design, and man was redeemed in order to be re-instated in his original rank and to resume his role and function in the Creation. And only by doing this can he become what he was designed to be, not only in the sense that he should display obedience, but also in order to accomplish the task which was appointed by God in his creative design precisely as *the task of man.*[25]

At first glance, Schmemann thinks in the same framework, but unlike Florovsky, he does not try to ease the contradiction between faith and culture even theologically. On the one hand, it may seem that this radical contradiction does not exist for him at all because both faith and culture belong in his theological system to "heavenly realities" and both set over against "religion" and "platitude" as "worldly things." "The Word of God, prayer, art" are equally capable to reveal that divine reality that cannot be presented by the most sophisticated "words about God."[26] While on the other, the tension created by the mutual challenge of faith and culture do not need to be eased, because it is productive for both sides:

> Verification not of Christ, of Gospel or Church in its ultimate realty, but of the historical forms of Christianity by culture, created and inspired by them . . . Culture of every age is a mirror, in which Christians ought to see themselves and a measure of their faithfulness to "one thing is needful." The idea of God's Kingdom can explode culture, but out of culture it would be impossible to discern, to hear and to accept it.[27]

Relations, usually described as an irreconcilable opposition that can be solved only in favor of one side, Schmemann transforms into a creative possibility, nourishing the life of both.

What does Schmemann's apology of culture consist of? Generally, three basic arguments cam be pointed out: kerigmatic ("the argument of message"), eucharistic ("the argument of offering and thanksgiving"), and eschatological ("the argument of Kingdom").

25. Ibid., 21.
26. Schmemann, *Journals*, 10.
27. Shmeman, *Dnevniki*, 110.

As far as *The Journals* include the most detailed elaboration of the first argument, it would make sense to enlarge upon it. The point of it becomes clear in the context of one of the principal Schmemann's oppositions of "religion" and "faith."

Being "the best" in its reference to an unbelief, inside Christianity religion quite often turns into a false substitution for faith:

> one can love religion like anything else in life: sports, science, stamps collecting; one can love it for its own sake without relation to God or the world or life. Religion fascinates. It has everything . . . : ethics, mystery, sacred and the feeling of one's importance and exclusive depth etc. This kind of religion is not necessarily faith. People expect and thirst after faith—and we offer them religion,

he wrote on November 1, 1974, in connection with the recently read biography of Sartre.[28]

While faith for him is by no means theoretical (or speculative), recognition of a certain set of doctrines, not an "idea" and not only a "conviction of things not seen" (Heb 11:1), but

> the experience of world and life literally in the light of Kingdom of God revealed through everything that makes up the world: colors, sounds, movements, time, space—concrete, not abstract. When this light, which is only in the heart . . . falls on the world and on life, then all is illumined, and the world becomes a joyful sign, symbol, expectancy.[29]

It is always utterly personal response to both the message and question of "who are you?" addressed to the person only. Generalizing, it would be possible to say that faith in Schmemann's theology is an utterly personal experience of eschatologism of life born as a response to the message. Being "inside" religion phenomenologically, the same time it "overcomes religion," checks the conventional forms of the religious tradition for truthworthness and sensitiveness to the personal questionings. It is in this ability of faith to put religion "under a question" the essence of the "gospel conflict," which makes the foundation of Christianity, lies: "The Gospel is quite clear: both saints and sinners love God. 'Religious' people do not love him, and whenever they can, they crucify him."[30]

28. Schmemann, *Journals*, 52.

29. Ibid., 20.

30. Ibid., 132.

> Being too "ideological," tending to sacralize words thus releasing from the necessity to ponder into their meanings, conventional religious language is not capable of expressing both message and response to it. Faith as a message requires a herald, who is also the witness, while ideology needs a propagandist, affirming "unreal and non-existing world as real and existing" and passing ethical and behavioral rules of survival in this false reality. According to Schmemann's belief, neither academic theology nor "religious chatting" is capable of proposing language equal for strength and trustworthiness to this perfect message. Inside the Church it is fully expressed only by the Eucharist, while on the border of the Church and the world it can be conveyed by culture as a domain of images, creative questioning and symbolic expression. It is culture, born from the experience of "referral . . . to the Other" every word,"[31]

can give true witness of God and His Kingdom, which shines through it. "I think about the words of a Russian poet: "But them the words: a flower, a child, a beast. . ." while looking at the golden trees pierced by an afternoon sun behind my window, at a wandering cat, at children . . . returning home from school. It returns me to God so much more than theological and religious thoughts."[32]

The eucharistic argument is based, first of all, on Schmemann's idea of the commonality of culture and the Eucharist as a pure offering and thanksgiving, in which the priestly vocation and "Eucharistic nature" of humans is realized. Symbolism of culture is very close to liturgical symbolism—both are transparent, pointing (even in the negative, "rebelling" forms of culture) to the "meaning, beauty, value, to the experience of Kingdom," to the profound "eschatological character of life itself and all that in it."[33] Both for him are theophanies revealing the presence of God in the visible beauty, as well as in the longing for Him that penetrates modern culture and can fully be quenched only in the Eucharist as a highest point of human creativity. It provides the key for reflection on both eucharistic and eschatological arguments in the context of Schmemann's idea of culture as an overcoming of mortality: "What is real culture? Communion. Participation in that which conquering time and death."[34]

More reasons for the justification of the eschatological argument in the apology of culture can be found in Schmemann's idea of culture as the

31. Shmeman, *Dnevniki*, 58.

32. Schmemann, *Journals*, 131–32.

33. Ibid., 24.

34. Ibid., 27.

interpretation of the prophesies, as well as in his conviction that "all culture and all in culture is about the Kingdom of God, for or against. Culture consists of bringing into real existence the treasures of one's heart."[35] However, the last two arguments, new and challenging for Russian theological thought (and, maybe not only for it) would require more detailed and profound consideration.

## Bibliography

Averintsev, Sergey S. *Ad Fontes!* Kiyev: Dukh i Literatura, 2006.

Basil the Great, Saint. "Address to Young Men on the Right Use of Greek Literature." In *Essays on the Study and Use of Poetry by Plutarch and Basil the Great*, edited by Frederick Morgan Padelford, 99–120. New York: Henry Holt, 1902.

Florovsky, Georges. "Faith and Culture." In *Christianity and Culture*, 19–30. Collected Works of Georges Florovsky 2. Belmont, MA: Nordland, 2002.

Justin Martyr, Saint. "The Second Apology." In *The First Apology; The Second Apology; Dialogue with Tripho; Exhortation to the Greeks; Discourse to the Greeks; The Monarchy of the Rule of God.* Translated by Thomas B. Falls. Washington, DC: Catholic University of America Press, 2008.

Nikitin, Aleksandr I. "VII godichnyy s'yezd Dvizheniya." *Vestnik Russkogo studencheskogo khristianskogo dvizheniya* 11 (1930) 26–30.

Quintius Tertullian. "The Prescription Against Heretics." Translated by Peter Holmes. In vol. 3 of *The Ante-Nicene Fathers*, edited by A. Cleveland Coxe, 243–365. Buffalo: Christian Literature Publishing Company, 1885.

Schmemann, Alexander. *The Historical Road of the Eastern Orthodoxy.* Crestwood, NY: St. Vladimir's Seminary Press, 1963.

———. *The Journals of Father Alexander Schmemann. 1973–1983.* Translated by J. Schmemann. Crestwood, NY: St. Vladimir's Seminary Press, 2000.

Sedakova, Ol'ga A. "Poeziya kak vesti." *Vestnik Russkogo studencheskogo khristianskogo dvizheniya* 195 (2009) 19–20.

Shmeman, Aleksandr. *Dnevniki 1973–1983.* Moscow: Russkiy put', 2005.

———. "O Pushkine." In *Beseda na Radio "Svoboda."* Vol. 2. Moscow: Svyato-Tikhonovskiy Bogoslovskiy institut, 2009.

Surat, Irina Z. "Pushkin kak religioznaya problema." *Novyy mir* 1 (1994) 217–22.

Zen'kovskiy, Vasiliy V. "Puti Dvizheniya i Rossiya." *Vestnik Russkogo studencheskogo khristianskogo dvizheniya* 1 (1931) 11–16.

35. Ibid., 79.

# PART II

Historical Focuses

# 9

# Catholicity as an Ideal Foundation of Social Life

*Gregory Skovoroda and His Concept of the High Republic*

—VICTOR CHERNYSHOV

IT IS A WIDELY acknowledged fact that Gregory Skovoroda stands at the very beginning of modern Russian and Ukrainian thought. Although Russian and Ukrainian scholars fervently dispute whether he belongs to the Russian or the Ukrainian cultural trend, very few of them have ever dared to deny his importance and the key role he played in the history of both Russian and Ukrainian philosophy.

Most of the ideas we find in the texts of prominent Russian thinkers of the nineteenth and twentieth centuries were already present in Skovoroda's writings, although sometimes in a very specific or imperfect form. One of the ideas is the idea of catholicity (*sobornost'*), which in the nineteenth century drew considerable interest from Slavophiles. Slavophiles (as well as many others afterwards) saw in catholicity the true archetype and ideal foundation of social and political life, sanctified by the authority of the Christian Church—as the concept became widespread and well known from the ninth article of the Nicene Creed.

There is no such term as "catholicity" (*sobornost'*) in the writings of Skovoroda. Actually, abstract terms were quite alien to him—he did not like them, and therefore used them rather rarely. It was the Slavophiles (e.g. Ivan Kireevsky, Alexei Khomiakov), who initially introduced the concept of "catholicity" to the Russian intellectual tradition. Later, in Russian philosophy and theology, it continued its triumphal procession throughout the writings of Russian thinkers until the end of the Russian Era of philosophy and the beginning of the Soviet one. However, the most brilliant and showy representation it had in the writings of thinkers of the Russian Diaspora (e.g. Nicolai Berdyaev, Semen Frank, and many others), who devoted themselves for different (but equally enthusiastic) studies of the idea, in which they saw the only foundation for any normal social life. Although the issue itself was not altogether alien to Skovoroda, since he described the same reality though in other terms which later Russian thinkers would have usually described with the concept of "catholicity."

Skovoroda begins from afar. Although it seems altogether natural in order to penetrate into the mystery of human social life, first, we should give us an account of the nature of human beings, as the philosopher considers it to be. Therefore, it is quite natural that the study of social life begins with the issues rather peculiar to anthropology and ethics.

Gregory Skovoroda believed that people are created to be happy. The very source of his philosophy is the aspiration for happiness. The quest for happiness and happy life is an existential foundation of Skovoroda's teaching: "There is nothing more pleasant for a Pilgrim as talking about the City, which all his Toils will crown with Rest. We were born for True Happiness and Travel to it. And our life is the Way, flowing as a River,"[1] says one of the personages of his dialogues. Thus, Skovoroda says that human life is like a pilgrimage towards a city of rest, comfort and happiness. A guideline on this way is that we can call the basic human instinct, which is the human craving for happiness—everyone wants to be happy. It is, as Skovoroda puts it, the most powerful motivation for any human activities.[2]

People strive (blindly, and almost madly) for happiness, but in the majority of cases do not obtain the desired goal. Why does it happen? What is the reason for all of these human failures? Skovoroda answers that for a separate human being in itself there is no hope at all, and the battle for happiness is altogether lost. There is a showy image in one of Skovoroda's works: a dog who is carrying a piece of meat across a river in its jaws happens to catch sight of its reflection. Wishing to take the piece of meat away from the (imaginable) adversary, the poor thing loses its own.[3] Thus the life of

1. Skovoroda, *Zbirka tvoriv*, 503.

2. Ibid., 502.

3. Ibid., 404, 437, 513, 791, 958.

ordinary people is very much like this fable. People who want to gain more, lose even that which they had. The human pursuit of happiness may easily turn (and in the majority of cases it does so) in a bitter state of unhappiness.

Skovoroda sees the main source of this pitiful state of human unhappiness as human folly[4] or naughtiness, which hinders people from happiness: "The source of all our troubles is our naughtiness [*bezsovetie*][5]: it takes us, putting bitter for sweet, and sweet for bitter."[6] The collection of naughty people make a society of unadvised people who are almost unable to decide for themselves; Skovoroda calls them "the crowd," "low people," or "the unadvised world." We may recollect his words:

> O world! The world unadvised!
> Thy hope thou in princess puttest?[7]

The unadvised world is the source of disorderly passions, tumults, wicked ideas, opinions, and prejudices, which hinder people from happiness. For a concrete human being this state is like a deep sleep: the ordinary unadvised people live as in a sleep, dreaming the dreams, which are very far from the real state of things: "All the world sleeps. . ."[8] Their life is rather unreal, but the unreal, dreamy life, Skovoroda supposes, can hardly become a happy one, since eventually there will come the time for them to wake up. The basic human instinct can do nothing even against the ruinous activity of time,[9] yet lesser in face of death.[10] Therefore, an empirical human being is altogether helpless to realise this main instinct and attain happiness—the waves of time, and eventually the death, it seems, are able to take everything, wherein usual people put their trust for happiness.

The only way to avoid unhappiness is to get rid of the collective illusion which the unadvised world offers. Life in this illusion Skovoroda likens to that in Sodom, as well as the people of the crowd he likens to the wicked inhabitants of the biblical city.[11] Therefore, to avoid wickedness

---

4. It seems, here, as in many other places of Skovoroda's works, we may hear an echo of ideas of Skovoroda with those of Desiderius Erasmus of Rotterdam, who was one of Skovoroda's favourite authors. Desiderius wrote an entire book on the subject of folly, which title is *Stultitiae Laus*—"The Praise of Folly."

5. Literally, the word means the state of being unadvised. The concept comes from the Church-Slavonic translation of the biblical book of Prov 11:6.

6. Skovoroda, *Zbirka tvoriv*, 507, see also: 560, 571, 654, cf. Isa 5:20.

7. Skovoroda, *Zbirka tvoriv*, 70.

8. Ibid., 200, 966, cf. 960.

9. Ibid., 163.

10. Ibid., 60.

11. Ibid., 440, 603, 788–94, 796, 798, 800, 879; cf. Gen 19:1–29.

and unhappiness (and gain happiness and felicity instead) a human being leaves the wicked city. The departure from Sodom is an urgent task, since the entire human life and happiness depend upon it. It must be proceeded immediately, without any further delay, and glancing back[12] to the hell from which the exodus is made: "Remember Lot's Wife!"[13] Skovoroda reminds us. The only way to do this is the way of self-knowledge. Self-knowledge is the only way to overcome the false opinions and prejudices of the crowd, and to overcome them is the only way to put the beginning for pilgrimage toward happiness. Leaving a settled place is not an easy thing, leaving a settled place it is to become a pilgrim and stranger (of that who yet long not ago was a settled and neighbour), taking the road towards the invisible (but intelligible) end of the journey. For Gregory Skovoroda endows the ancient imperative "Know yourself!" with a predominant significance. It is a call for spiritual revival, dehypnotization, and the beginning of the recovery from the illness with which the unadvised world is heavily tormented in its dreamy unhappiness. The revival is the "second birth"[14]—the "birth from above" that Christ once upon a time spoke about to Nicodemus (John 3:1–21). Self-knowledge is ultimately necessary. It reveals the things of which an "inhabitant of Sodom"—"the man of flesh and blood" is completely ignorant. The only sign, which reveals the calling (which is generally unconscious) is intuition, deeply rooted and buried in the depths of human nature—the aspiration and craving for happiness.

Describing the metaphysics of self-knowledge as a second birth, Skovoroda insists definitely that self-knowledge is to reveal the reality which the "Sodom man" is absolutely ignorant and unaware of. The reality is the inner life of a person. In many places in his writings, Skovoroda invites us to divide everything "in two," "to perceive two in everything."[15] For him the whole, empirical world (and everything in it) must be divided in two, since the world is twofold in itself, since such is his nature. Considering each particular human being to be a "little world" (microcosm), Skovoroda insists upon using the same principle as with the large world (macrocosm). This division is important enough as it helps to make a distinction between the carnal and spiritual, temporal and eternal, phenomenal and ideal, il-

---

12. There are at least three widely known cases of "looking behind (back)" in the European culture: that of Orpheus on his way from the netherworld, the second one of the wife of biblical Lot (Gen 19:26), and the third one about which Christ warns in the Gospel of Luke (9:62).

13. Skovoroda, *Zbirka tvoriv*, 786–800.

14. Ibid., 784, 789, 790, 791, 798, 1284.

15. Skovoroda, *Zbirka tvoriv*, 309–12, 320, 324, 332, 343, 388, 393–407, 440, 461, 528, 578, 604, 666, 928, 1355.

lusion and reality. The division—Skovoroda supposes—is to reveal the inner beauty of the human self, making the spectator interested in his/her spiritual life, and eventually leading the person to reveal the hidden image of everlasting God in their own self.[16]

In relation to human nature, the division is presumably to represent the difference between general human nature (i.e. the human substance) and the particular human nature (i.e. the person, the mind or heart), which form the empirical reality of a concrete human being. Following Apostle Paul's footsteps (2 Cor 4:16), Skovoroda recognises in a human being two "men"—an "inward man" and an "outward man."[17] The "inward man" is a spiritual part of human being, turned to God, as the "outward man" is another part of the same (empirical) human being, but turned towards the world and the temporary existence of the transitory life. This distinction enables Skovoroda to make a few substantial conclusions. Only the "inward man" is able to communicate with God and inherit God's Kingdom, while the "outward man" must "exhaust himself" in doing the job which he is intended (and called) to do in this world. This apparent loss of the outward man will contribute greatly to the "inward man." The people who are seeking to find happiness after the "outward man" will eventually suffer greatly and ultimately lose while those, who are seeking happiness in their own "*serdechnyya peshchery*" ("caves of heart")[18] will be given the everlasting joy and felicity of the Kingdom of God. Moreover, having at its foundation the image of everlasting God, the "inward man" can easily overrun the boundaries of created nature that enables him for direct and immediate personal communion with God. The communion takes its place immediately within the holy of holies of a human being—within the human heart. Gregory Skovoroda is discoursing much—it is one of his favourite topics—on the human heart, which he understands as an existential core of any human being. The predominant significance for it has its intentions and values, everything a human being values, craves and strives to attain. On these grounds, there is an opportunity to speak about "the earthly heart" (or "the old heart") and "the new heart:" the appearance of the latter is due to the second birth, which is, in its own turn, a result of self-knowledge.

The call to "Know yourself!," for Skovoroda, is an aspiration for the discovery in the depths of one's personal being the voice of God calling. and eventually obtaining in the fullness of its light the understanding of

---

16. See, e.g., ibid., 231.

17. See, e.g., ibid., 176, 200–202, 205, 249, 294, 310, 339, 1237, 1270, 1271, 1277, 1279.

18. Ibid., 82.

God's will concerning the concrete human being that is the personal voca-tion (*srodnost'*), i.e. the call for a kindred activity unto which a person is predestined by God's Providence.

Yet the most important fruit of the self-knowledge is the discovery of the mystery of Divine Providence in relation to the universe in general[19] as well as to any concrete creature in particular.[20] This revelation of the mys-tery of Divine Providence leads the person to be thankful, feeling a deep gratitude to the Creator and Preserver of all humankind, which Gregory Skovoroda supposes to be the only adequate response to it.[21] This deep gratitude and thankfulness transforms the person, making him or her God's child, ascending from the state of slavery to the most perfect state of kinship with God. It is also noteworthy that Skovoroda stresses that the connec-tion is altogether spiritual that removes any suspicions and disapproves any charges of pantheism: "The unity is neither in a bodily likeness, nor in the same state, nor in likeness of clothes, nor in a number of years, nor in the same age, nor in a clannishness, nor in a sharing of the same lands; it is neither in heaven, nor in the earth, but in hearts which are connected in the unity of Christ's philosophy."[22]

Ultimately, the call for self-knowledge is a call for a personal holiness, which is to be realized in a person of the concrete representative of the hu-man race. The mystery of holiness drew the attention and keen interest of Skovoroda many times throughout his writings. The typology of holiness is not easy for the reader to understand. It seems that its main feature is its individual character, a certain setting apart from the rest, a distinct indi-viduation from everything connected with the crowd or even a "mass (or public, collective) conscience." The rest of necessary features are truth,[23] stability (or immovability),[24] goodness,[25] mysteriousness,[26] detachment and uncommonness (set towards the God alone),[27] remoteness from corruption

19. Ibid., 218.

20. Ibid., 654, 902, 1365, 1373.

21. Ibid., 874, 927, 1046, 1048, 1364.

22. Ibid., 1270.

23. Ibid., 231.

24. Ibid., 389.

25. Ibid., 656.

26. Ibid., 736, 780–81.

27. Ibid., 736, 751.

(immutability),[28] love of virtue(s),[29] the greatness.[30] All these, Skovoroda supposes, purport to create the "saving harbour,"[31] a new heart,[32] which is the abiding place for the Holy Spirit himself. Apparently, Skovoroda was convinced that human holiness is a result of a deeply personal activity, which is in accord with God's will. Most people are not holy since they live on their own, pursuing worldly lusts and desires of their own carnal heart, as those, who are holy live in communion with God, after God's will, keeping his commandments. All of those who feel this kinship with God make up a particular people—a holy nation, a chosen generation of God's offspring, a city (or commonwealth, or a republic) of God.

The most important means on the way of self-knowledge is the Holy Scripture—the Holy Bible. For Skovoroda the Bible is the third world— along with the great world (i.e. the macrocosm or the Universe) and the little world of a particular human being (i.e. the microcosm). Formulating his teaching on the basis of the three worlds—the macrocosm, the micro-cosm, and the symbolical world of the Bible, Skovoroda apparently follows in the footsteps of Saint Maximus the Confessor.[33] For Skovoroda (as with Maximus ten centuries before[34]) there is *Scriptura homo mysticus*—"the Holy Scripture is a mystical human being." It means that the Holy Scripture offers to any human being a perfect archetype of being, which is apparently an ideal model of being for both the great world and any particular human being. Therefore, the Bible comes to be something like the thread of Ariadne, guiding through a labyrinth of the inward world of human beings (microcosm), governing and directing a particular human being towards the way of happiness and salvation, which is the way of communion with God and the other people of God.[35] The Bible shows clearly "the face of the Almighty," it is a clear symbolical representation of God and his plan for the world. This Skovoroda's teaching echoes the Pauline doctrine ("Pauline panentheism") that everything which is there is in God, and there is God in everything, that is because he is called *the Almighty*.[36]

28. Ibid., 780.

29. Ibid., 1063.

30. Ibid., 141–42.

31. Ibid., 1233.

32. Ibid., 1284, 1359.

33. See, e.g., Maximus the Confessor, "Mystagogia."

34. Ibid., cols. 683–84.

35. Skovoroda, *Zbirka tvoriv*, 201, 796.

36. Cf. Rom 11:36; 1 Cor 2:10; 8:6; 2 Cor 2:18; Eph 1:23; 3:9; Col 1:16–17; 3:11.

It is no wonder then that the showiest and the most original of Skovoroda's images, representing an ideal human society, appears in his tract *Lot's Wife* dedicated to principles of reading and interpretation of the Holy Scriptures, being used in relation to the Bible—it is the concept of the High Republic (*Gornyaya respublika*).

> You must know, my friend, that the Bible [it] is a New World and a People of God, a Land of the living, a Country and a Realm of Love, the High Jerusalem, since, beyond the low Asiatic, there is the High one. There is neither hostility nor discord. There is no old age or gender, or difference either in this Republic. Everything is common there. The community is in love. Love is in God. God is in the community. Here is the Ring of eternity![37]

A few pages later the term reappeares, Skovoroda reprises the idea: "In the High Republic, there are all things new: the new People, the new creatures, the new creature. It is very much unlike to that what we have here, under the sun, wherein everything is odds and ends and vanity of vanities."[38]

It is usually remarked upon that Gregory Skovoroda borrowed the idea of the High Republic from Desiderius Erasmus of Rotterdam (and the early Slavic spiritual writers, e.g. Theophanous Prokopowicz, who also used the term borrowed from Erasmus), but made some changes in its meaning.[39] However, whatever the immediate source of this concept was for Gregory Skovoroda, he substantially changed its meaning, complicated the semantics of the term, supplemented the concept with new features, stressed the personalistic aspect, which is rather typical for the theological tradition of the Eastern Orthodoxy.

It can be easily observed that the quoted passages are not directly connected with the (so to say) "empirical problematic" or an empirical social context, as the concept has sometimes been interpreted as being taken out of its proper context.[40] Skovoroda's purpose is quite far from it, though it is hard to deny that in developing the concept he purports to give substantial grounds for understanding the ideal social model which, doubtlessly, is not to be limited within the narrow bounds of the fleeting earthly life.

Skovoroda is aware enough that the goodness of social life is one of the mysteries of being, which is rather the gift of God's mercy and grace, depending completely on Divine Providence although, to some extent, he

---

37. Skovoroda, *Zbirka tvoriv*, 788.

38. Ibid., 790.

39. See, e.g., ibid., 815.

40. See, e.g., Mishanich, "Skovoroda," 405; Tolstov, "Dukhovni zasadi," Shevchuk, *Piznaniy i nepiznaniy Sfinks*, 457–72.

wishes to penetrate this mystery, perceiving the principles of the ideal human society (a commonwealth).

The first principle is set towards God and the perennial truth. Skovoroda calls it "the remembrance of Eternity." Taking for his starting point the teaching on the twofold nature of the being (seen and unseen, visible and invisible, creating and created, false and true), Skovoroda states the twofold character of human memory. There is memory which set towards remembrance of the things perishable (and which have already perished indeed), while there is also the memory which is set towards remembrance of things everlasting—the Eternity which is the Holiness. For Skovoroda, this distinction between the memory unto death and the memory unto life is a fundamental one and which has a powerful impact on social life. The remembrance of the holiness and the set towards the life, Skovoroda believes, is the only subject of all the Sacraments of the Church, which purpose the sanctification and renewal of memory (and through it the whole human being) pilgrims to the Eternal City.[41]

As there are two kinds of human memory, so there are two kinds of social organization: one is set towards the perishable, while another towards the imperishable and eternal. Among the symbols of human collectives of these two kinds of organization, for Skovoroda (as well as, yet earlier before him, for many thinkers since Apostle Paul (e.g. Heb 12:22–23; 13:14–15) and Saint Augustine[42]) there are the biblical cities and toponyms—Sodom, Segor (Zoar), Jerusalem, Sion (Zion), etc. Sodom is the city of sin, which should be left since it is to perish. Segor (Zoar) is the city of refuge, which shelters those who flee from Sodom. Sion (Zion), as well as Jerusalem, are the mountain and the city of the great King, the High Republic, which is the place of the ultimate salvation. It is easy to observe that only Sodom is a place of perils, perishing and destruction, as the others are places that are more positive. The organizations of these two types of human collectives are very contrary to each other, though they have some parallels. These parallels represent the other principles Skovoroda observes throughout his studies on this problematic.

41. Skovoroda distinctly says about the Baptism, which is the sign of the second (spiritual) birth, and the pledge of the new, spiritual life. He also mentions the Eucharist a number of times, interpreting it as a visible sign of invisible relations, connections and communion between God and human beings, i.e. the Church. First of all Eucharist for him, it is the Sacrament of thanksgiving for God as Maker, Preserver, and Savour, as well as for the fellow-brethren.

42. For instance the main idea of his famous work *De civitatis Dei* that there are two cities throughout human history: one which perishes and another which is to be saved.

The second principle is that of human intention. The crowd of Sodom is concerned merely with their selfish (carnal) lusts, as the intentions of citizens of the High Republic or a commonwealth, which Skovoroda directly calls the Church—"the commonwealth, . . . the fruitful orchard of the Church, saying even clearer, the garden of Society"[43]—is towards the common good.

The third principle is the principle of spiritual kindred or affinity (*srodnost'*). Any normal social life is rather to be founded on spiritual affinity than carnal kindred. This spiritual affinity is the result of an intensive inner activity of self-knowledge. That is why the symbols of this deeply spiritual unity are the city, commonwealth, republic, society (but, it seems, never a family!). The personal vocation (*srodnost'*) of the people of God is directly contrary to those enforcements or vain motivations, which are peculiar to the states of the Sodom type.

From the third principle stems the fourth. It is the principle of the "unequal equality" (which is opposed to the illusory, but popular principle of "equal equality"). The principle makes it evident that every member of society is valuable and good, when used in an appropriate way, i.e. according to the vocation that, in its turn, depends upon God's Providence.

The fifth principle is rather a summary of the preceding four. It is the principle of happiness or the happy, godly and virtuous life, the principle of catholicity as the only foundation of any normal social life. The only pattern and pledge to it is the lively unity of the Catholic Church.

To conclude this brief overview of Skovoroda's social teaching it should be said that developing his teaching on catholicity as an ideal foundation of social life, Skovoroda goes from the concrete personal reality and the basic human instinct (which is the aspiration instinct for happiness) to an ideal abstraction of social organization (city, commonwealth, republic, society), and from the abstraction of social organization to the lively and real being of the Catholic Church. Self-knowledge (which turns in the knowledge of God), personal vocation (*srodnost'*) of each human being are the very foundation stones of the High Republic, which is understood as a real, mystical unity of those, who are obedient to God's will. Therefore, there is no other way to form a social organization as an organic whole, but by the voluntary unity of those who are godly and good. Any other unions cannot be but merely accidental ones, mechanical compositions, which are hardly able to be the foundation of any real social life.

<hr />

43. Skovoroda, *Zbirka tvoriv*, 651.

# Bibliography

Maximus the Confessor. *"Mystagogia."* In vol. 90 of Patrologia graecae, edited by J.-P. Migne, cols. 658–718. Paris: Migne, 1863.

Mishanich, Oleksa V. "Skovoroda." In *Istoriya vsemirnoy literatury v devyati tomach*, 5:404–7. Moscow: Nauka, 1988.

Skovoroda, Grigoriy. *Povna akademichna zbirka tvoriv*, Kharkiv: Maydan, 2011.

Tolstov, I. V. "Dukhovni zasadi ukrayins'kogo gromadyans'kogo suspil'stva i 'Gornya respublika' G. S. Skovorodi." In *Grigoriy Skovoroda u svitli filologiyi, filosofiyi ta bogoslov'ya*, 266–70. Kharkiv: Vidavets' Savchuk O. O., 2013.

Shevchuk, Viktor O. *Piznaniy i nepiznaniy Sfinks: Grigoriy Skovoroda suchasnimi ochima: rozmisli.* Kiev: Pul'sari, 2008.

## 10

# Religiosity and Pseudo-Religiosity in Russia's Nineteenth-Century Liberation Movement Preceding Bolshevik Quasi-Religiosity

—Katharina Anna Breckner

Nineteenth-century revolutionary Russia is a perfect example of how pseudo-religiosity comes into being in—or, perhaps better, by—the denial of Christian religion. As is well known, Russia's revolutionary nineteenth century was begun by the so-called "Decembrists." Pavel Pestel' (1793–1825), author of the legendary *Russian Truth (Russkaya Pravda)*—an incomplete draft of the constitution to the transitory first Russian Republic envisioned after the abolition of tsarism by a *coup d'état*[1]—was one of the five revolutionaries hanged in 1825 who became important martyrs guiding the next generation of revolutionaries in their fight for liberation from serfdom and for the abolition of tsarism[2] even if the contents of this wording of a law remained unknown for almost a century because it was hidden in the archives.[3] Pestel,' a Freemason, had tried to reformulate "veritable Christendom"

1. Pavlov-Sil'vanskiy, "P. I. Pestel,'" 233.
2. Florovskiy, "Iskaniya molodogo Gerena," 278.
3. Nechkina, "Russkaya Pravda," 9.

(*istinnoye khristianstvo*)—a legacy of Russian Freemasonry[4]—into a state doctrine. His *Truth* prescribed a peculiar theocratic "welfare state" desirable in order to continue Russia's political fate.[5] Russian Orthodoxy would have made part of Russia's governmental machinery and was to proselytize non-believers and members of non-Orthodox confessions:[6] censorship would have been no less considerable than as under the Bolsheviks, only based on another ideological paradigm.

The following account of Alexander Herzen's, Nikolai Chernyshevsky's, and Nikolai Mikhaylovsky's vision of so-called "Russian socialism"—all three of them are acknowledged trend-setting revolutionaries—highlights the pseudo-religious myth inherent in their campaigns which created and/or amplified the pseudo-religious atmosphere within the ranks of the Russian *intelligentsiya* (intellectual elite). The omnipotent presence of censorship exercised under the triple slogan *narodnost'* (populism), *pravoslaviye* (or-thodoxy), *samoderzhaviye* (autocracy), as it were, created a constant threat of persecution, bringing forth a certain atmosphere of apocalyptic crisis: already this historical situation seemingly called for Biblical metaphors.

Alexander Herzen (1812–70) had become familiar with European Enlightenment philosophy via his French private teacher, who himself was proud of having been one of the judges of Louis XVI. This teacher cautiously prepared Hercen's future as a revolutionary and his "new religion" contained an apotheosis of personal liberty and independence; in fact, Herzen became the "Russian Voltaire."[7] In 1848 he chose exile in order to bypass censorship. His journal *The Bell* (*Kolokol*, 1859–70) was extremely successful. Russian intellectuals from the 1860s onwards were educated by Herzen's prophecies:[8] his writings indeed created the myth of a renewed form of Christianity, which was to launch Russia's golden age within a very short time. New Christianity (*nouveau christianism*), promulgated first by early French socialists such as Pierre Leroux,[9] was reinforced as a core idea of "Russian socialism" that was based on the pseudo-religious myth of the Russian *obshchina* (rural community). As Herzen maintained, in comparison to European civilization demoralized by capitalism, Russian rural social life had not undergone this fundamental mental change, but had conserved a particular form of broth-erhood and communism. Seen from here, the problem left was to abolish

4. Voronitsyn, *Dekabristy i religiya*, 14; Semevskiy, "Dekabristy-masony," 2.

5. Pestel,' "Russkaya Pravda," 137, 114.

6. Ibid., 153.

7. Tschizewskij, *Hegel bei den Slawen*, 263.

8. Breckner, "Vor-, anti- und postmarxistische Sozialismusideen," 11.

9. Koyré, *Études*, 183; El'sberg, *Gertsen*, 31.

feudalism and, of course, all its political, juridical, and social consequences: the fabulous *obshchina* was to become the cellular sociological setting of the future Russia and evolve into a loose federation of local self-governmental unities.[10] Within the ranks of the Russian revolutionary intellectual elite this prophecy was widely accepted as creed of "Russian socialism." It stimulated Russian populism in the 1870s, 80s, and 90s.[11] This pseudo-religious myth then blurred animosities amongst religious Slavophiles and non-religious Westernizers.[12] Herzen then used the title "apostles" with reference to all of the populists engaged in enlightening Russian folk:[13] enlightenment was to make them fully realize their privileged historical situation.[14]

Nikolai Chernyshevsky (1828–89), a student at the seminary of Saratov until 1844,[15] did not in fact continue in his father's footsteps as a priest himself, but by the end of the 1840's had instead become an enthusiastic follower of Ludwig Feuerbach. His early journal entries discuss the question of whether there exists a personal God or whether God rather is a myth,[16] yet, later writings clearly document that Chernyshevsky may righteously be considered the "Russian Feuerbach."[17] In 1848–49 he belonged to the conspiratorial circle propagating French socialism.[18] In 1863 he was banished for the rest of his life. Via his publications as editor-in-chief of the *Sovremennik* (*The Contemporary*) he had become a sort of "politician"[19] of "Russian socialism," one of the "apostles" of "new Christianity." He may righteously be considered one of Herzen's most important disciples. To be sure, the type of socialism they propagated has never been a systematic ideological program, but rather a special type of prophecy basing on the pseudo-religious myth axiomatically turning around the *obshchina*. From 1856 onwards Grigoriy Eliseyev, a member of the Old-Believers, assisted Chernyshevsky in spreading this prophecy, a matter of fact that inspired intense cooperation between religious and non-religious forces. Herzen and Chernyshevsky both called for the joint action of believers and non-believers in defending this

10. Gertsen, "Russkiy narod i sotsializm."

11. Breckner, "Vor-, anti- und postmarxistische Sozialismusideen," 11.

12. Gertsen, "Ne nashi," 298.

13. Gertsen, "K staromu tovarishchu," 172.

14. Gertsen, "Rossiya," 187.

15. Dukhovnikov, "Chernyshevskiy," 540.

16. Cf. Chernyshevsky's Diary entries of July 11, 1849 and January 20, 1850, Chernyshevskiy, *Polnoye sobraniye sochineniy*, 297, 358.

17. Lyatskiy, "Chernyshevskiy."

18. Anikin, *Put' iskaniy*, 273.

19. Venturi, *Roots of Revolution*, 129.

pseudo-religious myth as to represent the nucleus of golden times ahead.[20] In the early 1860's Afanasiy Shchapov, one of Elseev's students, successfully recruited Old-Believers to the first revolutionary combat unit of Zemlya i volya (*Land and Liberty*).[21] The second unit of this type in the beginning of the 1870's followed this example. At this time, the New Testament had become the most frequently used statement of defense; the saying of a man facing arrest that he respected as "teachers" solely "Christ, Saint Paul, and Chernyshevsky"[22] has become famous. In the 1870's, "revolutionary" and "seminarist" (student of theology) were used as synonyms and the *Sovremennik* was called a "consistory."[23]

Nikolai Mikhaylovsky (1842–1904) admitted to having been educated by Herzen and Chernyshevsky.[24] Like his brothers in arms he became journalist, reviewer, essayist, in short, a revolutionary of the word. When in 1868 Eliseyev asked him to join the staff of the *Otechestvennyye zapiski* (*National Notes*) he had already become familiar with early French socialism, for in 1867 he had translated *De la capacité de la classe ouvrière* by Pierre-Joseph Proudhon into Russian.

Mikhaylovsky was extremely popular amongst the active and passive participants of Russian Populism, the *narodnichestvo*,[25] for he highlighted conjoint views instead of insisting on dissent between the three fractions: the first followed Mikhail Bakunin in his belief in violent uprising, the second trusted the concept of enlightenment by words as Herzen had preached it, and a third recalled the French Jacobins. Yet, by the end of the 1870's Mikhaylovsky clearly positioned himself in favor of Herzen's concept of "enlightenment."[26] Especially his work *Pis'ma o pravde i nepravde* (1877) witnesses to the fact that Mikhaylovsky also shared the myth about the Russian *obshchina* as the cornerstone of all ideal visions of future Russia. He, himself a non-believer, nonetheless acknowledged the Slavophiles' discourses on knowledge of the self as not being comprehensible beyond the "we," or otherwise said as to always connote the existence of the next within

20. Cf. Chernyshevskiy, "Slavyanofily i vopros ob obshchine," 737 and Gertsen, "Russkiy narod i sotsializm," 307, and also in many other writings by both authors.

21. Venturi, *Roots of Revolution*, 253.

22. Billington, *Mikhailovsky*, 120.

23. Ibid., 123.

24. Vilenskaya, *Mikhaylovskiy*, 23.

25. Kolosov, *Ocherki mirovozzreniya*, 63.

26. Rusanov, "Politika Mikhaylovskogo," 125.

oneself in metaphysical and in terms of existence.[27] The above-cited work is extremely important with respect to his heuristics, too.

Refusing the disconnectedness between "theoretical truth" (*istina*) and "practical truth" (*pravda*) he intended "subjective truth" (*pravda sub"yektivnaya*) to be the focus of his discourses.[28] Referring to August Comte, he also believed in a three step development of history. He saw those three phases distinguished by means and modes of the division of labor. This discursive view represents the *istina*, the theoretical discourse he upheld. The first period was then epitomized by total absence of division of labor and belief in non-personal God, the second by increasing division of labor and Christianity plus increasing capitalism, whereas in the third phase of history civilization would return to a situation where people would live and work collectively and not divide their labor into branches of production isolated from one another. Capitalism would necessarily end and be substituted by some sort of socialism, with the socializing of property and labor.[29] This decisive turn of history would arise out of people's immense psychological strain caused by growing poverty, but even more importantly by the growing isolation from each other. He called this assessment of the historical situation *pravda*.[30] In order to bypass the risks of capitalism augmenting both negative developments, he recommended also the Russian rural community, the *obshchina*, to set the example of how labor and property could be organized also with respect to growing modern industries.[31] This vision denotes the *subjective truth*—a mixture of *pravda* and *istina*—he defended. In his eyes this pseudo-religious myth represented the appropriate basis for debates on Russia's future. He considered Marxism dreadful, for he feared a "new terror" if social revolutions replaced political reform.[32]

I hold that in the nineteenth and twentieth century Russian Orthodoxy did not significantly react either to the ongoing resistance against tsarism and its institutions or to the Bolshevism. The destiny of Russian Orthodoxy differs fundamentally from the fate of the European Christian Churches. By the nineteenth century, the latter had already gone through many centuries of constant religious adjustment and change in the Renaissance, Reformation, and Enlightenment to guide themselves and make them formulate

---

27. Mikhaylovskiy, "Pis'ma o pravde i nepravde."

28. Mikhaylovskiy, "Predisloviye k 3-mu izdaniyu."

29. Mikhaylovskiy, "Iz literaturnykh i zhurnal'nykh zametok," 719, and "Chto takoye progress?" 103.

30. Mikhaylovskiy, "Geroi i tolpa," 174.

31. Frangian, *Michailovsky*, 41.

32. Kolosov, *Ocherki mirovozzreniya*, 66, and Ziemke, *Marxismus und Narodnichestvo*, 388.

and reformulate religious guidelines according to historical change. Con-trastingly, official post-Petrinian Orthodoxy did not even aspire to develop models of adjustment assistance in the face of modernity that step by step had also begun to take its rise in the feudal empire. As Fr. Sergey Bulgakov put it, Orthodoxy never developed such a thing as "autonomous ethics" which rather constitutes a "spiritual gift of Protestantism."[33] "The ideal foun-dation of Orthodoxy is not ethical, but religious, aesthetic; it is the vision of 'spiritual beauty.'"[34]

This essay was not to discuss the rightness or wrongness of his judg-ment, but drew a picture of how processes of secularization went in Russia's intellectual history in the nineteenth century until the Church's influence was reduced to nothing by the Bolsheviks. It seems of immense interest to follow up the development of today's Orthodoxy as it has gained new spheres of liberty and new importance. One of its new assignment of tasks might be to examine closely spheres and impact of pseudo-religiosity that seeks analogies with Christian thought and differs from quasi-religiosity in this point. What I call quasi-religious thinking is when eschatological anal-ogy is *not* intended, yet nevertheless appears so to say unconsciously as a constituting feature of a sentence, a comprehensive discourse, an ideology etc. Consequently I agree with Nikolai Berdyaev,[35] Sergey Bulgakov,[36] and other prominent thinkers in their point that Marx declaring "the sum of proletarians" to fulfill history's purpose comes down to a quasi-religious vision. Marxism really was Hegelianism with a new face. Hegel's saying that the world's history is progress in the consciousness of freedom was, in Bulgakov's eyes, borrowed and vulgarized by Marx and Engels when they spoke of a leap from the kingdom of necessity into the kingdom of freedom. The "economic base" substituted what had been *die letzte Instanz* ("the final instance") in Hegel, and just as the World Spirit uses human desires and in-terests for its own ends, so in Marx's historical ontology the leap to the king-dom of freedom originates in the *List der Vernunft* ("cunning of reason"), too. People fulfill, as if against their will, history's intentions. This infamous "cunning of reason" comes into play, because otherwise the metamorphosis from "wolf" to "brother," the sudden leap from "social Darwinism" to so-cialism, to paradise on earth, is inexplicable. Historical materialism, devoid as it is of any suitable concept of man, cannot justify the introduction of

33. Bulgakov, *Orthodox Church*, 153–55.

34. Ibid., 154.

35. Berdyayev, *Filosofiya neravenstva*, 155, and many other places throughout his works.

36. Bulgakov, *Christentum*, 28.

socialism.[37] Adam Smith and Marx defended the same "hedonistic" end, yet whereas Smith introduced, as Bulgakov asserts, the dogma of the *homo economicus* merely in terms of a "hypothetical presumption" Marx made it an axiomatic, fundamental thesis.[38] Yet, the Leviathan Marx had created was much "worse," since a collective entity devoid of personal character was to take over the rule of the world:[39] a "pit of wolves" was to work its way up to a crowd of "brothers, loving and kissing each other."[40] This metamorphosis from "wolf" to "brother" constituted, as far as Bulgakov was concerned, the central weakness of Marx's historical materialism. He, just like his ideological friend Berdyaev, suspected it of being a disguised religious faith of quasi-chiliastic character: in fact, Marxism—which is also true with respect to Bolshevism—is a "secularised chiliastic teaching" about the 1000 years long Sabbath to come.[41]

## Bibliography

Anikin, Andrey V. *Put' iskaniy. Sotsial'no-ekonomicheskiye idei v Rossii do marksizma.* Moscow: Izdatel'stvo politicheskoy literatury, 1990.

Berdyayev, Nikolay A. *Filosofiya neravenstva. Pis'ma k nedrugam po sotsial'noy filosofii.* Paris, 1970.

Billington, James H. *Mikhailovsky and Russian Populism.* Oxford: Oxford University Press, 1958.

Breckner, Katharina Anna. "Vor-, anti- und postmarxistische Sozialismusideen und ihr Postulat eines Sonderweges Russlands." *Die Ostreihe* 10 (1998).

Bulgakov, Sergej N. "Christentum und Sozialismus." In *Sozialismus im Christentum?,* translated by Hans-Jürgen Ruppert, 135–71. Göttingen: Vandenhoeck und Ruprecht, 1977.

Bulgakov, Sergey N. "Apokaliptika." In *Dva grada,* 1:207–48. Moscow: Put', 1911.

———. "Ob ekonomicheskom ideale." In *Ot marksizma k idealizmu,* 231–50. Moscow: Obshchestvennaya pol'za, 1903.

———. "Religiya chelovekobozhiya u L. Feyyerbakha." In *Dva grada,* 1:51–71. Moscow: Put', 1911.

Bulgakov, Sergius. *The Orthodox Church.* Translated by Lydia Kesich. Crestwood, NY: St. Vladimir's Seminary Press, 1988.

Chernyshevskiy, Nikolay G. *Polnoye sobraniye sochineniy v pyatnadtsati tomakh.* Vol. 1. Nendeln, Lichtenstein: Kraus Reprint, 1971.

37. Bulgakov, "Religiya chelovekobozhiya," 58, and many other places throughout his works.

38. Bulgakov, "Ob ekonomicheskom ideale."

39. Bulgakov, *Christentum,* 37.

40. Ibid., 28.

41. Bulgakov, "Apokaliptika," and many other places throughout his works.

———. "Slavyanofily i vopros ob obshchine. Opyt izlozheniya glavneyshikh usloviy uspeshnogo sel'skogo khozya'stva Strukova." In *Polnoye sobraniye sochineniy v pyatnadtsati tomakh*, 4:737–61. Nendeln, Lichtenstein: Kraus Reprint, 1971.

Dukhovnikov, Flegont V. "Nikolay Gavrilovich Chernyshevskiy. Iz ego zhizni v Saratove." *Russkaya Starina* 67 (1890) 531–74.

El'sberg, Yakov E. *A. I. Gertsen. Zhizn' i tvorchestvo*. Moscow: Gospolitizdat, 1951.

Florovskiy, Georgiy V. "Iskaniya molodogo Gertsena." *Sovremennyye zapiski* 39 (1929) 274–306.

Frangian, E. *N. K. Michailovsky als Soziologe und Philosoph. Eine sozial-philosophische Studie*. Dissertation. Berlin, 1913.

Gertsen, Aleksandr I. "K staromu tovarishchu." *Literaturnoye nasledstvo* 61 (1953) 159–73.

———. "Ne nashi. Slavyanofily i panslavizm. A. S. Khomyakov, I. Kireyevskiy, K. Aksakov, P. Ya. Chaadayev." In *Byloye i dumy*, 284–305. Leningrad: Gosudarstvennoye izdatel'stvo khudozhestvennoy literatury, 1946.

———. "Rossiya." In *Sobraniye sochineniy v tridtsati tomakh*, 6:187–224. Moscow: Goslitizdat, 1955.

———. "Russkiy narod i sotsializm." In *Sobraniye sochineniy v tridtsati tomakh*, 7:307–40. Moscow: Goslitizdat, 1955.

Kolosov, Evgeniy E. *Ocherki mirovozzreniya N. K. Mikhaylovskogo. Teoriya razdeleniya truda kak osnova nauchnoy sotsiologii*. St. Petersburg: Obshchestvennaya Pol'za, 1912.

Koyré, Alexandre. *Études sur l'histoire de la pensée philosophique en Russie*. Paris: Vrin, 1950.

Lyatskiy, Evgeniy A. "Nikolay Gavrilovich Chernyshevskiy i Sh. Fur'ye." *Sovrennyy mir* 2 (1910) 161–88.

Mikhaylovskiy, Nikolay K. "Chto takoye progress?" In *Sochineniya*, 1:9–165. St. Petersburg: Russkoye bogatstvo, 1906.

———. "Geroi i tolpa." In *Sochineniya*, 2:95–190. St. Petersburg: Russkoye bogatstvo, 1907.

———. "Iz literaturnykh i zhurnal'nykh zametok 1872 g." In *Sochineniya*, 1:685–722. St. Petersburg: Russkoye bogatstvo, 1906.

———. "Pis'ma o pravde i nepravde." In *Sochineniya*, 4:381–463. St. Petersburg: Russkoye bogatstvo, 1897.

———. "Predisloviye k 3-mu izdaniyu." In *Sochineniya*, 1:v–vii. St. Petersburg: Russkoye bogatstvo, 1897.

Nechkina, Militsa V. "Russkaya Pravda i dvizheniye dekabristov." In *Vosstaniye dekabristov. Russkaya Pravda P. I. Pestelya i sochineniya, ey predshestvuyushchiye*, edited by Militsa V. Nechkina, 7:9–75. Moscow: Gospolitizdat, 1958.

Pavlov-Sil'vanskiy, Nikolay P. "P. I. Pestel.'" In *Sochineniya. Vol. 2: Ocherki po russkoy istorii XVIII–XIX vv.*, 206–39. The Hague: Europe Printing, 1966.

Pestel', Pavel I. "Russkaya Pravda. II redaktsiya." In *Vosstaniye dekabristov. Russkaya Pravda P. I. Pestelya i sochineniya, ey predshestvuyushchiye*, edited by Militsa V. Nechkina, 7:113–69. Moscow: Gospolitizdat, 1958.

Rusanov, Nikolay S. "Politika Mikhaylovskogo." *Byloye* 7 (1907) 124–38.

Semevskiy, Vasiliy I. "Dekabristy-masony." *Minuvshiye gody. Zhurnal, posvyashchennyy istorii i literature* 2 (1908) 1–51.

Tschizewskij, Dmitrij. *Hegel bei den Slawen*. Darmstadt: Wissenschaftliche Buchgesellschaft, 1961.

Venturi, Franco. *Roots of Revolution: A History of Populist and Socialist Movements in Nineteenth Century Russia*. London: Weidenfeld and Nicolson, 1960.

Vilenskaya, Emiliya S. *N. K. Mikhaylovskiy i ego rol' v narodnicheskom dvizhenii 70-ykh i nachala 80-ykh godov XIX veka*. Moscow: Nauka, 1979.

Voronitsyn, Ivan P. *Dekabristy i religiya*. Moscow: Ateist, 1928.

Ziemke, Thies. *Marxismus und Narodnichestvo. Entstehung der Gruppe "Befreiung der Arbeit."* Dissertation. Kiel, 1978.

# 11

# Tolstoy and Conrad's Visions of Christianity

—Brygida Pudełko

For Joseph Conrad, whose family had been exposed to political persecution in Russia, it was "a country, a system of government, and a people; it was also, and very importantly, a literature."[1] On October 20, 1911, Conrad wrote to Olivia Rayne Garnett: "I know extremely little of Russians. Practically nothing. In Poland we have nothing to do with them. One knows they are there. And that's disagreeable enough . . . I crossed the Russian frontier at the age of ten. Not having been to school then I never knew Russian."[2] Six years later he repeated his denial of Russian in a letter to Edward Garnett: "The trouble is that I too don't know Russian; I don't even know the alphabet."[3] To George T. Keating in 1922 Conrad protested against H. L. Mencken's "harping on [his] Slavonism:" "If he means that I have been influenced by so-called Slavonic literature then he is utterly wrong. I suppose he means Russian; but, as a matter of fact, I never knew Russian. The few novels I have read, I have read in translation."[4] In his letter to Charles

---

1. Najder, *Conrad in Perspective*, 126.

2. Conrad, *Collected Letters*, 4:490.

3. Ibid., 248.

4. Jean-Aubry, *Joseph Conrad*, 2:289.

Chassé on 31 January 1924, Conrad also expressed his opinion on Russian language and literature:

> I must point out that I do not know the Russian language, that I know next to nothing of Russian imaginative literature, except the little I have been able to read in translations; that the formative forces acting on me, at the most plastic and impressionable age, were purely Western: that is French and English: and that, as far as I can remember, those forces found in me no resistance, no vague, deep-seated antagonism, either racial or temperamental.[5]

Nevertheless, although Conrad denied his knowledge of the Russian language[6] and declared a limited knowledge of Russian literature, the latter is the third, after English and French, most frequently mentioned in his letters. This was largely due to Conrad's friendship with Edward Garnett who had many Russian friends, and whose wife Constance was a well-known translator of Turgenev's novels into English.

The great Russian novelists of the nineteenth century aroused mixed feelings in Conrad. Although Leo Tolstoy was considered by Conrad "perhaps . . . worthy"[7] of Constance Garnett's translation, he was treated with reserved respect and suspicion as being too mystical for Conrad's taste. His chief antipathy was reserved for Dostoevsky—"the grimacing, haunted creature, who is under a curse"[8]—in contrast to the civilized, liberal and humane Turgenev, who was one of Conrad's literary predecessors and masters, next to Flaubert, Maupassant and James. The contrast is crucial for it shows how Conrad viewed Turgenev as a pure artist tragically caught between his apollonian gifts and the mire of the world, while he viewed Dostoevsky as a grim, graceless writer who lacked all that Turgenev possessed. We may also agree that avoiding being accused of rejecting all "things Russian" and all

---

5. Ibid., 336.

6. On Conrad and Russian language, see Morf, "Conrad Did Not Know Russian," 61; Najder, "More on Joseph Conrad's Knowledge of Russian," 94. Najder in *Conrad's Polish Background*, 60, 170, quotes the circumstantial evidence for Conrad's knowledge of "the Cyrillic alphabet and a few Russian words, since he was able to send telegrams to his uncle, but he certainly neither spoke nor read Russian." Karl in *Joseph Conrad*, 91 notes that "Conrad always insisted he did not know either German or Russian—especially the latter, the language of the hated Dostoevsky—but it is hard to see how he grew University Press among these language clusters, in which Polish, German and Russian were intermingled politically, without becoming aware of vocabulary and even grammar."

7. Conrad, *Collected Letters*, 5:71.

8. Jean-Aubry, *Joseph Conrad*, 2:192.

Russian writers, Conrad found it easiest to praise Turgenev, who combined in himself and in his writing national and universal values in a satisfactory balance.

As for Conrad's complex relation to Leo Tolstoy (1828–1910) it needs to be pointed out that although on one or two occasions granting him as an artist a grudging tribute and considering "Turgenev (and perhaps Tolstoy) the only two worthy"[9] of Constance Garnett's talent as a translator,[10] Tolstoy's works were censured severely by Conrad. When he wrote about Stephen Crane, he alluded to Tolstoy's *War and Peace* having nothing better to say about the book than that "the subtle presentation of Rostov's squadron under fire for the first time is a mere episode lost in a mass of other matter, like a handful of pebbles in a heap of sand."[11] Nor could Conrad see any merit in other works by Tolstoy. Having declared his friend John Galsworthy "a humanitarian moralist," Conrad writes:

> I don't believe that it will ever lead you into the gratuitous atrocity, of, say, Ivan Illyitch [*sic*] or the monstrous stupidity of such thing as the *Kreutzer Sonata*, for instance; where an obvious degenerate not worth looking at twice, totally unfitted not only for married life but for any sort of life is presented as a sympathetic victim of some sort of sacred truth that is supposed to live within him.[12]

Clearly, Conrad feels that, within the works he cites, Tolstoy is moralizing. Conrad, an artist who wanted to arrive at his meanings immediately through the sensuous renderings of passionate experience, and not merely to define meanings in abstraction as didacticism or moralizing, was suspicious about Tolstoy—the humanitarian moralist. In a letter to Edward Garnett of 23 February 1914, Conrad sums up his view on the Russian novelist: "*Dislike* as definition of my attitude to Tolstoy: is but a rough and approximate term. I judge him not—for this reason that his anti-sensualism is suspect to me. In that matter (which is not worth the fuss which is made about it) the pros and the antis seem to me tarred with the same brush."[13]

---

9. Conrad, *Collected Letters*, 5:71.

10. Conrad was eagerly interested in getting Constance Garnett's translations of Tolstoy's books. In a letter to Edward Garnett he added in a postscript: "Remember me to your wife. I did not know she translated Tolstoy. I shall get it at once from L[ondon] L[ibrary]." Conrad, *Collected Letters*, 1:366.

11. Wright, *Joseph Conrad*, 112.

12. Conrad, *Collected Letters*, 4:116.

13. Ibid., 5:358.

Having spoken of the Russian's anti-sensualism, which is an important ingredient of *The Kreutzer Sonata*, Conrad elaborates on what he especially dislikes in Tolstoy:

> The base from which he starts—Christianity—is distasteful to me. I am not blind to its services but the absurd oriental fable from which it starts irritates me. Great, improving, softening, compassionate it may be but it has lent itself with amazing facility to cruel distortion and is the only religion which, with its impossible standards, has brought an infinity of anguish to innumerable souls—on this earth.[14]

## Tolstoy's Vision of Christianity

At the end of the 1870s Tolstoy was at the peak of his glory, wealth and family happiness, but at the same time he was suffering a deep existential crisis. This crisis took him from a position of secular indifferentism towards the search and discovery of his own belief in God, which appeared to be quite different from the official doctrine of the Orthodox Church. Throughout the 1880's, the great Russian novelist decided to abandon the narrative fiction at which he excelled, and within a decade he began to produce religious and didactic writings which were to bring him equal fame as a Christian moralist and philosopher. Tolstoy's works of the 1880s and 1890s—*A Confession, What I Believe, A Critique of Dogmatic Theology, The Kingdom of God, On Life, What is Art*, and others—reflect the evolution of his ideas and record his agonizing search for the essence of true Christianity. The stimulus for Tolstoy's "awakening" became his reflections upon death, in which there can be found motifs developed later on by existentialism. Death for Tolstoy is inseparable from life. Life itself is a kind of dying, and death appears to be the sum total of life. It throws merciless light on all the previous life, separating genuine things in life from those that are false, i.e. truth from lies. A horrible and agonizing death is the punishment for an idle and empty life, whereas a decent death is for Tolstoy a reward for a plain, Christian life full of hard work. In general, Tolstoy's highly rationalized Christianity has much in common with Kant's *Religion Within the Bounds of Mere Reason*. They agree in their reduction of Christianity to moral teaching, in the refusal of setting hopes on God in earthly affairs and in excluding everything supernatural and miraculous from Christianity. For Tolstoy, Jesus Christ is not God-man, but the greatest moral teacher of mankind, the embodiment

14. Ibid.

of man who has recognized his filiations to God. The purpose of "a religious person's actions," according to Tolstoy, "is to satisfy everything demanded of him by the laws of God." That law is not to be found in "some theological doctrine, but rather to become manifest as that state of consciousness Tolstoy calls 'religious.'"[15] In other words, moral reality resides for Tolstoy not in action, but in perception. The quest for it consists of "progressive withdrawals from conventional constructs penetrating to purpose, meaning and reality."[16]

The unifying keystone of Tolstoy's Christian teaching is the idea of non-resistance to evil.[17] In *The Kingdom of God* he examined Christ's moral teachings to demolish the familiar objection that they were too idealistic and impractical for humanity to follow, and made the doctrine of non-resistance a criterion for a revaluation of all human institutions. He condemned the Christian churches for turning the meaning of Christ's message into meaningless verbiage and dogmas offering no satisfactory direction to the community of the faithful. Christianity, Tolstoy argued, actually thought that non-violence was the only proper foundation for the blessedness and perfection all religions preached. Although Tolstoy did not provide many convincing examples of the successful practice of non-resistance, he was convinced that it was not an abstract moral imperative, but a mode of daily living promoting individual survival and the improvement of society.[18] The major part of *The Kingdom of God* was devoted to the exposition of Christian anarchism, although the word was never mentioned because of its late nineteenth-century association with violence. Tolstoy was amazed and indignant at a government's ability to murder and destroy with impunity when violence was so obviously incompatible with Christian discipleship

15. Huneker, *Ivory, Apes, and Peacocks*, 261.

16. Ibid.

17. Wacław Lednicki writes that Tolstoy's doctrine of non-resistance was very close to the teachings of the Polish romantics who were persistently and consistently advocating the principles of pardoning for inflicted sufferings, being faithful to the best traditions of Polish political thought of the fifteenth and sixteenth centuries and of the end of the eighteenth century, and preaching the Christianization of politics, even of the Church itself; see Lednicki, *Tolstoy*, 139. Whereas Jayme A. Sokolov and Priscilla R. Roosevelt claim that in the late 1880's, when Tolstoy became increasingly obsessed with his theory of Christian non-resistance, he began studying the writings of two prominent New England pacifists, William Lloyd Garrison (1805–79) and Adin Ballou (1803–90). According to Tolstoy, these men's ideas helped him reinforce and order his own pacifist principles, broadening and deepening his evolving philosophy of non-resistance, and providing the inspiration and model for his monumental work on the ethics of nonresistance, *The Kingdom of God is Within You*, see Sokolov and Roosevelt, "Leo Tolstoi's Christian Pacifism."

18. See Tolstoy, *Polnoye sobraniye sochineniy*, 28:165–293.

and universal morality. For Tolstoy, military conscription, military expenditures, and the burgeoning coercive powers of the state symbolized the total corruption of contemporary civilization and the evisceration of Christianity.[19] Tolstoy also criticized private property, social and economical inequality, love, science, and art.

Three years later after publishing *The Kingdom of God*, Tolstoy wrote an ethical treatise on the creative process entitled *What is Art*, in which he eloquently described the sense of universality produced by great art. According to Tolstoy's view, a work of art must be morally good if it induces morally good feelings in the audience.[20] Truth and sincerity, then, are the plumblines of any work of art, Tolstoy maintains. When those inspire the author, a fair creation is bound to be born.[21] Good alone occupies the supreme position in Tolstoy's hierarchy of values. Truth is dissolved in good as one of the means of its realization, and beauty is opposed to it as an inferior value. Good coincides with the victory over private predilections with beauty forming their basis. Good is objective while beauty is subjective. In the sphere of human relations, beauty only prevents one from seeing the moral nature of man in a non-biased way. The pursuit of beauty in the sphere of art leads to counterfeit art which is incomprehensible and unnecessary for common people. Good art, therefore, should be universal in its appeal which means that like ethics it should not be based on enjoyment because every human activity has a meaning which lies deeper than mere enjoyment. Art, in order to cease being a mere toy and amusement, must renounce totally the notion of beauty. The high predestination of art is to be the means of human communication. Real art must be intelligible and accessible to everybody. Being intelligible in form, art must convey a moral and Christian content.[22] The main objection to Tolstoy's teaching about art is that he wishes to make it too exclusively moral and social claiming that all beauty and intellectual splendour are reflections of the nature of God.[23]

19. Ibid.

20. Diffey, *Tolstoy's "What is Art?,"* 69–70.

21. Kvitko, *Philosophical Study of Tolstoy*, 99.

22. The application of this criterion to the history of art leads Tolstoy to biased and absurd evaluations. He insists that *Uncle Tom's Cabin* deserves its place in the treasure house of world art unlike the works of Shakespeare, Goethe, Beethoven, and his own great novels.

23. Craufurd, *Religion*, 183.

## Conrad and Christianity

About his attitude towards Christianity, it is clear that Conrad was not a practicing believer and, indeed, would not follow institutional religion, which would come under the heading of "formulas" he could not accept. Despite his Catholic upbringing, Conrad presents a view of man that is entirely secular, for whom the universe was man-directed. His attitude to Christianity, Cedric Watts writes, resembles "not an agnostic's nostalgia for certitude (a common Victorian attitude) but rather an Augustan's distaste for fanaticism."[24] Conrad's comments about religion, particularly those contained in his letters to R. B. Cunninghame Graham and Edward Garnett, attack Christianity for duping man into believing that life is meaningful. For instance, to Graham he writes that "Faith is a myth and beliefs shift like mists on the shore"[25] and "I don't care a damn for the best heaven ever invented by Jew or Gentile,"[26] while he complains to Garnett of "the idiotic mystery of Heaven."[27] Clearly, Conrad doubted Christianity's mystical beginnings and disliked certain of its doctrines, especially if they hinted at a *quid pro quo* arrangement with the Deity, encouraged latent hypocrisy, brought about anguish by insisting on impossible standards, or led to the exploitation of devoted individual followers. During Christmas 1920, he told his fellow-sceptic Garnett: "It's strange how I always, from the age of fourteen, disliked the Christian religion, its doctrines, ceremonies and festivals . . . Nobody—not a single Bishop of them—believes in it. The business in the stable is not convincing; whereas my atmosphere (*vide* reviews) can be positively breathed."[28]

However, Conrad, who also claimed that "Everyone must walk in the light of his own heart's gospel. No man's light is good to any of his fellows,"[29] does not offer a total disavowal of Christianity, but rather debunking of its dogma and extremism. Some of these are elements of the formula, some, simply, the faults of the followers. For instance, as in the above quoted letter when criticizing Leo Tolstoy, Conrad says that it is not Christian "services but the absurd oriental fable from which it starts"[30] which is not acceptable to him. In Conrad's eyes, then, Christianity needed to be less mystical, less

---

24. Watts, *Preface to Conrad*, 52.
25. Conrad, *Collected Letters*, 2:17.
26. Ibid., 2:238.
27. Ibid., 1:268.
28. Ibid., 2:468–69.
29. Ibid., 1:253.
30. Ibid., 5:358.

demanding and more realistic in its appraisal of human frailties and emotions. That Conrad's critique of Catholicism and Christianity in general is a complex one is noted by John Lester, who points out that Conrad's comments on religion are very often tailored to suit his addressee.[31] Thus, the religious scepticism in the letters to Cunninghame Graham is extenuated by the suggestion of Christian succour in correspondence with Marguerite Poradowska: "For charity is eternal and universal life, the divine virtue, the only manifestation of the Almighty which can in some way justify the act of creation."[32] This letter is intended as a rebuke to Poradowska for carrying her self-sacrifice too far. Conrad asks rhetorically, "have you found the peace which is the reward of these sacrifices accepted by the master of our souls?"[33] but it simultaneously—and contradictory—acknowledges the existence of such aspects of Christian doctrine as "the Almighty" and "master of our souls." This is no impasse, but rather a reasoned middle path that eschews the excesses of Christian dogma. Conrad is equally wary of the claims of science, whose advances in the nineteenth century, more than anything else, rendered traditional religious belief untenable. Conrad was far from going to the extremes of disbelief and extolling science and material progress as substitutes for dwindling spirituality.

Conrad's general scepticism of Christianity is pervasive and many of his novels reveal the blind fanaticism abounding within institutionalized religions. It extends to the presentation of hypocritical religious zealots, like the ostentatiously professing Protestant, the bigoted Podmore in *The Nigger of the "Narcissus."* Therese in *The Arrow of Gold*, and the French Catholic clergy living off the peasant villagers in *The Idiots*, and implicitly to the influence of a priest-father, upon the Professor in *The Secret Agent*. Added to this, the despair his characters experience is often the metaphysical anguish born of a faithless age. Taminah in *Almayer's Folly* knew no heaven to send her prayer to while Heyst in *Victory* regretted that he had no heaven to which he could recommend Lena. Conrad's atomic view of sin and salvation, the necessity for the individual to be aware of his rights and wrongs, makes each person accountable only to himself not to the dictates of God. There is no squaring of accounts with heaven. Rewards are on this earth, and hell exists solely as a conscience in each man's heart. In *Under Western Eyes*, Razumov's sin and salvation are secular: his are never considered sins against God; they are not even in their strict sense religious sins. Similarly, Nostromo's remorse of conscience is connected with his fears for his reputation;

31. Lester, *Conrad and Religion*, 20.
32. Conrad, *Collected Letters*, 1:107.
33. Ibid., 107–8.

and Heyst's dilemma is purely one of personal decision. Jim, also, must get back into normal society through self-discovery and not through prayer; his salvation, which is of this world, can come only when he redeems his sins of omission through self-sacrifice. If God exists, as Conrad never denied, then He exists in the individual and not as an ambiguous force whose ways man can never ascertain. Man is, in a sense, autonomous; society does not make decisions for Razumov or Winnie Verloc. Similarly in *Chance*,[34] which also illustrates Conrad's secularity, Flora can fall back only on herself; Captain Anthony is an egoistic knight, not a Christian gentleman; the governess is motivated by selfishness with no thought of heavenly retribution; and the Fynes live the good life in the sight of earthly rewards. By secularising the matter of the novel, Conrad was carrying into English the freedom of the French novel. He de-emphasized that amorphous sense of religious morality that had marked the nineteenth-century novel, a morality that was in essence a Christian morality responsible to the Christian God. Carleon Anthony, the deceased poet of *Chance*, wrote extensively of chivalrous Christian love, but his daughter, Mrs Fyne, advocated, as if in rebellion against her father's doctrine of womanly acquiescence, that "no consideration, no delicacy, no tenderness, no scruples should stand in the way of a woman."[35] This view, of course, indicates self-reliance and independence. Consequently, although the narrator Marlow sardonically scorns this kind of feminism and pours contempt on female insincerity, Conrad has nevertheless broken from the idea of women placed according to a strict Christian morality. Flora's decision must be made from the standpoint of personal happiness and personal salvation. By choosing Anthony, she selects sanity; the way of her father, she recognizes, is self-destructive. The very fact that she can embrace her husband while rejecting her father shows the cracks in the traditional family structure based on Christian precept. Each individual, Conrad stresses, must choose their own salvation. By de-emphasizing the relation between man and some murky God, or between men and an organized Christian

34. The most famous assessment of *Chance* is Henry James's review-essay of *The Younger Generation* first published in the "Times Literary Supplement" on 19 March and 2 April 1914, and then revised and expanded into *The New Novel* in *Notes on Novelists*, excerpted in Sherry, *Conrad*, 263–70. Although James described Conrad as a genius and granted him a high place in the middle generation of English writers, he criticized *Chance* for its artificial construction and excessive subordination of content to form. Interestingly, James placed Conrad on the opposite side to Leo Tolstoy, in whose method of writing he condemned the dominance of content over form, a subordination of the means of presentation to the subject. James's confrontation of the two writers appeared at about the same time when Conrad, too, spoke disapprovingly about Tolstoy; see Conrad, *Collected Letters*, 5:358.

35. Conrad, *Chance*, 47.

morality, Conrad subscribed to an atomistic view of morality in which self-responsibility determines individual action. Not only does this view of personal morality cut deeply into twentieth-century literary ideas, but it is also close to its general notions to the philosophical existentialism theorized by Sartre and Camus. Conrad's ideas also both parallel Gide's insistence on human liberty in their way, leading to the latter's notion of the gratuitous act in which the individual is at the zenith of his freedom, and give background to the work of Proust in which the individual with his recurring past is the very center of the only universe that counts.

The closest counterpart's of Flora's relatives, who are motivated solely by self-interest thinly disguised as Christian charity, and who are totally lacking in understanding and sympathy, are the ugly colonizers in *An Outpost of Progress* and *Heart of Darkness*. Marlow's evident scorn for them reflects a general distaste that Conrad himself felt for the products of Christianity.

## Bibliography

Conrad, Joseph. *Chance: A Tale in Two Parts*. Edited by Martin Ray. Oxford: Oxford University Press, 2002.

———. *The Collected Letters of Joseph Conrad*. Edited by Frederick R. Karl and Laurence Davies. Cambridge: Cambridge University Press, 1983–2008.

Craufurd, Alexander H. *The Religion and Ethics of Tolstoy*. London: T. Fisher Unwin, 1912.

Diffey, T. J. *Tolstoy's "What is Art."* London: Croom Helm, 1985.

Huneker, James G. *Ivory, Apes, and Peacocks*. New York: Sagamore, 1957.

Jean-Aubry, Gerard. *Joseph Conrad, Life and Letters*. 2 vols. London: Heinemann, 1927.

Karl, Frederick Robert. *Joseph Conrad: The Three Lives*. New York: Farrar, Straus and Giroux, 1979.

Kvitko, David. *A Philosophical Study of Tolstoy*. New York, 1927.

Lednicki, Wacław. *Tolstoy between "War and Peace."* The Hague: Mouton, 1965.

Lester, John. *Conrad and Religion*. London: Macmillan 1988.

Morf, Gustav. "Conrad Did Not Know Russian." *Joseph Conrad Today* 2 (1977) 61.

Najder, Zdzisław. *Conrad in Perspective: Essays on Art and Fidelity*. Cambridge: Cambridge University Press, 1977.

———. "More on Joseph Conrad's Knowledge of Russian." *Joseph Conrad Today* 3 (1978) 94.

Sherry, Norman, ed. *Conrad: The Critical Heritage*. London: Routledge and Kegan Paul, 1973.

Sokolov, Jayme A., and Priscilla R. Roosevelt. "Leo Tolstoi's Christian Pacifism." *The Carl Beck Papers in Russian and East European Studies* 604 (1987) 1–24.

Tolstoy, Lev N. *Polnoye sobraniye sochineniy*. Edited by Vladimir G. Chertkov. 90 vols. Moscow: Izdatel'stvo Khudozhestvennaya literatura, 1928–57.

Watts, Cedric. *A Preface to Conrad*. London: Longman, 1982.

Wright, Walter F., ed. *Joseph Conrad on Fiction*. Lincoln: University of Nebraska Press, 1964.

# 12

# Nikolai Fedorov and Godmanhood

## --Cezar Jędrysko

Nikolai Fedorov is the creator of a unique concept which goes far beyond the limits of theoretical philosophy. He proclaimed that mankind is under a moral obligation to overcome death and actualize the immanent, physical and universal resurrection of the dead. Humanity, united in a common brotherhood, ought to transform the blind forces of nature into life-giving powers in order to repay the debt of life to its ancestors and to fulfill the Gospel message of Christ the Redemptor. Fedorov's project, the so-called "common task," is an extraordinary mixture of practical indications, futurism and eschatology.

Despite the fact that Fedorov's common task is in the first place an imperative, a call to action, it contains a developed exposition of the metaphysics of Godmanhood. This paper is an attempt to look at Fedorov's project through the prism of Godmanhood. It aims to show the significance of the Godmanhood component in Fedorov's thought and to depict its impact on the understanding of the whole project.

Godmanhood is the mutual relationship between the divine and the human. It describes: (1) the internal union of two natures—divine and human—within a person; (2) the relationship between man and God in terms of complementarity and interdependence; (3) and the indirect reference of God to the cosmos.

The concept of Godmanhood is derived from the Christological dogma endorsed at the Council of Chalcedon in AD 451, which explains how Jesus could be both God and a man at the same time. It says that two perfect, complete and inseparable natures—the human and divine—coexist united in the person of Christ. They are not merged or mixed together, each is different and distinct, and each retains its own properties and autonomous being. It is, as the theologian Sergey Bulgakov explains, a hypostatic union:

> The unity of the hypostasis guarantees the unity of the life, and the duality of the natures guarantees the complexity and duality of the life; but the union of the natures, headed by the one divine hypostasis, establishes a new and particular bi-unity, which exists neither in Divinity nor in humanity. For in Divinity we have unity of nature in the case of hypostatic trinity, with each hypostasis entirely possessing the nature; and in humanity we have unity of nature in the case of multiplicity of hypostatic centers, each of which has the nature in its personal possession.[1]

Hypostases are separate wills and freedoms united in one subsistence and cooperation, where the divine will have precedence—though not authority—leading and guiding the human will.

For Godmanhood, the assumption that manhood is Godmanhood is essential.[2] The Christological dogma determines orthodox anthropology, which means, in other words, that statements about Christ are statements about the ideal human. Every single man is a person like Christ, thus everyone is subject to the internal dialectics of man and the divine, which is expressed by the so-called "golden rule" of patristic soteriology: God became man so that man may become God.

Man was created in God's image, and therefore he possesses godlike powers, freedom and creativity, which have to be used in order to adjust his likeness to that of the Creator. The *imago Dei* in man demands to be realized through acts of human spirit. It is an appeal to imitate the way of Christ in a particular human life, to become a reflection of Christ. God, incarnated as a man, divinized his manhood, and so this shall be the destiny of all man.

Godmanhood refers not only to the internal relationship of elements in person, but expresses the external relationship of man and God. Man cannot exist without God, while God would not be God without man. We learn from the concept of Godmanhood that man and God are inseparable and complementary, supplying mutual needs, but still staying distinct—they are hypostasis. God is the most human of all man and man has to become

1. Bulgakov, *Lamb of God*, 181–82.
2. Berdyaev, *Divine and the Human*, 111.

the living God. Godmanhood implies the reality of the divinization of the human—it shows the reality of *theosis*.

For Russian thinkers such as Vladimir Soloviev, Nikolai Berdyaev and Sergey Bulgakov, the association of man and God has a principal meaning. It is a fundamental and basic relation, which underlies the cosmic relationship between God and the world. On the basis of the metaphysics of Godmanhood, the divine refers to the cosmos indirectly, through the hands of man, which implies that the burden of eschatological responsibility for *theosis* lies in mankind itself.

The Chalcedonian resolutions regarding the two natures of Christ outline not only the Christian ontology of the human being but also its deontology. They indicate the destiny of man—the divinization of its human nature and the entirety of existence. Yet another duality appears in the understanding of Godmanhood: on the one hand it is a profound description of the origins of a person, while on the other hand it is a presentation of a project, pointing out a potentiality that ought to be realized.

The concept of Godmanhood, which had been implicit in Russian religious thought, was officially incorporated into modern philosophy as an object of consideration by Vladimir Soloviev, the founder of the first Russian philosophical system. His deliberation on the idea, expressed especially in the *Lectures on Godmanhood*, became a signpost that oriented the next generation of philosophers, such as Nikolai Berdyaev, Semen Frank, Sergey Bulgakov, Pavel Florensky, Boris Vysheslavtsev, Nikolai Lossky, Evgeniy Trubetskoy, and Lev Karsavin.

Soloviev regards Godmanhood as a relationship between man and the divine, which was realized in Jesus Christ as the result of a dual act of humility and self-emptying. God manifests his love and becomes a human being, he renounces his omnipotence, omniscience and eternity as a means to overcome sin and the decline of the world in the limited and temporal form of earthly life. God's self-denying of his divine attributes in order to assume human form is complemented by man's self-denying of manhood in the pursuit of divinity. The rejection of the three temptations has a crucial significance for the process of divinizing Christ's human nature. Satan in the desert tests all the three aspects of Christ's human nature: body, soul and spirit separately. By rejecting all of Satan's offers, Christ receives power over all of the flesh, mind and the power in the Kingdom of Spirit. Incarnation and divinization mutually complete each other. The path of Godmanhood is a synchronization of two movements: the descent of the divine to earth and the ascent of man into the Kingdom of God. So Godmanhood is at the same time the Christology of man and the anthropology of Christ.

There are two ways of seeing Godmanhood, stressed by Soloviev, as static and as dynamic. In the first view, it is an ontological scheme of being, while in the second depiction it is a process, implied by an adopted plan, where all of mankind follows the path of Christ in the divinization of His human nature.

Godmanhood plays a dual role in philosophical thinking. On the one hand, it is a kind of religious supposition, even if it is not explicit. The concept resolves some classical philosophical problems, but generates others. On the other hand, the acceptance of this idea has a consequence for the method of doing philosophy. Theological terms and categories are adopted as the root of all further philosophical thinking.

Although Godmanhood is often considered, especially by those thinkers who continue to develop it, as one of those categories that marks out the specifically religious character of Russian philosophy, the essence of the concept seems to be universal for all Christianity, rather than limited to one specific nationality. This way of understanding the relationship between God and man has been present in Christian thought since its earliest stages.

There are several reasons why the name of Nikolai Fedorov is sometimes intentionally not included on the list of authors that develop the philosophical tradition of Godmanhood. Firstly, he lived and worked at the same time as Vladimir Soloviev, one of the most prominent philosophers in the history of Russian thought, who created the representative form or pattern of what we call the philosophical idea of Godmanhood. Despite the fact that both authors were in contact, Fedorov develop his concept independently. Fedorov did not publish a great deal and his views were simply not well known by his contemporaries. The concept of Godmanhood was associated mainly with Soloviev and his later followers, while Fedorov acquired the status of a mysterious thinker. Secondly, as was mentioned at the beginning of the paper, Fedorov had no intention of working out the metaphysics of Godmanhood. Fedorov founds his concept of Godmanhood by way of explaining the imperative requirement of the resurrection of deceased fathers. As opposed to Soloviev, he did not plan to build a philosophical system or theory; he was focused on the practice of his common task. Nevertheless his idea of Godmanhood was expressed fully and clearly. Thirdly, from its very beginning Fedorov's project has been highly controversial. Not only is the futuristic and utopian mechanism of the common task questionable, but also Fedorov's selective interpretation of Christianity and Christ's life has raised questions regarding its orthodoxy.[3]

3. These kinds of concerns have been raised by Georgy Fedotov, Georges Florovsky, Sergey Bulgakov, and even Nikolai Berdyaev, who criticizes the "magical" component of Fedorov's thought.

To introduce the issue of Godmanhood in the philosophy of the common task we must start with Fedorov's description of man. The anthropology assumed in his project is extremely dynamic. The humanity of the present is defined as something that ought to be upgraded. It contains in itself perfectness in terms of future prospects that appeal for realization. The term "mankind" has meaning only as a process of becoming, turning from one state into another. Fedorov's understanding of man has been expounded in three key characteristics:

First, mortality—man dies and in this moment this fact constitutes the condition of the human being. Mortality does not refer only to death itself, but also to all of its intermediate forms and consequences, such as illness, hatred, poverty and so on. The Russian thinker tries to reveal that all forms of evil and suffering are indirectly caused by the existence of death.[4] Although death is the ultimate form of evil, it is a denial of consciousness. This is a chaotic blind force, pure pointless destruction. Man as a part of the cosmos is dependent on this terrible power yet, however, he does not accept it. Mortality shows the defectiveness and weakness of the human being.

Second, "Son of man"—this biblical idiom is used to describe the interdependence of generations. It communicates several things. Firstly, that man cannot be considered simply as a single individual, because he is not self-reliant. Every man has a father to whom he owns the gift of life. Secondly, being a son carries an obligation—every man carries the burden of this afore-mentioned debt. How it can be paid off? For the value of a life the only equivalent is a life.[5] Children have a moral obligation to compensate for the glaring injustice between generations by resurrecting their deceased fathers. Thirdly, there is a blood kinship of all man due to common ancestors—Adam and Eve.

Third, the resurrector—the reaction to the death of an intimate is radical disagreement. Although reason justifies death as natural, some sort of power in man always stands opposite to death and questions its reality. These powers are responsible for grief and in fact they have shaped our culture. Man began to bury the dead with the intention of bringing them back to life.[6] The overcoming of death is a deeply rooted human need.

Man belongs to the universe by virtue of the substance out of which he is made. Flesh and soul consist of the same atoms and elements as dust, planets and stars. Particles of dead people circulate in the matter cycle creating new forms. However, man also exceeds the cosmos, which inertly evolves

---

4. Semenova, *Filosof budushchego veka*, 161.

5. Fedorov, *Sobraniye sochineniy*, 1:108.

6. Ibid., 1:142.

towards a state of entropy.[7] He has the ability to intentionally transform the world. Moreover, he does not have to be determined by its rules, even if they are considered by reason as beyond doubt. Fedorov calls into doubt the argument that death is certain. Our knowledge about this phenomenon is settled only by experience. We take the inevitability of death for granted based on inductive reasoning, which does not give absolute certainty.[8]

The physical and mental aspects of man's humanity are products of evolution, which was triggered by an initial shock following the death of the father. In that distant moment morality was born, when life was identified as good and death was named evil. Through the existence of humanity the universe gains self-consciousness.

All of the further history of mankind is the history of rebellion against death, which consists in attempts to replace natural processes, all things which man cannot change, with controlled activity, creativity. A first step in that direction was achieving vertical posture.[9] Man has freed his front limbs and turned them into organs of self-creation.[10] Straightening up against gravity delivered him from the horizon of annihilation and allowed him to sweep across the sky and notice that the world forms a unity. Adopting vertical posture gave the opportunity to learn about the interrelationship between objects and pioneered a series of discoveries

Man became a creator who "had to consider the use of this, that which was given, as the most shameful, while creation out of nothing as the greatest perfection."[11] Self-creation oriented on overcoming natural limits leads to the development of a manifold of talents and to culture. For Fedorov, to be human means to constantly develop in order to recreate life. The destiny of humanity is to reach the point where the primal trauma of death could be absolutely overcome by man's creativity, which demands the erasing of the phenomenon of death from the future, present and past.

The very origins of all culture lie in divine-inspired opposition against death. A culture, being a cumulative result of mankind's creativity, has its meaning only when it is directed toward the resurrection of all dead. Building an authentic Christian, eschatological and life-preserving culture is an aspect of divinizing man's nature, a manifestation of the Godmanhood process in history.

---

7. Ibid., 2:243–44.

8. Ibid., 1:258–59.

9. Lukashevich, *Fedorov*, 153.

10. Fedorov, *Sobraniye sochineniy*, 2:249.

11. Ibid., 2:253.

For man defined in this way Christ—a God who became a man in order to divinize his humanity—is a prodigy. In fact, there is no separation between the man and the God. Man was made in the image of God and has to strive for perfection in God's likeness. Creativity is man's godlike power. Mankind has to follow the path of Christ, who lived a human life and as a man resisted temptations in the desert, and to carry out Christ's command to do what He did—to resurrect the dead.

Fedorov's portrayal of Christ arouses ambivalent feelings among commentators. For example, Georges Florovsky underlines the lack of proper Christology in the common task project,[12] while Vladimir Il'in, in contrast to that opinion, emphasises the depiction of Christ as person, not a distant dogma.[13] Certainly, the picture of Christ in Fedorov's writings is very limited and selective. In fact, the author refers to only a few passages from the Gospels, mostly to those regarding the resurrection of Lazarus. Nevertheless, we would not be keen to say that philosopher reduces or even disavows the richness of its content. Fedorov conceives the significance of Christianity in the fact of resurrection. There is no interest for him in developing theology when it comes to the practical realization of the Gospel message.

Fedorov perceives three eminent moments in the history of salvation. The importance of the first one, the resurrection of Lazarus, consists in proving that the power of death can be broken. By the physical—not metaphorical—bringing of Lazarus back to life, Christ has shown what is to be done. It is a testimony of Godmanhood and a declaration of the common task. The act of resurrection itself is a manifestation of God's love and the union of man and God. The second is the redemption of humanity from sin through the sacrifice on the cross and resurrection of Christ, which founds the Christian faith. One individual died the death of all mankind and he overcomes it. This is an act of God's Holy Grace, which is the beginning of the common resurrection of the dead. The final transformation of the cosmos has a twofold nature, just as there are two inseparable natures in the person of Christ. There must be both an act of God's will, which has already taken place, and an act of human will.[14] God's act of redemption opens a space for mankind's respond. And the answer to Christ's resurrection can be only the common resuscitative-resurrection of deceased ancestors. That is the third and the ending point of our history—the realization of the common task that was established by Christ himself.

12. Florovskiy, *Puti russkogo bogosloviya*, 322.

13. Il'in, "Otvet Florovskomu," 728–9.

14. Fedorov, *Sobraniye sochineniy*, 1:142.

Father Florovsky accuses Fedorov of mistaking the provinces of man and God.[15] In his opinion, the project of resuscitative-resurrection is founded on the premise that mankind is capable of delivering itself from the power and penalty of sin without a divine and transcendental act. The common task gives us a falsified image of salvation, a salvation in the absence of grace. Through this misinterpretation of the nature of man Fedorov falls into the heresy of pelagianism.

However, Florovsky seems not to pay proper attention to the inclusion of Godmanhood in Fedorov's description of man's nature. Even when the author of *Philosophy of the Common Task* declares that there would be no other salvation than the immanent salvation accomplished by internal means of humanity, it is still a false conclusion to identify this statement with the exclusion God from participation in the process. Fedorov rejects the idea of a transcendental and immanent unravelling of history, understood as a supernatural act undertaken by a solitary God or mankind. Where he mentions internal human powers, we should remember the divine element that constitutes the person. Fedorov says, "The soul of the man is not a *tabula rasa*, it is not an empty sheet of paper, it's not a soft wax, which can be formed freely—it is made of two images, two biographies united in one person."[16]

A man's creative act—an act that brings life to the world—is concurrently an act of God. A man is an instrument of superhuman aims.[17] However this relationship is far from one of blind submission. The divine will establish a goal, while human will follows it by its own means. This cooperation of the human and the divine can be called synergy or God-man acting (*bogodeystviye*).

Since Christ's sacrifice, the salvation of mankind has been under construction. The act of God, which initiated the process and opened a space for further steps, has to be complemented and finalized by an equivalent act of man. The power needed for the ultimate transformation of man's nature has already been brought to this world. The instruction was given. It now comes to man to take the eschatological responsibility in hand and complete what was started. This would lead to the final divinization of all nature. The illusory difference between God and man will cease to exist with the redemption of sin through resuscitative-resurrection. In other words, the realization of the common task would be the arrival of the Kingdom of God.

15. Florovskiy, *Puti russkogo bogosloviya*, 319–20.

16. Fedorov, *Sobraniye sochineniy*, 1:282.

17. Ibid., 1:402.

# Bibliography

Berdyaev Nicolas. *The Divine and the Human.* Translated by R. M. French. London: Geoffrey Bles, 1949.

Bulgakov, Sergius. *The Lamb of God.* Translated by Boris Jakim. Grand Rapids: Eerdmans, 2008.

Bulgakov, Sergiy. "Zagadochnyy myslitel' (N. F. Fedorov)." In *N. F. Fedorov: Pro et contra. K 175-letiyu so dnya rozhdeniya i 100-letiyu so dnya smerti N. F. Fedorova. Antologiya. Kniga pervaya,* edited by Anastasiya G. Gacheva and Svetlana G. Semenova. St. Petersburg: Izdatel'stvo Russkogo Khristianskogo gumanitarnogo instituta, 2004.

Fedorov, Nikolay. *Sobraniye sochineniy.* 4 vols. Moscow: Progress, Traditsiya, Evidentis, 1995–2000.

Florovskiy, Georgiy. *Puti russkogo bogosloviya.* Minsk: Izdatel'stvo Belorusskogo Ekzarkhata, 2006.

Il'in, Vladimir. "Otvet G. V. Florovskomu." In *N. F. Fedorov: Pro et contra. K 175-letiyu so dnya rozhdeniya i 100-letiyu so dnya smerti N. F. Fedorova. Antologiya. Kniga pervaya,* edited by Anastasiya G. Gacheva and Svetlana G. Semenova. St. Petersburg: Izdatel'stvo Russkogo khristianskogo gumanitarnogo instituta, 2004.

Lukashevich, Sephen. *N. F. Fedorov (1828–1903): A Study in Russian Eupsychian and Utopian Thought.* Newark: University of Delaware Press, 1977.

Semenova, Svetlana G. *Filosof budushchego veka: Nikolay Fedorov.* Moscow: Pashkov dom, 2004.

# 13

# Catastrophism as a Manifestation of the Crisis of Consciousness in Russian and Polish Cultures

—Natalia Koltakova

DESPITE CERTAIN IDEOLOGICAL AND social differences, both Russian and Polish cultures share the same cultural space where the common ideological and aesthetic ideas of the day are expressed. One of these general trends is the so-called crisis of culture originating at the turn of the twentieth century—the times that were known as "fin de siècle." The thinkers of the time seem to have anticipated many of the social and cultural upheavals that manifested themselves in the twentieth century.

It is worth noting, however, that the concept of crisis should not only be limited to the time at the turn of the century. The crisis consciousness tends to display a high degree of "continuity" throughout the twentieth century, becoming not a temporary but rather a permanent issue. The Russian symbolists were one of the first who presaged the universal catastrophe. They pointed out that the crisis had outgrown the personality scale, becoming truly apocalyptic in its dimensions. The search for the unity in essays and poetry (Andrei Bely, Vyacheslav Ivanov) is followed by the awareness of its decay and disintegration (Polish catastrophism). Aesthetic catastrophism is closely associated with religion. People encroach on God's place and their conscience is split as a result. It is worth mentioning that the origins of Russian catastrophism actually predicted the disasters of the twentieth century. A philosophy of war begins to develop long before war breaks out. Vladimir Soloviev was one of the first to capture this mood in his "catastrophic" work *War, Progress and the End of History*. Completed in 1899–1900, this work is an expression of the borderline state of consciousness in all senses. However, the philosopher does not give us an apology for war, merely a warning. Even though the philosopher stresses the historical aspect of his thoughts because—in his opinion—history "had for its object not a universal cataclysm of creation but the conclusion of our historical process,"[1] he nonetheless takes catastrophism to a universal level.

Soloviev's thoughts on evil in the historical context, where evil grows to a cosmic scale, caused a lot of reflection both in the Russian (Andrei Bely's article "Apocalypse in Russian Poetry") and Polish cultures (Czesław Miłosz). Andrei Bely was deeply impressed by Soloviev's prophetic gift as well as the anticipation of future disasters. "Even back then I realized that the haze that obscured the spirituality is bound to befall Russia, revealing all the horrors of wars and revolutions . . . I knew: fireworks of chimeras were about to explode over mankind."[2]

The twentieth century illustrated those "fireworks of chimeras" foretold by Andrei Bely. It is therefore unsurprising that Soloviev's 1990 edition of *War, Progress and the End of History*, had a preface by Czesław Miłosz. The Polish poet and philosopher pointed out that this work "marks a turn in his thinking and, because it gives due attention to the power of evil, belongs already to our time."[3] Evil in the philosophical concept of "fin de siècle," of course, can be negated through Nietzsche's immoralism. Yet, in reality, a total crisis of consciousness of those times is still valuable for a reason. Besides, an attempt of an individual to leave the sphere of values and guidelines is always quite questionable. Even Nietzsche actually only seemingly transcends the axiological dimension. His "beyond" does not offer salvation but is simply an escape. An universal catastrophe appears to be inseparable from the madness of the individual. Thus, using an apt remark by Andrei Bely, Nietzsche saw early in his madness "a grimace that slid across the face of humanity."[4]

The Russian tradition in philosophy, influenced by Nietzscheanism (including Vyacheslav Ivanov), however, remains within the realm of ethics. Ivanov's Christianized ethics and aesthetics is nurtured by Nietzschean

1. Solovyov, *War, Progress and the End of History*, 193.
2. Belyy, "Apokalipsis v russkoy poezii," 136.
3. Miłosz, "Introduction," 11.
4. Belyy, "Apokalipsis v russkoy poezii," 136.

motives and pagan images. Perhaps one of the reasons for the crisis of consciousness in late nineteenth and the whole of the twentieth century lies in its reliance on controversy and contradictions. This also refers to Nietzsche's attempt to construct a system of immoralism, the logical conclusion of which is madness. Only madness is truly beyond good and evil. Christianized Nietzscheanism by Vyacheslav Ivanov can also be added to this list of contradictions because he is quite an interesting figure of the crisis epoch, last but not least because he adopted Catholicism. Thus, one person embraces two versions of Christianity. So, obviously, from a religious point of view the Russian and Polish cultures are not only opposed as Orthodox and Catholic, but also adjacent to a single Christian world. This adjacency is most noticeable not at the level of dogmas and rituals, but at the level of art.

It is impossible to explain total catastrophism using purely historical reasons. They are closely linked to much deeper reasons that tap into ideology and mindset. So, for instance, George Seaver defines Berdyaev's personalism as "a resolution of the apparent antinomy between Monism and Pluralism."[5] However, putting personality to the foreground is just as dangerous. The aesthetics of Russian Symbolism is based on blatant contradictions: on the one hand, it is deeply and intrinsically rooted in the Orthodox tradition. On the other hand, the unity of divine and human is broken because the balance is upset, because we now witness the power of individuals who may exceed their authorities and abilities. The crisis of consciousness rightly leads to the definition of art as hell by Alexander Blok, according to whom "art is an awful and majestic hell."[6]

It is worth noting the fact that the crisis of consciousness that is analyzed here, although largely stipulated by value reasons, must itself be devoid of negative connotations. Crisis is described as times of active quest, a sharp ideological change, a state of anguish that leads to discoveries. The word *catastrophe* itself is of Greek origin and it means an end of life, a death, an overturn, a change of laws. The concept of catastrophism is often associated with Polish literature and Czesław Miłosz. Vladimir Morenets, a researcher of Ukrainian catastrophism, suggests that catastrophism is not just a state of mind but a trend in the literature. However, following the researcher's observations, "the catastrophic element is the element of purification."[7] Accordingly, catastrophism puts an apocalyptic mood in the foreground. The Second Coming of Christ is manifested through a universal catastrophe which in turn leads to purification.

5. Seaver, *Nicolas Berdyaev*, 44.
6. Blok, "O sovremennom sostoyanii," 244.
7. Morenets,' *Natsional'ni shlyakhi poyetichnogo modernu*, 270.

Catastrophic motifs in Russian and Polish culture, in literature in particular, are surprisingly similar. No wonder language represents a form of culture, quoting Ernst Cassirer. Therefore, language-shaped manifestation of catastrophic poetics makes it possible to accentuate the whole picture of the crisis of consciousness. Obviously, the integration of literature and philosophy within a single cultural domain is a promising area of research. The involvement of Russian symbolism and Polish catastrophism shows the dynamics of the literary process in particular and the dynamics of culture as a whole. Therefore, the study of the crisis of consciousness must constantly take into account "the contradiction between an individual work and the historical process," as noted by Janusz Sławiński.[8]

The symbolist foreboding of disaster, an image of a haze that precedes it, can be found in pre-symbolist poetry by Nikolai Minsky. The vivid image of the city created by this poet ("The City Afar") appears to be not so much mysterious as timeless, hazy, and unreal:

> Live vapours of toiling and passionate cries
> Weave a darkening pall.
> Dust and smoke and the specks and the shadows that rise,
> And numberless hearts with their throbbing and sighs,
> Aloft weave a darkening pall.[9]

Timelessness ("and its load nor the morn nor the noon can upraise") already in itself is a powerful manifestation of the fact that personal consciousness has lost its foothold. Disaster at the turn of the century does not occur all of a sudden, it is foretold and foreboded.

These prophetic motifs quite naturally cause fear, which is existentially linked to disaster. These very motifs led to the concept of fear in a poem by Dmitry Merezhkovsky:

> A sacred awe through all the land,
> As of some secret thing is born.[10]

A prayer and a miracle can save us from this fear ("O pray then, and believing, see / a wonder from a wonder rise"). All of the aesthetics of Russian symbolism are based on expecting and predicting a miracle. It takes the shape of a beautiful but impossible Wonderland. The catastrophe is a kind of "miracle upside down." After all, art for art's sake does not save from fear. This aestheticism was aphoristically expressed by Nietzsche: "I was in love

---

8. Sławiński, "Synchronia i diachronia," 284.

9. Selver, *Modern Russian Poetry*, 51.

10. Ibid.

with art, passionately in love, and in the whole of existence saw nothing else than art."[11] In general, passion, fear, feelings of crisis are dominant within artistic consciousness of "fin de siècle."

So the crisis of consciousness is caused not only by existential ide-ology, but also by purely vital factors pushing the rapid technical process, which would gain considerable momentum in the twentieth century. Prog-ress and catastrophe are largely interdependent and interrelated concepts. Thus, even Zinaida Gippius celebrates electricity ("Electricity"):

> End unto end is taken,
> Fresh "yea" and "nay" ignite,
> And "yea" and "nay" awaken,
> Into the moulding shaken,
> And from their death comes, light.[12]

This poetry is of particular interest not even because of what it depicts but because of what it contains in its very heart. In fact, the glorification of trivial things like electricity is pretty close to the total mechanization and computerization of the twentieth century. The light bulb is not very far from the mobile phone. However, the age-old opposition of nature and civiliza-tion or culture and civilization remains fundamental and acute. It burns and reaches its peak to give rise to universal catastrophe.

Crisis motives of symbolist aesthetics and poetics blur the line between madness and prophecy. Valery Bryusov states pretty much in the spirit of "fin de siècle:"

> Ponder and dream, and be renown your quest!
> Tis one to me, or imbecile, or sage,
> Produce of wisdom or a merry jest.[13]

But poetry shaped as prophecy is no longer art of its own, it belongs to the domain of religion.

If Russian symbolism acutely senses disaster, Polish catastrophism is realistic in its perception and acknowledgment. It is not only about the chronology of a diachronic sequence but about a logical continuation of the trends noticed by the symbolists. In this context, the logical continuation and result of this trend is the Polish catastrophism of 1930s. So the Polish catastrophism as well as the Russian one are both escape routes out of an ideological and aesthetic crisis and the desire to solve it. Czesław Miłosz's

11. Nietzsche, *Complete Works*, 8:86.

12. Selver, *Modern Russian Poetry*, 33.

13. Ibid.

catastrophism takes root from this concept. He not only artistically represents catastrophic motifs but also conceptualizes the philosophical foundations of catastrophism. The prewar and postwar catastrophism of Czesław Miłosz is determined not only by social particularities that are naturally inherent in him as an artist. They are also largely due to the fact that he was born on the frontier. Using the poet's own definition, he "was born and grew up on the very borderline between Rome and Byzantium."[14] This positioning on the spot where cultures crisscrossed and merged turned out to accelerate the split of consciousness in the art world of Miłosz.

Indeed, Polish catastrophism is paradoxically associated with Polish symbolism not so much as assonance, but as a consequence and transition. Looking from this perspective, various trends in art lose their isolation, so that the poem by Leopold Staff sounds somewhat close to catastrophism by Czesław Miłosz. Leopold Staff reveals a situation where faith and a sense of reality in poetry are lost, naming one of his poems "The Bridge," a very telling image in terms of the borderline state of consciousness:

> I didn't believe that I would cross that bridge,
>
> And now that I am standing on the other side,
>
> I don't believe I crossed it.[15]

The crisis is always characterized by a loss of orientation and coordinates. Even if people do reach certain goals, they do so intuitively, feeling no boundaries between illusion and reality.The works of Czesław Miłosz are full of acute catastrophism. The English anthology of his prose and poetry edited by Raymond Soulard Jr. and Kassandra Soulard bears an eloquent title: *If There Is No God*. Talking about Miłosz, he is well known for giving his poems conceptual titles (e.g., "After Paradise"). The question of faith remains relevant for twentieth-century poetry, and it is manifested both in religious and atheist works. Miłosz is no exception to this "religiousness" of modern poetry. For him, "faith is in you whenever you look."[16] The phrase is especially telling due to the fact that this poem was written in 1943 in Warsaw at a time of total social disaster.

His personal religiosity is most clearly expressed in a sketch, "Churches":

> People go to church because they are divided beings. They wish,
> for a moment at least, to find themselves in a reality other than
> the one that surrounds them and claims to be the only true

14. Miłosz, *Witness of poetry*, 4.

15. Miłosz, *Postwar Polish Poetry*, 2.

16. Miłosz, *If There Is No God*, 10.

reality. This daily reality is unyielding, brutal, cruel, and hard to bear. The human "I" is soft in the center and feels every moment that its adaptation to the world is doubtful.[17]

Indeed, the doubtful world requires adaptation not because it is cruel, but because of the separation of the person ("they are divided beings"), which is perceived particularly painfully in times of crisis.

In Miłosz's works personal consciousness loses its center ("there is no capital of the world, neither here nor anywhere else"), whereas "the time of human generations is not like the time of the earth." The human and universal time are not the same, they only partially overlap, bringing forth motifs of pain and suffering. On the contrary, in times of crisis universal pain and individual human pain are united.

Civilization devastates, and the human mind cannot stand the feeling of crisis for too long. That is why in one of the later poems by Miłosz ("After," 1999) we read the following:

> Convictions, beliefs, opinions,
> certainties, principles,
> rules and habits have abandoned me.
> I woke up naked at the edge of a civilization.[18]

The dream disaster ends in an insight, which is why for Miłosz "a devout and God-fearing man is superior as a human specimen to a restless mocker who is glad to style himself an 'intellectual.'" Intellectualism and technicism do not provide the fulfillment that is so needed in the post-crisis era. Every crisis is followed by renewal and rebirth, but to reach it one must first fully experience the crisis state.

Crisis, disaster, catastrophism—these are the dominant themes that determined the development of cultural awareness in Russia and Poland at the turn of the century. It all comes down to a complete paradigm shift, when some laws are displaced and other ones are introduced.

The time at the turn of the centuries is "borderline time;" these are hard times in all senses. This decay first takes shape of hopelessness and frustration, and only afterwards evolves into pronounced apocalyptic motives. Thus, catastrophism is a common ideological trend for Russian and Polish cultures. It is deeply rooted in the common Christian both Orthodox and Catholic eschatology. The thinkers of the time perceived the world as

17. Ibid., 11.
18. Ibid., 27.

a pre-apocalyptic one. Following Christian teachings, the Apocalypse still offers hope for redemption.

## Bibliography

Belyy, Andrey. "Apokalipsis v russkoy poezii." In *Kritika russkogo simvolizma*, edited by Nikolay A. Bogomolov, 2:134–49. Moscow: Olimp, 2002.

Blok, Aleksandr A. "O sovremennom sostoyanii russkogo simvolizma." In *Kritika russkogo simvolizma*, edited by Nikolay A. Bogomolov, 2:236–46. Moscow: Olimp, 2002.

Miłosz, Czesław. *If There Is No God: Selected Poetry and Prose*. Seattle, WA: Burning Man, 2007.

———. Introduction to *War, Progress and the End of History*, by Vladimir Solovyov. Hudson, NY: Lindisfarne, 1990.

———, ed. *Postwar Polish Poetry: An Anthology*. Berkeley: University of California Press, 1983.

———. *The Witness of Poetry*. Cambridge: Harvard University Press, 1983.

Morenets,' Volodimir P. *Natsional'ni shlyakhi poyetichnogo modernu pershoyi polovini XX st.: Ukrayina i Pol'shcha*. Kiev: Osnovi, 2002.

Nietzsche, Friedrich. *The Complete Works*. Edited by Oscar Levy. Vol. 8. New York: Macmillan, 1911.

Seaver, George. *Nicolas Berdyaev: An Introduction to His Thought*. London: J. Clarke, 1950.

Selver, Paul, ed. *Modern Russian Poetry: Texts and Translations*. London: Kegan Paul, Trench, Trubner, 1917.

Sławiński, Janusz. "Synchronia i diachronia w procesie historycznoliterackim." In *Problemy teorii literatury*, edited by Henryk Markiewicz, 2:284–99. Wrocław: Ossolineum, 1987.

Solovyov, Vladimir. *War, Progress, and the End of History: Three Conversations, Including a Short Story of the Anti-Christ*. Hudson, NY: Lindisfarne, 1990.

# 14

# Nikolai Berdyaev and the Transformations of the Idea of Humanism

—Ovanes Akopyan

In the thought of the great Russian philosopher Nikolai Berdyaev, the term *humanism* (*gumanizm*) seems to have an important place. Although he focused on the very notion of humanism in his essays (especially in "The End of the Renaissance and the Crisis of Humanism,"[1] in *The Meaning of History*[2] and other major works, he opposed the humanistic mode of thinking which, according to him, had determined the development of European thought, especially of its secular aspects, since the Renaissance to the so-called New Middle Ages (*novoye srednevekov'ye*).

Explaining the rise of humanism in Italy and then in the whole of Europe, Berdyaev argued that its nature was non-religious because of the crisis of Christianity in Western Europe. He assumed that in the era of Middle Ages, with its aspiration for self-concentration and immersion into religious practices, it had been possible to preserve creative and mental power, which was later frittered away during the Renaissance and subsequent eras.[3] Hence, the Renaissance might be considered as a period of a gap between two large parts of Western Christian history. On the one hand,

---

1. Berdyayev, "Konets Renessansa."

2. Berdyaev, *Meaning of History*.

3. Berdyayev, "Konets Renessansa," 541.

146

medieval contemplation gave rise to the creativity of Renaissance artists. On the other hand, the "humanistic period of history," during which the influence of irrational forces upon human life was firstly denied and then totally abolished was characterized by the wasting of this creative power, the further atomization of society and, as opposed to the very doctrine of humanism, the loss of freedom and dignity.[4] For Berdyaev, the peak of this "secular humanism" was reached in the philosophy, literature and politics, first of all in its socialist component, of the late nineteenth and early twentieth centuries. It is important to note that Berdyaev explained the origin of socialism, fascism and communism in relation to the crisis of humanistic "know-how." According to him, the notion of socialist society is the reverse angle of the development of humanistic individualism, while the two most radical doctrines of the twentieth century should be examined as a response to the deadlock reached by humanistic history.

Let us turn our attention to several aspects of Berdyaev's doctrine. Firstly, it seems obvious that for him there was no difference between humanism and the Renaissance as such. Traditionally related to each other, these two concepts are in close agreement in Berdyaev's thought. The Renaissance, as opposed to the Middle Ages, is considered to be the very beginning of "new," individualistic era of European history, which by the end of the nineteenth century, according to Berdyaev, faced crisis. However, the very opposition of two periods of European history was not a central subject of speculation of the most prominent Renaissance thinkers. Despite the criticism of medieval Latin (which gave rise to the very term "Middle Age" or *medium aevum*),[5] by Petrarch and his followers we know several significant examples of the continuity of medieval and scholastic tradition in subsequent epochs. One of the best apologies of medieval thought was the famous letter of Giovanni Pico della Mirandola to Ermolao Barbaro which quickly became widespread not only in Italy, but throughout Europe.[6] Most probably, the idea to oppose the Middle Ages to the Renaissance should be regarded as the legacy of the philosophy of the Enlightenment: the former, based on scholasticism and religious beliefs, was severely criticized, while the latter was praised as the era of *dignitas hominis* and new science instead of theology and "popular superstitions." Thus, it is possible that some of the important concepts Berdyaev was dealing with had nothing to do with the

---

4. Ibid., 540–42.

5. See Mommsen, "Petrarch's Conception"; see also Gray, "Renaissance Humanism."

6. Pico della Mirandola, "Ioannes Picus Mirandulanus Hermolao Barbaro suo salute."

Renaissance and humanism and were introduced several centuries later by French philosophers.

Finally, Berdyaev's attack on humanism was, without doubt, provoked not by the Renaissance itself but by the philosophical views on humanism and anti-humanism of his own epoch, perfectly described in Henri de Lubac's *The Drama of Atheist Humanism*.[7] Strongly influenced by Fyodor Dostoevsky and worried about "the spiritual situation of the time" (to use Jaspers's definition), Berdyaev obviously tried to overthrow atheistic ideas on humanism in the context of the philosophy of the *Übermensch*, opposing Nietzsche and his followers. It is quite symptomatic that in his essays on Dostoevsky, dedicated especially to *The Demons* and to the figure of Stavrogin,[8] Berdyaev underlined the significance of the collapse of such a doctrine. Yet, as it was suggested above, Berdyaev's *gumanizm* had nothing to do with the Renaissance. Thus, Berdyaev's attack on humanism in the Renaissance seems to be not only radical, but, in some respects, rather unfair. Moreover, in the two leading contemporary historiographic theories of Renaissance humanism, described by Eugenio Garin and by Paul Oskar Kristeller, there are no traces of the humanistic disputes of the late nineteenth and early twentieth century. My task is to reveal the complexity of the term *humanitas* in Renaissance Europe, especially in Marsilio Ficino's works, and to show its further development in modern European thought up to Berdyaev's "The End of the Renaissance and the Crisis of Humanism."

The notion of humanismus was "invented" around 1800 by Friedrich Immanuel Niethammer, friend and disciple of several great German philosophers including Fichte, Kant and Hegel.[9] A fervent admirer of Ancient culture and educational theorist, Niethammer intended to create an ideal system of classical education based on a Greek and Latin legacy. Labeled *Humanismus* and described in his *Der Streit des Philanthropinismus und des Humanismus in der Theorie des Erziehungs-Unterrichts unsrer Zeit*,[10] this new educational concept was opposed to the philanthropinism cultivated by Johann Basedow and his disciples. Completely rejecting *Philanthropinismus*'s orientation toward the priority of physical education, Niethammer insisted on the development of classical studies which, according to him, were in a better position to advance liberty as the central idea of human being. Niethammer's intention to restore "classicism" found several supporters and gave rise to the formation of classical schools. Niethammer's ideas, however,

7. Lubac, *Drama*.

8. Berdyayev, "Stavrogin."

9. Toussaint, *Humanismes/Antihumanismes*, 1:68.

10. Niethammer, *Der Streit des Philanthropinismus und des Humanismus*.

were intended exclusively for practical educational use. Only in the late nineteenth and early twentieth centuries did the aspiration for Antiquity attain some ideological and political implications. While Werner Jaeger's *Paideia* can be regarded as a theoretical update of Niethammer's views, some of his contemporaries tried to prove that between the Ancient (first of all Greek) and German cultures there was a relation of continuity—in other words, that German culture was a direct heir to Antiquity. As is well known, the making of such a mythology had far-reaching effects. It seems rather more important that Paul Oskar Kristeller's philological and rhetorical interpretation of Renaissance humanism as *studia humanitatis* obviously developed in the context of Niethammer's educational reform and Jaeger's *paideia*, without any political references.[11]

Garin's vision of the Renaissance *humanism* arose from another source.[12] Firstly, Garin's intellectual background was formed by the circle of Giovanni Gentile, the Neo-Hegelian philosopher and one of the most influential Italian thinkers of that period. According to Gentile, the significance of the Renaissance was marked by the turn toward the idea of *dignitas hominis* and anthropology as the most specific element of the Renaissance culture. It is unsurprising that the famous *Oratio de hominis dignitate* by Giovanni Pico della Mirandola received a special and honored place in the concept of the Renaissance of Gentile and his followers. However, as Brian Copenhaver has shown, the expression *de hominis dignitate* was added to the title several years after Pico's death and the very aspect of human dignity was not a key problem of the treatise.[13] However, this "progressive" vision of the Renaissance found its supporters, and Garin was among them. In 1947 he published his major work on Italian humanism which was later republished more than once.[14] It was commissioned before World War II by Ernesto Grassi, one of the leading ideologists of Italian fascism, to glorify Italy as the homeland of modern thought and culture. Although Garin's book is free of these political connotations, it is quite interesting that after the fall of Mussolini's regime Garin became a supporter of communist doctrine.

Formed by different sources, Kristeller's *humanism* as a philological *studia humanitatis* and Garin's *humanism* as a new vision of the world still determine two opposite interpretative approaches to one and the same culture. While Kristeller's definition of *humanism*, influenced by Niethammer

11. On Kristeller, see Monfasani, "Paul Oskar Kristeller," Kristeller, King, "Iter Kristellerianum," Fubini, "L'umanesimo italiano."

12. On Garin see J. Hankins, *Humanism and Platonism*, I:576–81.

13. Copenhaver, "Secret of Pico's Oration" and "Magic and the Dignity of Man."

14. Garin, *Der italienische Humanismus*, recent Italian edition: *L'umanesimo italiano*.

and partly by Jaeger, was diffused in the Anglo-Saxon world, Garin's characterization is still accepted in Italy, France and other European countries, including Russia. Yet curiously, both Garin and Kristeller seemed to disregard
the use of the term in the periods closely preceding their work, especially
in the late nineteenth and early twentieth century. We can just wonder if
such a gap can be understood as an attempt to reconsider the very notion of
*humanitas* and purify it of the "anti-humanisms" of Nietzsche, Heidegger,
and Sartre.

However, the great Florentine Quattrocento philosopher Marsilio Ficino gave another definition of *humanitas*, which transcends the limits of
standard historiographic concepts. In his letter to Tommaso Minerbetti[15]
and some fragments of *Theologia platonica de immortalitate animorum*,[16]
Ficino represented *humanitas* with the triad *erudition—philanthropia—unitas*. If Ficino's *eruditio* is rather close to *studia humanitatis* and the ancient
ideal of *homo humanus* perfectly described in the twentieth century in
Heidegger's "Letter on 'Humanism,'"[17] the *philanthropia*, which is usually
nowadays used as a substitute for humanism as such, is closely related to
the *unitas*, i.e. the unity of individuals. According to Ficino, such an eternal
*humanitas* unifies the whole of mankind and all people, those who are alive,
dead or as yet unborn.[18] It is obvious that by *humanitas* Ficino described
the idea of Church with its mystical component and, thus, enlarged the
significance of the term without limiting himself to anthropology, *dignitas
hominis*, and other well-known concepts.[19] For years absorbed in "reforming" traditional Christianity with new ideas and sources and creating the
doctrine of *prisca theologia*,[20] Ficino gave rise to new religious speculations
in Renaissance Italy and then in the whole of Europe. Yet Ficino's idea of *humanitas* as an analogy and synonym of the Church for "literati" was quickly
found nonviable: after the Reformation it became impossible.

15. Ficino, "De humanitate," 107.

16. Ficino, *Platonic theology*, 2:263–72.

17. Heidegger, "Letter on 'Humanism,'" 244.

18. Ficino, *Platonic Theology*, 2:266: "Ergo in his tribus una est communis humanitas per quam aeque sunt homines, una pulchritudinis natura, una etiam bonitatis,
per quas aeque pulchri sunt et aeque boni. Humanitas ipsa quae his communis est,
innumerabilibus quoque aliis qui sunt, fuerunt eruntve, quocumque in tempore et
quocumque in loco nascantur, communis existit; similiter pulchritudo et reliqua: sed
quod loquor de humanitate, de reliquis etiam dictum puta. Si ergo humanitas singulis
personis, locis, temporibus se aeque communicat, nulli est astricta personae, nulli loco,
nulli etiam tempori."

19. Toussaint, *Humanismes/Antihumanismes*, 47.

20. The most important text concerning Ficino's religious studies is *La religione
cristiana*.

Obviously, Nikolai Berdyaev, one of the most severe opponents of humanism, was wrong to criticize the Renaissance for the non-religious nature of its major philosophical doctrines; his main opponents were his own contemporaries who tried to replace humanism with "anti-humanism." Deeply involved in polemics with Nietzschean philosophy and its aftermath, Berdyaev did not realize that the intentions of Ficino were in fact close to his own.

# Bibliography

Berdyaev, Nicolas. *The Meaning of History*. Translated by George Reavey. London: Geoffrey Bles, 1936.

Berdyayev, Nikolay A. "Konets Renessansa i krizis gumanizma. Razlozheniye chelovecheskogo obraza." In *Smysl tvorchestva*, 531–44. Moscow: AST, 2004.

———. "Stavrogin." In *Smysl tvorchestva*, 5–14. Moscow: AST, 2004.

Copenhaver, Brian. "Magic and the Dignity of Man: De-Kanting Pico's Oration." In *The Italian Renaissance in the Twentieth Century: Acts of an International Conference. Florence, Villa I Tatti, June 9–11, 1999*, edited by A. J. Grieco et al., 295–320. Florence: L. S. Olschki, 2002.

———. "The Secret of Pico's Oration: Cabala and Renaissance Philosophy." *Midwest Studies in Philosophy* 26 (2002) 56–81.

Ficino, Marsilio. *La religione cristiana*. Roma: Città Nuova Editrice, 2005.

———. *Lettere. Epistolarum liber I*. Florence: L. S. Olschki, 1990.

———. *Platonic Theology*. Translated by M. J. B. Allen and J. Warden. 6 vols. Cambridge: Harvard University Press, 2001–6.

Fubini, Riccardo. "L'umanesimo italiano. Problemi e studi di ieri e di oggi." *Studi francesi* 51 (2007) 504–15.

Garin, Eugenio. *Der italienische Humanismus, Philosophie und bürgeliches Leben in Renaissance*. Bern, 1947.

———. *L'umanesimo italiano. Filosofia e vita civile nel Rinascimento*. Roma-Bari, 2008.

Gray, Hanna H. "Renaissance Humanism: The Pursuit of Eloquence." *Journal of the History of Ideas* 24 (1963) 497–514.

Hankins, James. *Humanism and Platonism in the Italian Renaissance*. Vol. 1, *Humanism*. Roma: Edizioni di Storia e Letteratura, 2003.

Heidegger, Martin. "Letter on 'Humanism.'" In *Pathmarks*, translated by W. McNeill, 239–76. Cambridge: Cambridge University Press, 1998.

Kristeller, Paul Oskar, and Margaret L. King. "Iter Kristellerianum: The European Journey (1905–1939)." *Renaissance Quarterly* 47 (1994) 907–29.

Lubac, Henri de. *The Drama of Atheist Humanism*. Translated by Mark Sebanc. San Francisco: Ignatius, 1995.

Mommsen, Theodor E. "Petrarch's Conception of the Dark Ages." *Speculum* 17 (1942) 226–42.

Monfasani, John. "Paul Oskar Kristeller." *Proceedings of the American Philosophical Society* 145 (2001) 208–11.

Niethammer, Friedrich Immanuel. *Der Streit des Philanthropinismus und des Humanismus in der Theorie des Erziehungs-Unterrichts unsrer Zeit*. Jena: Friedrich Frommann, 1808.

Pico della Mirandola, G. "Ioannes Picus Mirandulanus Hermolao Barbaro suo salutem."
    In *Prosatori latini del Quattrocento*, edited by E. Garin, 804–24. Milan: Ricciardi,
    1952.
Toussaint, Stéphane. *Humanismes/Antihumanismes. De Ficin à Heidegger*. Vol. 1. Paris:
    Les Belles Lettres, 2008.

# 15

# Between Idol and Icon

*A Critical Appraisal of the Mystery Project of Culture by*
*Vyacheslav Ivanov in the Context of the Thought of Jean-Luc*
*Marion*

—Marta Lechowska

The subject of the following reflections is the unique position of culture in the system of values of a human defining him—above all—religiously. We are of an opinion that it is in the context of thorough religious self-awareness that the problem of affection towards such a different matter as culture takes its visible shape.

The structure of the following considerations is to discuss—on the base of the analysis by French phenomenologist Jean-Luc Marion—two types of religious self-awareness: iconic and idolatrous, and to relate them to the "erotic" concept of culture by the Russian poet, philologist and philosopher Vyacheslav Ivanov; and finally, to decide what point of view on culture phenomenon is proposed by the Russian thinker.

Let us begin with a short phenomenological juxtaposition of the two mentioned areas of interest: culture and religion. The area of culture, naturally different to that of religion, has been founded upon extremely dissimilar to religious rules (setting up a completely different human attitude). The culture element assumes affirmation, not renunciation; affirmation of life, creativity and physicality. Culture is not about fasting; it is about having a feast of aesthetic forms. It is not about poverty but the splendour of the fruits of human creativity and ecstasy coming from tasting the world rather than suffering. The incompatibility exposed here of the two areas poses a question of coexistence of the two elements within one radically religious awareness.

Jean-Luc Marion's concept draws on two types of human perception of religious culture: iconic and idolatrous ("icon and idol" for short). The theoretical proposal of the French philosopher is based on two theses: First, idol and icon are not distinct, fixed classes of objects but rather manners of the existence of these objects. The second thesis, which opens up a broad perspective for anthropological and culturological analysis commands searching for an "ontological" foundation of being for idol and icon; not as a result of human made object definitely, once and for all classified (as an idol or an icon) but as an object continuously being established as an icon or an idol by human perception. "The gaze makes the idol, not the idol the gaze."[1]

Let us ask what the being of an idol is. According to Marion it means that an invisible mirror reflects the perception of human himself. The human, craving The Invisible, holds the perception on what is visible. "The idol with its visibility fills the intention of the gaze, which wants nothing other than to see."[2]

It is worth asking why the philosopher talks about an invisible mirror. The answer is: "The idol masks the mirror because it fills the gaze."[3] The mirror—as Marion explains—fills up the whole human intention to the point that it becomes impossible to notice that in supposititious revelation of sacrum there is nothing more than the one who longs for it. In all honesty, the searching for The Other (what is absolutely transcendent) human gets satisfied with the creation of his own eyes, his own—intellectual, aesthetic and ethical—intention.

> The idol testifies to the divine, but each time the divine thought starting from its aim, limited to a variable scope by *Dasein*. Therefore, the idol always culminates in a "self-idolatry" . . . The idol: less a false or untrue image of the divine than a real, limited, and indefinitely variable function of *Dasein* considered in its aiming at the divine.[4]

1. Marion, *God without Being*, 10.
2. Ibid., 11.
3. Ibid., 12.
4. Ibid., 28.

Idol is the "point of failure" of seeking infinity in human perception or in other words it's "fallen perception." The French philosopher largely describes this archaic movement of idolatry:

> In each visible spectacle, the gaze found nothing that might stop it; the gaze's fiery eyes consumed the visible so that each time the gaze saw nothing. But here the idol intervenes. What shows up? For the first (and last) time the gaze no longer rushes through the spectacle; it is fixed in it, and far from passing beyond, remains facing what becomes for it a spectacle to *re*-spect. The gaze lets itself be filled: instead of outflanking the visible, of not seeing it and rendering it invisible, the gaze discovers itself as outflanked, contained, held back by the visible. The visible finally becomes visible to the gaze because, again literally, the visible dazzles a gaze until then insatiable. The idol offers to, or rather imposes on, the gaze, its first visible—whatever it may be, thing, man, woman, idea, or god.[5]

This description reveals an idol's characteristic attitude: without creating distance, hence without causing any pursuit in human, it turns out to be safe, familiar; it turns out to be "the found Eden." An idol does not hold any secret, but is perfectly visible. What does it mean? It means as much as: it measures up to human: "It is an experience of the divine in the measure of a state of *Dasein*."[6]

In the above context, the words about the "murderous role of idol"[7] are not just a coincidental play on words. They signalize real, based on idolatry danger: an idol, striving towards becoming the ultimate appeasement of the human desire for God, wants to kill the desire and eventually—God Himself. The idol category—as a certain way of existence, as opposed to a specific being—could serve as a tool for insightful reflection on all displays of human cultural activity. If beings as "ontologically subtle" as ideas could become idols, it seems that all phenomena, theories, and objects linked with religion are at risk of bearing this identity as well. Does it mean that the whole religious culture should be rejected in case it is defeated by idolatry? Not at all. If human perception alone validates idolatry, it is enough to apply vigilance and constant effort to transgress from the idolatrous towards the iconic. For the human as a transcendent being can never rest. This great truth, although difficult for humans, is voiced by an icon.

---

5. Ibid., 11–12.

6. Ibid., 28.

7. Cf. Tarnowski, "Jean-Luc Marion," 11.

An icon is a sign of divinity in a completely different than an idol's manner; an icon exists in a different way.

> Icon is also a mediatative image of God, however the one in which the basic intention does not come from us but comes down from God Himself and captures our sight guiding it towards The Invisible. An Icon is an image, which in the most paradoxical way represents The Invisible as The Invisible, not trying to replace Him with our, even the most pious and sophisticated, images and concepts of God. That is the reason why upon this day we are so fascinated by Byzantine icons.[8]

An Icon does not "consume," does not "constrain" human perception, just the opposite: in its essence it pushes further, pushes upwards. An Icon does not withhold, because it respects what the unsellable for human to stay human: his continual "journey." Icon does not expect it is viewing, but seeing as deep as the seeing of its own eyes. An Icon causes the Visible only by stimulating infinite perception.

Iconic existence, hence iconic culture, is far from, characteristic to idolatry, fanaticism. This is because the icon takes the human out of his comfort zone every time, coming from the belief of completion of the religious quest. The Icon always first encourages humans to verify their own attitude, their own "being towards," before starting the fight for their own God. In that sense an icon never allows human to say that he possesses absolute knowledge about God. This phenomenon protects from fanaticism and the hypocrisy linked to it.

Marion's phenomenological analysis—as far as we believe—enabled the exposure of the constitutive base of idolatry, in which human perception, failing, creates idols. The great institution of idolatry is based each time on individual appreciation; in other words, being an idol is always a result of idolatrous perception. What does it mean? It means that the power of idol creation lies in nobody else's hands—but ours. An Idol cannot exist on its own, even if we were flooded by a sea of tacky objects aspiring to religious status. An Idol would not arise (because it does not possess the power to arise), if humans did not open up to its "anaesthetic" (speaking of "anaesthesia" of human's metaphysical quests) action. This way of putting the matter—although it establishes the existence of idolatry—brings a hope based on the truth about idol's manner of existence: humans can always change perception. Humans can bounce from where their religious intention "solidified" so far and search for the real recipient of their religious

---

8. Ibid., 12.

susceptibilities. All that matters is making effort to espouse the iconic rather than idolatrous perspective.

Ivanov undoubtedly makes that effort, prioritizing in his anthropology and philosophy of culture the category of Eros—as the metaphysical desire always present in human. This aspect of philosopher's thinking places him within the philosophy of desire for The Impossible. This category opens up the space for a unique rationality which refuses to be driven by common sense. Humans sense God as a "presence of absence" and this absence (The Other) is an object of his desire. What's more, this desire is not accidental, it establishes the essence of a human being. This means that human is in a way secondary in relation to his desire (although he is the subject of that desire at the same time). Desire is the category which enables the revealing of general endeavour of a religious human and—at the same time—sourcefully deter-mine his condition. The essence of the above mentioned condition could be described in words being the reaction to encounter between religious existence and the world: "The true life is absent."[9] This, coming from the discord between the inside and the outside world reality, statement signal-izes the basic direction of religious existence: towards what is "out of this world" ("What we live from and enjoy is not the same as that life itself"[10]), what is in relation to that world—trancendental. The religious human never settles down within the world; just the opposite: he would constantly strive for justifying it against the object of his desire. So what does desire call on? The Platonian Eros as a paradigm of religious desire commands humans to long for the world of Idea hence to long for absolute, divine reality. Ivanov describes this similarly when he writes: "Plato's Ideas—the essence of *res*."[11] It is worth mentioning that Eros—according to Plato's *Symposium*—is "the son of Plenty and Poverty and partakes of the nature of both."[12] The above paradox reveals the dynamics of the described category: in order to desire something, one has to what is desired—already in some way "own." A re-ligious human, calling on The Other, already The Other knows due to his internal experience. Hence, based on paradoxical dynamics of desire, term: "presence of absence." Let us emphasize that desire—as opposed to the eas-ily to fulfil need—can never be fulfilled.[13]

It means that a religious human unsatisfied with the easily achievable possibilities of the world, constantly stays in front of what in its essence

9. Levinas, *Totality and Infinity*, 33.

10. Ibid., 122.

11. Ivanov, "Dve stikhii," 549.

12. Plato, *Symposium*, 10.

13. Levinas, *Totality and Infinity*, 114–15.

is impossible. Therefore, Eros means constant openness to "The Impossible" (*Eros Nevozmozhnogo*[14]). So does Ivanov—linking culture with desire for The Impossible—bind humans to communing only with idols? Surely cultural phenomena, satisfied out of necessity with the concreteness of the world, never fulfil metaphysical desire.

Let us have a look at Ivanov's mystery project (pointing out at The Mystery) which, according to the author, would meet the requirement of iconic reference to The Impossible. The focus of this project is on theatrical drama, as much as possible similar to its ritual source—a dithyramb. Let us emphasize that a dithyramb—as a ritual hymn sung in honor of Dionysus as a core of Dionysian mystery festivals—implies a certain anthropological and culturological vision, based on leading culture out the most intimate for human source—religion. This everlasting source causes humans to be "doomed" to what is beyond them. This is why various disciplines of culture can be defined by pointing out at them, but at the same time they do not dissipate in their ocularity; they are much more than just empirically visible objects. This way of thinking is close to Ivanov's: theatre to him is not "just theatre," aesthetics is not "just aesthetics." "Theatre exists beyond aesthetics,"[15] he writes. For theatre, being very concrete cultural reality, pertains to something beyond itself, beyond "aesthetic information." "The real content of an artistic image always goes far beyond its physical boundaries. The work of genius tells us about something else; something deeper, more beautiful, more tragic, more divine, more than what a piece of art work directly represents."[16]

A dithyramb as a core of Ivanov's project is a paradigm of the whole—founded within choral, communal awareness—an act of creation which should become the framework of all areas of culture, not just theatre. Dithyramb is the manifestation of the level common to all human race; it's a proof of deep, common to all mankind awareness—universal "The Self" (*vsechelovecheskoye Ya*[17]). Creativity is therefore closely linked to religiousness,[18] understood as universal "religious disposition," not as positive religion. According to Ivanov, the depth of human religiousness is based on dialogue relationship with The Other, identical with an everlasting desire for The Other. The continuously renewed movement of sanctifying of oneself

14. Ivanov, "Ideya nepriyatiya mira," 90.

15. Ivanov, "Esteticheskaya norma teatra," 213.

16. Ivanov, "Predchuvstviya i predvestiya," 92.

17. Ivanov, "Novyye maski," 76.

18. "The common ground of art and asceticism is the mystical experience, which reveals the noumenal or transcendental." Bird, "Tender Mystery," 303.

and the world, caused by the permanent incompatibility with the object of desire (which determines human's erotic condition), guarantees cultural *energeia*—the everlasting vitality present in culture threads and ideas.

Summarising, let us say that theatre based on a dithyramb is, according to the Russian author, a cultural correlate of the religious aspect of humanity; its model would be a ritual or a liturgy in which humans are not spectators but involved participants, and the communal awareness defines it deeper than individual awareness. ("Personality grows out of the community, not the other way around"[19]). The demand to overstep the latter—as one of the most profound moments of Ivanov's thought—has been expressed by the poet with a formula from the writings of Saint Augustine: *Transcende te ipsum.*[20] The imperative is of course related to art as well. Art in its essence (religious sources) cannot withhold the perception of the spectator on itself (the risk of idolatry), but it has to send it deep, towards the source. Only under the above condition would the area of aesthetics gain its iconic sense. "A piece of art, if it is to have aesthetical impact, needs to be impossible to be understood and processed fully. Hence longing for the inarticulate; which is a soul and a core of any aesthetic experience."[21]

Ivanov's vision seems to be an example of iconic perception on cultural reality, especially since the poet certainly realized how unreachable The Idea is and how longing for it awakens creativity in humans. In the face of this incompatibility—between the presence of The Idea in desire and its unbearable absence in the world—Ivanov proposes a radical thesis: every attempt to reach for the ideal fulfilment (the attempt of expressing it in the cultural and social world) is not only the sign of weakness, but most of all—it is a sin. If so, it means that the thinker has perfectly realized the ubiquity of idols and their mortal power.

In order to justify the above hypothesis, let us quote the two fragments of Ivanov's writings drawing on the fact that every activity, including cultural, which leads to implementation of The Idea is—according to human capabilities ("'The possible' lies within human capability"[22])—bound to end up as the ultimate disaster. "To do the possible means to betray the sacrum of 'the impossible' or in other words: 'the implicit,' 'the unconditional.'"[23] "It is pure profanity and cruelty to rip the perfect Idea out of its peaceful homeland of true being just to throw it into a stream of endlessly craving

---

19. Ivanov, "Esteticheskaya norma teatra," 219.

20. Ivanov, "Dve stikhii," 553.

21. Ivanov, "Predchuvstviya i predvestiya," 92.

22. Ivanov, "Prometey," 112.

23. Ivanov, "O deystvii i deystve," 159.

but never fully achieved 'existence.'"[24] If so, it means that the culture does not hold the power of sending back to the metaphysical world. The human as a creator of culture is situated in a tragic position between Scylla and Chabrydis of the aspects of his own condition. "An imprint of an eternal tragedy of human and humanity striving for the divine but never achieving it."[25] Confronted by The Impossible, everything that belongs to the area of possibility (human world) is sacrilege.

We have shown that "the ideal type" of sacrilege is the idol which does not deny the existence of the sacrum (just the opposite: the idol also grows out of religious experience), however it takes the sacrum away from the human perception focusing that perception on itself (the idol). According to Ivanov, even the biggest personalities, which could, as the common sense suggests, have the biggest chances to bring The Idea "down to Earth," out of necessity create new, disguised as icons, idols. So it is clear to see that Ivanov's point of view—against optimistic "erotic" characteristic of culture open to the ideal world—is closer to Nikolai Berdyaev's concept, in which relation between the inner intention of creativity and its cultural objectifications is called the tragedy of culture.

Furthermore, one should take into account another type of inconsistency. The insightful thinker, who recognizes the "original sin" of man and culture, like a prophet[26] presents his vision of the forthcoming organic (synthetic) era. An era in which—through the theatre, based on dithyrambic paradigm—the mysterious truth about human and culture will be revealed. Is it possible, therefore, that the thesis of the tragedy of culture, which lies in its continuous falling into idolatry, does not apply to its own creator? Had the vigilance of the cultural theorist been put to sleep in relation to himself, just because of the theoretical—and thus not subjected to the allegations of idolatry—nature of his activity? Did Ivanov consider his speculations to be a metatheory, which does not belong to the realm of culture and is not compromised by its frailties? At this point, one should recall the first of the thinkers in question. Jean-Luc Marion knows very well that, due to the human gaze, both tangible objects and—even more effectively hiding the truth about themselves—more subtle entities like notions and theories become idols. And only then do they have the power to refer us to the Transcendence, when no one (neither the author, nor the recipient) absolutizes them.

24. Ibid.

25. Kondakov, "'Vertikal' i 'gorizontal,'" 271.

26. Ivanov, "Predchuvstviya i predvestiya," 87.

# Bibliography

Bird, Robert. "The Tender Mystery: Romanticism and Symbolism in the Poetry and Thought of Viacheslav Ivanov." PhD diss., Yale University, 1998.

Ivanov, Vyacheslav I. "Dve stikhii v sovremennom simvolizme." In *Sobraniye sochineniy*, 2:536–61. Brussels: Foyer Oriental Chrétien, 1974.

———. "Esteticheskaya norma teatra." In *Sobraniye sochineniy*, 2:215–18. Brussels: Foyer Oriental Chrétien, 1974

———. "Ideya nepriyatiya mira." In *Sobraniye sochineniy*, 3:79–90. Brussels: Foyer Oriental Chrétien, 1979.

———. "Novyye maski." In *Sobraniye sochineniy*, 2:76–82. Brussels: Foyer Oriental Chrétien, 1974.

———. "O deystvii i deystve." In *Sobraniye sochineniy*, 2:156–69. Brussels: Foyer Oriental Chrétien, 1974.

———. "Predchuvstviya i predvestiya." In *Sobraniye sochineniy*, 2:86–104. Brussels: Foyer Oriental Chrétien, 1974.

———. "Prometey." In *Sobraniye sochineniy*, 2:107–55. Brussels: Foyer Oriental Chrétien, 1974.

Kondakov, Igor' V. "'Vertikal'' i 'gorizontal'' v kul'turfilosofii Vyacheslava Ivanova." In *Vyacheslav Ivanov. Materialy i issledovaniya*, edited by Vsevolod A. Keldysh, 262–73. Moscow: Naslediye, 1996.

Levinas, Emmanuel. *Totality and Infinity: an Essay on Exteriority*. Translated by Alphonso Lingis. Dordrecht: Kluwer, 1991.

Marion, Jean-Luc. *God without Being*. Translated by Thomas A. Carlson. Chicago: University of Chicago Press, 2012.

Plato. *Symposium*. Translated by Benjamin Jowett. Stilwell, KS: Digireads, 2005.

Tarnowski, Karol. "Jean-Luc Marion, fenomenolog miłości większej niż bycie." Introduction to *Bóg bez bycia*, by Jean-Luc Marion, 8–19. Krakow: Znak, 1996.

# 16

# Ivan Il'in on the Foundations of Christian Culture
—Yury Lisitsa

## Biographical and Historical Sketch

Ivan Aleksandrovich Il'in (1883–1954) was a Russian religious philosopher, legal and political theorist, philosopher of Russian national identity, orator and publicist. Born in Moscow on March 28 (April 10, new style), 1883, of a noble family, he developed his patriotism directly in the Kremlin. His grandfather Ivan Ivanovich was a colonel in the army and a civil engineer who built the Great Kremlin Palace, also serving as its commandant and living there with his family. The grandfather was given the special title "Major of the Great Kremlin Palace Gate" (i.e., Keeper of the Gate) by Emperor Alexander II. The Emperor had served as godfather to the philosopher's father Alexander, who was named after him. The philosopher's mother was of German descent. Her father Julius Sweikert von Stadion was raised in a doctor's family. He was educated at Leipzig University, in the Faculty of Medicine, graduating in 1831. In 1832 he and his wife immigrated to Russia, where he became a private doctor for Prince Kurakin. Later he became the head physician of the Imperial Home for Widows in Moscow. Alexander Ivanovich and Ekaterina Julievna Il'in had five sons; the third was the future philosopher Ivan.

He completed the famous First Moscow Gymnasium with the gold medal on May 31, 1901. Like his father, he entered the Faculty of Law of

Moscow Imperial University, receiving his diploma with a First on May 25, 1906. He was a student of the remarkable philosopher-jurist Professor Pavel Ivanovich Novgorodtsev, who conveyed a lively interest in the history of philosophy, in natural right and the rule of law to his students, and also inculcated in Ivan Il'in a love of philosophy, especially of Socrates and Plato. On September 22 of the same year he was retained at the university to undertake a master's degree. On August 27, 1906, he married Natalia Nikolaevna Vokach who had just graduated from the Higher Women's School and was interested in philosophy, art criticism and history. She came from an ancient noble family and was one year older than Il'in. The two were spiritually very close throughout their lives together.

In 1909 he was appointed *privat-dozent* in the Faculty of Law at Moscow University. He spent the years 1911 and 1912 in Germany, Italy and France, studying philosophy and preparing his dissertation on Hegel. He worked at Heidelberg (with Jellinek), at Freiburg (with Rickert), at Göttingen (with Husserl and Nelson) and at Berlin (with Simmel). After his return he delivered lectures and courses at the University and other Moscow institutes, published papers on the history of philosophical doctrines (Fichte, Hegel) and some works on the rule of law, ethics and social psychology (e.g., *On the Essence of Right, The Spiritual Meaning of the War, On Friendship*). He initially regarded the February revolution of 1917 as a "temporary disorder" and tried as a political and legal theorist to aid his Russian homeland. He published five sharply-worded brochures and several outspoken articles against the revolutionaries, particularly against the *Bolsheviks*. Their coup d'état on October 25, 1917 he apprehended as a "Russian catastrophe" and commenced his struggle against the Bolshevik regime. In 1918 he was arrested by the *Cheka* (secret police) three times and was taken to court, but was released because of an unproved accusation. While this trial was in process, he defended his dissertation on Hegel and on May 19, 1918, he received both a master's and doctoral degree at once, because his dissertation was seen as an extraordinary scholarly achievement. The two volumes of his published dissertation, *The Philosophy of Hegel as a Doctrine of the Concreteness of God and Man* (1918), have been described as one of the more significant commentaries on Hegel published in that century in any language.[1] Soon afterward he was appointed a Professor at Moscow University.

As a resolute foe of the Bolsheviks, he was arrested three more times during 1919–1922 and at last on September 26, 1922, he was exiled from Soviet Russia under threat of execution along with many other scholars, philosophers, theologians and writers irreconcilably opposed to the

1. Grier, "Speculative Concrete."

Bolshevik regime. Il'in and his wife left Russia for Germany on the board the *Oberbürgermeister Hacken*, the so-called "philosophers' ship" of exiles. Arriving in Berlin, he actively involved himself in the life of the Russian émigré community. He became a professor at the newly opened Russian Academic Institute in Berlin, also delivering hundreds of speeches, lectures and talks in Russian, German and French during the years 1923–1938, not only in Germany but also in many other European countries (France, Italy, Latvia, Switzerland, Belgium, Czechoslovakia, Yugoslavia and Austria). He published numerous articles in *Vozrozhdeniye* (Paris), *Russkiy Invalid* (Paris), *Rossiya i Slavyanstvo* (Paris), *Novoye Vremya* (Belgrade), *Slovo* (Riga), and published a journal of his own *Russkiy Kolokol* (Berlin). He was one of organizers of the Russian Émigré Congress (1926); he was an active member of the International Anti-Communist League (Theodor Ober's League). He published several books and many brochures.

Although he was a renowned anti-Bolshevik and anti-communist, which suited the Nazis, his critique of totalitarianism was not at all appreciated by the Nazi regime. Moreover, in 1934 he refused to accept their orders to spread Nazi propaganda in the Russian Academic Institute, was removed from his post by them and banned from all further employment. Finally in 1938 he was forbidden to speak in public, his most recent brochure was seized, and he himself was about to be arrested by the Nazis and sent to a concentration camp. At the last moment, with some friends' help and an extraordinary bit of luck, he and his wife escaped from Nazi Germany and wound up in Switzerland. The Swiss government forbade him the right to work or to engage in political activity, and demanded a "security" fee of 4000 CHF for the right to enter the country. The necessary money was contributed by the famous Russian composer Sergey Rachmaninov, who was a friend of Il'in living in Switzerland. Up until his death on December 21, 1954, Il'in continued working intensively on many books, lectures, projects and programs dedicated to "The Russia Yet to Be."[2]

## The Main Ideas and Works

*Philosophy as a spiritual deed.* In his book *The Religious Meaning of Philosophy* (1925) Il'in charged his readers with a task: "To find authentic, spiritually objective environments." The term he uses for "environments" (*obstoyaniya*) is an uncommon one in Russian. These *environments* are the invisible and intellectual world. Il'in wishes to tell us that the visible world,

---

2. Details see in Poltoratskiy, *Ivan Aleksandrovich Il'in*, and Lisitsa, "Ivan Aleksandrovich Il'in."

the world of the senses, came into existence only after the invisible and in-tellectual world. Hence "the philosopher," according to Il'in, "is the only one among the scholars who is going to settle *what the truth is*; he, like a priest, faces the *good*, searching its nature and revealing it to others; he, like an artist, is concerned with *beauty* itself, investigating its essence and finding means of realization, vision and comprehension." The spiritual deed of such a philosopher approximates that of the monk. The only difference is that the former is in the realm of cognition, while the latter concerns redemption. Both comprehend that the world is "really the school where reasonable souls exercise themselves, the training ground where they learn to know God."[3]

## The Doctrine of Legal Consciousness

Convinced that Hegel's doctrine of right and the state was ultimately a failure, Il'in began creating his own in 1918, while still in Soviet Russia. It was eventually published only posthumously as *On the Essence of Legal Consciousness* in 1956. The central notion in it is *pravosoznaniye*, from *pravo* (right or law) and *soznaniye* (consciousness), which can perhaps best be translated as "*legal consciousness.*" He formulated three *axioms of legal consciousness* and added nine *axioms of authority*. Then he joined *natural law* and *positive law* in an appropriate way: "A rational system of positive law would reflect the structure of natural law."[4] His book *On the Essence of Legal Consciousness* contains a number of uncommon but profound observations, useful to any national leader who wishes to have *a deeper religious and moral motivation* for ruling.

## On Resisting Evil with Force

In 1925 Il'in published his polemical book *On Resisting Evil with Force*, con-cerning an important ethical double-problem: "May a human being who is trying to achieve ethical perfection *resist* evil by force, using the sword?" and "May a human being who believes in God and accepts His creation, and who knows his place in this created world *not resist* evil by force, using the sword?"[5] Il'in gives a single direct answer to both: that one not only *may*, but *must* resist evil by force!

---

3. Saint Basil the Great, "Homilies on *Hexaemeron*," I, 6.

4. Il'in, *Sobraniye sochineniy*, 4: 204.

5. Ibid., 5:176.

Physical intervention and coercion may become the direct religious and patriotic duty of a human being; and then he must not
evade it. Meeting this duty turns him into a participant in the
great historical battle between God's servants and the forces of
the underworld; and this battle will force him not only to draw
his sword but to take upon himself the burden of homicide.[6]

This book produced a furore not only in the Russian émigré community but
in the Soviet Union as well.[7]

## The Russia Yet to Be

Il'in lived and worked with the single-minded purpose of reconstructing
Russia in an authentic way in the aftermath of the Bolshevik regime. He
wrote *A Proposal for the Fundamental Law of the Russian Empire* as a post-
Bolshevik constitution. During 1940–1954 he produced 215 anonymous
bulletins for a restricted list of readers only, and these were published together in two volumes *Our Tasks: Articles 1948–1954* only after Il'in's death.
This two-volume work is nothing other than an "Axiomatics of Political
Life," analogous to his *Axioms of Religious Experience*; it is clearly intended
to treat the disease of "*political nihilism.*"

## The Contemplative Heart

Between 1938 and 1945 Il'in created in German a wonderful literary *trip-
tych*: Ich *schaue in Leben. Ein Buch der Besinnung, Das verloschollene Herz.
Ein Buch stiller Betrachtungen, Blick in die Ferne. Ein Buch der Einsichten
und Hoffnungen* and described it as "devoted not to theology, but to a quiet,
philosophical praising of God." Despite all the striving of humanity to unveil the mystery of world creation, it has been losing a access to this mystery
on the path that it has selected. "Because the world remains as before, i.e.,
a great mysterious wonder, created by a reasoning inner Authority, carried
by a reasoning inner force, and moving toward a certain inner goal."[8] And
this "lost mystery" might be returned to humanity through a contemplative
heart, but only if the heart is open, loving and marvelling.

6. Ibid., 177.

7. Lisitsa, "O soprotivlenii zlu siloy."

8. Il'in, *Sobraniye sochineniy*, 3:529–30.

## Pneumatology

In 1953 Il'in published in Paris his main work *Axioms of Religious Experience* in two volumes which he had been preparing for 33 years. It was a profound and original investigation of the personal "religious act." One of its axioms, "The autonomy of religious experience," and the motives connected with it, "*loneliness*" and "*tragedy in the world*" were received somewhat critically by the Russian theologians, e.g., Archimandrite Kostantin Zaitsev. However this axiom was taken from one of the Church Fathers, Petrus Chrysologus, who wrote that only God "*solus est, sed non solitarius*" (is alone, but is not lone).

# Il'in on Foundations of Christian Culture

Among Il'in's vast heritage there is a small booklet *Foundations of Christian Culture* (1937), in which, however, as in other works of the philosopher, one can see the core of all his work. It consists of seven small chapters: "The crisis of modern culture," "The problem of Christian culture," "The right way," "Foundations of Christian Culture," "On acceptance of the world," "Culture and the Church," "On Christian nationalism" and "Conclusion."

The importance of this Russian Christian philosopher's work for our conference is undeniable, and I intend to present here briefly the contents of this brochure.

The first chapter of "The crisis of modern culture" says that in the twentieth century and we are confident we can add that in this twenty first century, "Christian humanity is experiencing a deep religious crisis."[9]

The cause of this crisis is that large sections of people have lost a living faith and moved away from the Christian church. Many people who have departed from Christianity carry in their souls a mood of alienation, condemnation and hostility to the church and faith. Therefore, even within Christianity itself, leaving the other religions—Judaism, Islam, Buddhism and others—formed a broad *anti-Christian front*, trying to create (and has in fact created) *unchristian* and *antichristian culture*.

Most people (Christians) lost the perception of religion as the *center of spiritual life*, as its *chief*, and perhaps the only *source*. But the Christian church used to be the guardian of their religion for them. Humanity has not only ceased to nurture and cherish the church-Christian experience, but does not bear it and *any other religious experience*. It is a growing and expanding *world-view* that avoids the *contemplation of God*. The culture of

---

9. Il'in, *Sobraniye sochineniy*, 1:285.

our time increasingly stands apart without Christianity, but not only has it—culture even loses the religious spirit and meaning, and the gift.

Humanity in our day follows, first, *materialistic science* that makes such research successes (thanks, as expected, to the exclusion of the "hypothesis" of God and rupture with all religion), leading to practical and technical results that come not only from a religious foundation, but also an ethos-threatening science of self-destruction.

Second, modern humanity follows *secular irreligious statehood*, not realizing that this state has missed its highest goal, is not it, does not see it, since the aim of this is (always has been and always will be) to prepare people for the "good life" (Aristotle), to life "by God" (Saint Augustine). The Godless state leads the nation as "the blind lead the blind, both shall fall into the ditch" (Matt 15:14).

Third, modern humanity is attracted by *acquisitive instincts* and *economic laws* that rule over them and over which it has itself no power because people have lost in their souls the living God.

Fourth, modern humanity betrayed *irreligious* and *godless art*, which becomes fun and unnerving "performance."

The *problem of Christian culture* in the sense of Il'in is to answer the following questions:

1.  How can Christian culture exist today, when the educated strata of humanity is running away from Christianity and is trying to win over the masses of the uneducated and semi-literate?

2.  How can Christian culture exist when Christianity has not found hitherto true reconciliation and creative combination with the great secular forces which enthrall people: *science*, *art*, *economy* and *politics*?

3.  How can Christian culture exist when the very first positive support, awakening in humanity, the power of *nationalism* is still not accepted and blessed by Christianity itself as well as it not having realized its Christian roots?

There is an alternative: either to *create a non-Christian culture*, or to *reject the culture* of Christian motives.

There is no doubt that the non-Christian culture of the people of the possible non-Christian faith is the culture of Islam, Confucianism, Buddhism, Shinto's, etc. But the nations that were long Christian and have lost that faith can only make futile attempts to create a culture *beyond belief and God*.

To properly solve the problem of Christian culture, one must understand once and for all, that the spirit of Christianity is not a literal, pedantic, or regulatory one but one which *renews* and *releases*. To create a Christian culture, it is necessary according to Christians to *regenerate* and *accept the world*, and it is necessary to implement this *acceptance* of a perfect law of freedom. That is why the Gospel gives us "the perfect law of liberty" (James 1:25).

So, according to Il'in, "*Culture* is a phenomenon of *internal* and *organic*: it captures the depths of the human soul and lives on the tracks composed, mysterious expediency. This differs from a *civilization* that can be assimilated and surface appearance, does not require the participation of all the fullness of soul."[10]

Il'in formulates the fundamentals of Christian culture in five principles. First, the spirit of Christianity is the spirit of the *innermost*. "The kingdom of God is within you" (Luke 17:21). According to this, all external, material, sensual *itself* has no unconditional value and is not justified before the face of God.

Second, the spirit of Christianity is the *spirit of love*. "For God is love" (1 John 4:8). This means that Christ showed that love is the ultimate and unconditional primary source of any creativity, and hence any culture. For culture creates and approves; culture utters some *acceptable* and *abiding* "yes." But love is the first and greatest ability—to accept, approve and create.

Third, the spirit of Christianity is the *spirit of intuitive* contemplation, he teaches us to "see" in a sensually "invisible" (2 Cor 4:18, Heb 11:27) and promises us that "pure in heart," living in the "world" and "holiness," "see the Lord," "face to face" (Matt 5:8; 1 Cor 13:12; 1 John 3:2; Heb 12:14; John 12:45; 14:7). God opens the eye of the spirit. He is the light (John 9:5; 1 John 1:5). This light must be seen internal sensuous vision, is not a bodily sight (2 Cor 5:6–8) takes us to God. Christianity teaches to pray to God not in an abstract way or logical theorizing and not by volitional stress trying to impel ourselves to the faith, but by the direct contemplation carried out in the *eye of the heart*. God reveals himself to the one who draws the eye of his love to him.

Fourth, the spirit of Christianity is the *spirit of the living creative content* rather than the form, not of abstract measures and "the oldness of the letter" (Rom 7:6). Not in a sense that the principle of "form" could not be appreciated, i.e., the limit of the law, and the commission of completion, but in the sense that swept aside the beginning blank abstract, self-contained form, devoid of saturating and sanctifying its content. The Christian is not looking for a blank form but a completed one; he is not looking for a dead mechanism but organic life in all its mystery, in all its ordinances; he craves form born out of a deep, spiritually rich content. He is looking for a

---

10. Ibid., 300.

*sincere form.* He wants *to be,* rather than *to seem.* He commanded liberty, not legalism, and that is why legality, which is out of the spirit, sincerity and freedom, does not touch his heart.

Fifth, the spirit of Christianity is the *spirit of perfection.* "Be perfect as your heavenly Father is perfect" (Matt 5:48). This means that a Christian before his *mind's eye* has *the perfection of God* by which he measures all worldly affairs and life of environment.Anyone who wants to create a Christian culture should accept Christianity, enter his breath in the depths of his soul and turn to the world of this new *wholeness* and *freedom.* To put it in philosophical language, we can say that it is intended to carry in itself a *religious "act" of Christianity* and from the start the creative work on the transformation of the world in a new spirit. It is natural that he should *accept this very world* created by God and bestowed upon them. We have to accept this world *as Jesus Christ accepted it.*

## Culture and the Church

Il'in wrote: "In the creation of Christian culture there is the task set before humanity two thousand years ago and it unresolved. This task cannot be solved by *one era, one people, one generation,* once and for all, for every age and every nation and every generation must seek to resolve it in his own way—in their own way reaching and not reaching."[11]

Il'in clarifies the role of the church and the state in solving this problem. Neither the church nor the state can and should *require* the creation of Christian culture; it must be created freely. This free creative act can and should begin *within the church itself,* and then *transmits* and nation-building, and in all areas of secular culture. We need to create a Christian culture *not in the church*: for this would mean leading the church from its direct purpose—to guard the faith, the sacraments, hierarchy and the Spirit of Christ—and broaden its scope and responsibilities to absorb the entire life. Earthly culture has been created not by the state and the church, but by the people: many sets of free-breathing and contemplating individuals. To sum up: people do; the state rules; the Church teaches.

## On Christian Nationalism

Culture is created not by one person. It is the heritage of many people, spiritually connected to each other. Most people have a profound unity of their

11. Ibid., 316.

*spiritual homogeneity* of similar psycho-spiritual *way of life*, of *love*, similar to a common and general, from a single *fate*, linking people in life and death, of the same *contemplation*, of a common language, of *faith* and of uniform joint *prayer*. This is precisely the *national unity of people*. Il'in wrote:

> National feeling not only contrary to Christianity but it receives from its highest point and the base, because it creates a unity of people in the *spirit* of *love* and heart and attaches to the highest on earth—the gifts of the *Holy Spirit* bestowed each nation and in their own implements each of them in history and cultural creativity. That is why Christian culture is feasible on the grounds of exactly how national culture and nationalism are not subject to condemnation, but the joyful and creative acceptance.[12]

The problem can be solved only by *true nationalism* in connection with a spiritually understanding homeland: because *nationalism is the love of the spirit of his people and specifically for his spiritual identity*. Anyway: "Nationalism is love to his people, *leading a spiritual life*."[13]

## Bibliography

Grier, Philip T. "The Speculative Concrete: I. A. Il'in's Interpretation of Hegel." In *Hegel, History, and Interpretation*, edited by Shaun Gallagher, 169–93. Albany: State University of New York Press, 1997.

Il'in, Ivan A. *Sobraniye sochineniy*. Edited by Yuriy T. Lisitsa. 10 vols. Moscow: Russkaya Kniga, 1993–99.

Lisitsa, Yuriy T. "Ivan Aleksandrovich Il'in. Istoriko-biograficheskiy ocherk." In Ivan A. Il'in, *Sobraniye sochineniy*, 1:5–36. Moscow: Russkaya Kniga, 1993.

———. "O soprotivlenii zlu siloy: pro et contra. Polemika vokrug idey I. A. Il'ina." In Ivan A. Il'in, *Sobraniye sochineniy*, 5:289–556. Moscow: Russkaya Kniga, 1996.

Poltoratskiy, Nikolay P. *Ivan Aleksandrovich Il'in—zhizn,' trudy, mirovozzreniye: sbornik statey*. Tenafly, NJ: Hermitage, 1989.

12. Ibid., 323–24.
13. Ibid., 196.

# 17

# Religious Realism and Historical Challenges

*Vasily Zenkovsky and Russian Youth Abroad*

—Natalia Danilkina

The establishment of the school system abroad played a vital role for the first wave of Russian emigration. It was regarded not only as a chance to provide education, but also as the key opportunity to preserve the national culture in children. The common religion, along with the language, were regarded as the strongest factors of the spiritual revival.

In order to prevent denationalization, the Russian Pedagogical Institute was opened in 1923 in Prague—the academic center of emigration, as teachers with a good knowledge of "Russian culture and life, and Russian pedagogical tradition" were strongly required.[1] From 1923 to 1926 the Institute was headed by Vasily Zenkovsky, one of the most influential figures of Russian education in exile.[2] Zenkovsky contributed to the organization of the Russian Student Christian Movement (together with Sergey Bulgakov, Nikolai Zernov, and others) and remained its leader afterwards. From 1923 to 1927 he chaired the Pedagogical Bureau of Secondary and Primary Russian School Affairs Abroad in Prague; took part in foundation of Ven.

1. Gessen, "K otkrytiyu."
2. See Zhukov and Maslin, "Zen'kovskiy."

172

Sergey of Radonezh Theological Institute in Paris (1925) and launched the Religious-Pedagogical Cabinet there and edited a number of pedagogical periodicals.

The "otherness" of Russian youngsters growing up in emigration could be ascertained already in the late 1920s, when the Pedagogical Congress of Russian Emigration was held. In many respects, this fact was a result of the new cultural environment. Zenkovsky reported: "We must be aware that our youth is not the same, as we knew it ten years ago: in addition to the profound upheavals brought with living in exile, some features in it are probably resulting from the overall historical situation, so it brings together our youth and the youth in other countries."[3] However, it was not just the normal process of socialization that caused his concern.

The research conducted by the Pedagogical Bureau in 1923–25[4] proved the impact of the three major groups of facts on children's minds: the destruction of the common way of life, the civil war, and the evacuation from their homeland to a new land. Zenkovsky wrote then: "just the effects of one group of facts would be enough to cause the most serious shock in the soul. But the lives of our children—of course, in varying degrees, depending on age and living conditions—had to go through the triple test, the soul had to be pierced through thrice."[5]

There was practically no chance for the families of ex-landlords, military officers, government officials and public figures to continue their regular life after their escape from Russia. Moreover, the old *normal order* fell into ruins before their eyes, and in the eyes of their children, in turn, all this appeared to be something uncontrollable, rapid and sudden, comparable with a terrible natural disaster. The intuitive perception of *order*, which is so critical for the development of children's psyche at the pre-school age, as stated by Zenkovsky, faded in many of them at the period described in the essays. In some of the older child refugees, the observations of the *new* (revolutionary) *disorder* and the atrocities of the war evoked the loss of reasonable meaning of events and emotional obtundation: "The extinction of meaning is conveyed truthfully and in relief here: the very foundations of life were shaken and almost destroyed."[6]

3  Zen'kovskiy, "Problema shkol'nogo vospitaniya," 355. This is a published version of Zenkovsky's speech at Pedagogical Congress of Russian Emigration in Paris in 1929.

4.  The research covered 15 Russian schools in Europe. In total, 2403 children's essays containing their memories beginning from the year 1917 were gathered and analyzed. The results were partly reported in the course of the research and finally presented in the book edited by Zenkovsky, *Deti emigratsii.*

5.  Zen'kovskiy, "Detskaya dusha v nashi dni."

6.  Ibid.

Some suppositions were made regarding the features of the actual existence of young newcomers. The feelings of homelessness and remoteness, typical for refugees, were quite common in them. Their "temporal" status made them hardly able to build any plans for their adult future. At the same time, the nightmare of the past had its reverse side in the behavior of many teenagers—their particular craving and affection for everything new: new acquaintances, places, contacts, and besides, an unusually strong attachment to their schoolmates and teachers, not in orphans only but also in those, who came from two-parent families. The deepest roots for both phenomena are perceived by the thinker in the acute need of homeland, mystical, unconscious, irrational:

> There is a specific mystique in connection of every soul with the whole, from which it took its language and religion, in which it was growing and matured . . . These very "mystical" connections with homeland remain without any food in exile, and the soul is looking for something like a surrogate of this food, oversensitively attaches itself to everything that at least partially satisfies the need of the soul for homeland.[7]

Zenkovsky analyzes the life of young emigrants, observes their spiritual confusion and quite numerous cases of escape to "cynicism, anguish of amorality, melancholic pessimism and cult of nonsense,"[8] and formulates their basic setting as follows: all that cannot be shown as a reality is a fiction, rhetoric, and lies. "Vladimir Soloviev wanted to show that the good was a cosmic and historic force, whereas our youth needs another kind of 'justification' of the good, namely the actuality of the good in the social-historical sense."[9] In other words, the good had to prove its real force, needed to be shown as an actual factor in life.

The thinker believes that the only saving grace for the spiritual quest of the young people would be the acknowledgment of the fact that the unreality of the good in their actual lives and in their historical time does not eliminate its Higher reality. The Good has such Higher reality in God as the Absolute Basis of existence.[10] Religion is regarded by Zenkovsky as the immediate abidance in the world of the supreme reality, from the personal experience of which, all spiritual values obtain their real sense. A religious life "that imparts to the soul the deep and invincible sense of power and truth of the Good, that shines to the soul in the darkest, most terrible life

7. Ibid.

8. Zen'kovskiy, "Problema shkol'nogo vospitaniya," 365.

9. Ibid., 364–65.

10. Ibid., 365.

conditions,"[11] is only able to maintain morals, and thus preserve the integrity of the person in a vulnerable situation.

According to Zenkovsky, the true religious life is possible in connection with the Church, and this connection expects to become the factor of historical reality. He notices the religious revival among the intelligentsia as compared to the pre-revolutionary years, and particularly in the youth who accumulated religious energy even more vividly.[12]

In spite of some considerable achievements in pedagogics, both religious and secular, the thinker urges intrinsic changes with respect to the needs of the youth. In his opinion, it is insufficient to introduce the so-called religious approach in work *with* children. For Zenkovsky, it is important to show that the time of religiously neutral pedagogics has passed, the Russian culture has taken a dualistic turn—it can be either religious or anti-religious, and the relation to the Church spirit can be the basic distinguisher in this matter. Christian pedagogy, in his view, is characterized primarily by proceeding from the integrity of the religious worldview, which is embodied in the life of the Church. Precisely because of this integrity, the principles delivered to pedagogics by anthropology, philosophy and religion acquire their meaning. Moreover, in this system of integral worldview, the meaning, objectives and conditions of the development of personality can be understood properly.

The particular attention to the problem of personality appears to be the main driving force of the evolution of Zenkovsky's views: "In the early years, I was greatly influenced by Vladimir Soloviev and Lev Lopatin, but gradually my views began to change—and the reflections on the concept of personality were decisive for me here."[13]

The metaphysics of the person becomes prior to the thinker. Zenkovsky seeks to develop his Christian anthropology as a kind of philosophical system. It is clearly reflected in his pedagogical concepts that he also intends to present *in the light of Orthodoxy*. The concepts of *personality, freedom*, and *self-consciousness appear to be in the focus of his considerations.*

Zenkovsky puts forward the development of personality as the main goal of education. He argues though against making personality the supreme and ultimate principle of pedagogy: "Personality both metaphysically and ethically is not closed in itself—it is included into the system of

---

11. Zen'kovskiy, "Korennaya problema."

12. In the mid-1920s the activity of the Orthodox youth circles became especially notable, see Zen'kovskiy, "Religioznoye dvizheniye," 121.

13. Zen'kovskiy, "Ocherk," 37.

the world, is subject to its laws, is associated with higher principles, standing over the world."[14]

The principles mentioned here, for Zenkovsky, are apparently embedded in Divine transcendence.

The thinker notes the general shift from matters of the intellectual sphere to that of the whole personality in the pedagogics of the first decades of the twentieth century.[15] He analyzes the major theories of personality, both the psychological and philosophical, and poses his own concept. In personality as a whole, he distinguishes between the "empirical *I*" and the "real *I*," which make an inseparable and unique unity.[16] The former is external, natural-social, involving all intellectual properties, psychic experiences, implies possible "crises" and "splitting." The latter is deep, spiritual, non-derivative from the former, not deducible from the natural being, nor from the social one.

*Self-consciousness* is the constitutive element of spiritual life. The presence of this over-empirical consciousness in man indicates his involvement in the self-existent (*samosushcheye*) being. The supranational in a human is attributed to the Divine gift, so the philosophical dualistic split between the natural and the spiritual does not affect the sphere of human gnosis. Self-consciousness, not inherent in the animal psyche, Zenkovsky poses, is given from *somewhere "above"—i.e. from God*, and appears to be the most direct expression of the image of God.[17] True religious education aims at revealing this image in man through the preparation for the temporal life and life in eternity.[18] This process, according to Zenkovsky, has no meaning beyond the development of freedom, which has become so crucial in pedagogical considerations of various directions: naturalistic, idealistic (based on philosophical transcendentalism), and religious.[19]

The notion of *freedom*, as it is conceived by the thinker, relates to the whole personality, both in its empirical and spiritual ("real") aspects. However, the naturalistic "external" freedom expressed in behavior and different external activities stays on the empirical periphery of the personality in his teaching. He also disagrees with the development of the theme of freedom in a way leading to the chaos of pedagogical anarchism (after Rousseau

14. Zen'kovskiy, "Problemy vospitaniya," 374.

15. Zen'kovskiy, "Korennaya problema," 133.

16. If this unity is disregarded, the anthroposophical mistakes of reincarnation take place. See Zen'kovskiy, "Problemy vospitaniya," 408–9.

17. Ibid., 408.

18. Cf. Zen'kovskiy, "Russkaya pedagogika," 217; "Problemy vospitaniya," 399.

19. See Zenkovsky's classification of Russian pedagogical trends in: Zen'kovskiy, "Russkaya pedagogika," 170.

and Tolstoy). "There is no need to be captious to the present, to admit that modern man cannot defend the good in himself, that he extremely easily gets tempted and seduced."[20] One should be prepared for freedom in the process of education—at this point Zenkovsky is in full consonance with other religious thinkers such as Ivan Il'in, who claimed: "We must educate ourselves to freedom, we should mature to it, grow up to it, otherwise it will become a source of temptation and perdition."[21] Discussing the same issue with the pedagogics based on philosophical transcendental idealism (Sergey Hessen), Zenkovsky argues: "to bind the freedom up with the principle of 'logos,' the laws of the spirit, which transcendentally straighten the 'mistakes' and 'rage' of freedom—is possible, but all this *presupposes readiness of the soul to take the path of morality and logos*."[22] The Orthodox thinker connects the idea of education *in* and *to* freedom with the idea of salvation.

We admit that Efim Osovsky is quite right when claiming that the understanding of freedom determined the interpretation of the major categories of pedagogics in exile.[23] For the Orthodox philosophers the notion of freedom included the dichotomy of good and evil, and historical and personal catastrophes were interpreted in terms of their confrontation.

According to Zenkovsky, many Russian pedagogues, apparently influenced by the early pedagogy of Leo Tolstoy,[24] erroneously ignore the problem of evil: "Evil has become so open, impertinent and often unpunished in contemporary life that it easily withdraws the good in the soul . . . the life is too full of tragedies, forces of self-destruction, to keep from thinking about it."[25] The freedom is not intrinsically associated with the good, "the gift of freedom" should be developed in the person, "enlightened from inside," filled with the positive content.

Thus, having put the issue of freedom in a metaphysical way, Zenkovsky approaches the following questions: "to develop freedom—does not that mean deepening in children the right of choice, and possibility to go to the side of the evil" and "how to ensure the connection of the freedom and the good."[26] For the thinker, it appears to be possible in the Church and on the base of Christianity that has left behind manifestations of fanaticism, and "preaches freedom in Christ . . . through love and respect for the free-

---

20. Zen'kovskiy, "Problemy vospitaniya," 395.
21. Il'in, "Put' dukhovnogo obnovleniya," 287.
22. Zen'kovskiy, "Korennaya problema," 134.
23. See Osovskiy, "Rossiyskoye zarubezh'ye."
24. Zen'kovskiy, "Russkaya pedagogika," 177.
25. Zen'kovskiy, "Problemy vospitaniya," 395.
26. Ibid.

dom of everyone."[27] In practice of education, the Russian schools should be included into the "oases" of Orthodox culture. Those should be initially created by groups of people, never by official decrees, as the education should be guided by the spirit of the Church, and not by its administrative power.[28]

In emigration, the theme of spiritual and cultural continuity acquired its particular tone. Conceptual reflection on the problems of education occurred in parallel with organization of the educational system. Zenkovsky was undertaking active steps in both fields.

As a matter of fact, the maintenance of the national culture was strongly inspired in the first years of the forced emigration, when children were expected to return to their Fatherland. Gradually, the task of *safeguarding and development of Russianness—the Russian element (russkaya stikhiya)* became more and more elusive. By the 1930s, the goals and content of education were significantly re-orientated, as the children of Russian emigrants needed an education which provided the opportunity to study at foreign universities and continue their life abroad. National culture and language were still cherished by many families and pedagogues, but these matters were no longer supported with the same force, especially at the institutional level. Nevertheless, Zenkovsky and his colleagues maintained an emphasis on the religious experience in educating children abroad, setting new claims to it.

The analysis of the thinker's works from 1920 to the 1940s shows that his pedagogical views crossed with other educational conceptions known at the time at many key points, though were at variance with the most of them regarding the role of the Church and its doctrine in the process of education. Zenkovsky's religious realism calls for brining pedagogics closer to the concrete life of children and youth, and that is not by means of joining the pragmatic trend becoming quite popular in western philosophy and worldview, but by paying closer attention to the necessity of the inner enlightenment of God's gift in the person.

## Bibliography

Gessen, Sergey I. "K otkrytiyu Russkogo Pedagogicheskogo Instituta v Prage." *Russkaya shkola za rubezhom* 1–3 (1923) 92–101.

Il'in, Ivan A. "Put' dukhovnogo obnovleniya." In *Put' k ochevidnosti*, 133–288. Moscow: Respublika, 1993.

Osovskiy, Efim G. "Rossiyskoye zarubezh'ye: pedagogicheskaya nauka v izgnanii (20e–50e gody XX veka)." http://pedagogics.narod.ru/obzor/zarub1.htm.

27. Zen'kovskiy, "Korennaya problema," 140.

28. See Zen'kovskiy, "Problemy vospitaniya," 386.

Zen'kovskiy, Vasiliy V., ed. *Deti emigratsii*. Moscow: Agraf, 2001.

———. "Detskaya dusha v nashi dni." In *Deti emigratsii*, edited by Vasiliy V. Zen'kovskiy. Moscow: Agraf, 2001.

———. "Korennaya problema sovremennoy pedagogiki." In *Pedagogicheskaya publitsistika Rossiyskogo zarubezh'ya*, edited by Efim G. Osovskiy et al., 133–40. Saransk: Mordovskiy gosudarstvennyy pedagogicheskiy institut, 2006.

———. "Ocherk moyey filosofskoy sistemy." *Vestnik Russkogo studencheskogo khristianskogo dvizheniya* 3–4 (1962) 37–39.

———. "Problema shkol'nogo vospitaniya v emigratsii." In *Pedagogicheskaya publitsistika Rossiyskogo zarubezh'ya*, edited by Efim G. Osovskiy et al., 351–67. Saransk: Mordovskiy gosudarstvennyy pedagogicheskiy institut, 2006.

———. "Problemy vospitaniya v svete khristianskoy antropologii." In *Pedagogicheskaya publitsistika Rossiyskogo zarubezh'ya*, edited by Efim G. Osovskiy et al., 368–525. Saransk: Mordovskiy gosudarstvennyy pedagogicheskiy institut, 2006.

———. "Religioznoye dvizheniye sredi russkoy molodezhi za granitsey." *Put'* 1(1925) 121–27.

———. "Russkaya pedagogika v XX veke." In *Pedagogika*, 164–222. Klin: Fond Khristianskaya zhizn', 2002.

Zhukov, V. N., and M. A. Maslin. "V. V. Zen'kovskiy o Rossii, russkoy filosofii i kul'ture." Introduction to *Russkiye mysliteli i Evropa*, by Vasilyi V. Zen'kovskiy, 4–9. Moscow: Respublika 1997.

# 18

## Russian Religious Thought in the Middle of the Twentieth Century

*Discursive Strategies in the Philosophical Diaries of Yakov Druskin and Alexander Schmemann*

—MARIA KOSTROMITSKAYA

AFTER THE REVOLUTION OF 1917, when the Soviet government headed for the promotion of militant atheism, it became almost impossible to study religious philosophy in Russia, at least, within official institutions. Religious thinkers had only two ways: to immigrate or to go underground. Therefore, it is possible to observe two opposite strategies, two views of Christianity and of the destiny of Russia: "from outside" and "from within." To analyze and compare them, I address Yakov Druskin's and Alexander Schmemann's diaries where, besides reflection on personal life experiences, the authors paid a lot of attention to various philosophical and religious issues. It is important to remember that the diary genre became a central one during the twentieth century; moreover, this genre stimulates contemporary Russian philosophy, drawing on the tradition of Vasily Rozanov, Nikolai Berdyaev and Sergey Bulgakov. At the same time, this genre corresponds to the tasks of today's reality.[1]

---

1. For an example of one extremely significant publication, demonstrating interest to the genre of diary see compilation: Bibikhin et al. *Dnevnik sovremennogo filosofa.*

Schmemann's works were broadly published and discussed in his life-time. In the early 1970s his work *For the life of the world* was even translated into Russian and distributed in the USSR through illegal channels. Today his works are equally admired both among academics and churchmen. Quite a number of authors analyze his philosophy in their publications.[2]

As for Druskin's diaries, they were published in 1999 for the first time as only "an academic print" project. At the same time, his philosophical heritage remains practically beyond the research interest with the exception of some minor articles, analyzing Druskin, first foremost, as an OBERIU member and interpreter of Vvedensky's and Kharms' poetry.[3]

Yakov Druskin (1902–80) is one of the most peculiar existential phi-losophers of the twentieth century. In the 1920s and 1930s he used to be a member of the esoteric artistic communities called "Chinary" and OBERIU. He was offered a vacancy at the philosophy department, but ignored it and instead Druskin made rather humble choice: a teacher in the correspon-dence schools in Leningrad. In fact, this was a kind of shelter, concealing his active creativity. Alexander Schmemann (1921–83), on the contrary, was an enthusiastic religious and public figure. He belonged to the "unnoticed generation" of immigrant youth. Many of them desired to "atone for the sins of the Motherland" and expand the influence of Christian culture. In 1962 Schmemann became the head of Saint Vladimir's Orthodox Theological Seminary in the United States. Under his leadership this institution trans-formed into one of the biggest theological schools in the Orthodox world; he used to be, in fact, permanent secretary of the Bishops' Council of the American Diocese; he travelled all over the land preaching and lecturing, keeping a keen eye on the political world outside.

Although the two philosophers were contemporaries, they belonged to absolutely different cultural and historical environments. To some extent (apart from objective reasons) it was partly determined by their individual choices, as a well as specific personal features. Druskin's diaries are quite compatible with a certain tradition: diaries, written by men of letters, hu-manitarians under strict ideological pressure. Nevertheless, in the early 1960's the USSR witnessed the advent of dissident movement (including the so-called "orthodox dissidents"), the formation of a new artistic avant-garde began (although mainly in Moscow), certain links with the West took place: radio *Liberty* (Schmemann was part of it!), the so called "*tam-*" and "*samizdat,*" etc. However, judging by the diary notes, Druskin had very little

2. See, e.g.: Pomerants, "Inkvizitor," Lyubimov, "Pravoslavnyy protestant," Parfenov, "Na nas nadvigayetsya," etc.

3. Jaccard, *Daniil Harms*; see also Roberts, *Last Soviet Avant-garde*; Kobrinskiy, *Poetika.*

interest in those "modern cultural trends." He was totally out of the "social system." "They ask him: do you work? The reply was: no, I write. Work—that's a service ('sweat' job)."[4] At the same time, he possessed enormous inner freedom, which incorporated non-stop intensive "mind work." Owing to his literary giftedness, the result was not just a diary, but a philosophical and religious *opus* of top quality. In view of the aforementioned work, Druskin may be justly ascribed as a bohemian representative; such people could be considered apolitical and, hence, "the idea of being engaged in the official establishment has always been hateful for them."[5]

Without a doubt, Schmemann was a creative person too, although he spread his wings beyond the limits of profession and ethnic entity. He was a man of "triple national embeddedness;"[6] firstly he perceived the Russian immigrant as well as French culture in his green years, later on, as a teenager, the American one. Such a kind of triple national identity was quite harmonious. In addition, Schmemann was an integral part of the social and clerical system: a protopresbyter, lecturer. However, all of these social and administrative activities were quite often a sort of burden for him—Schmemann's diary confessions describe them as such.

As for the choice of subjects touched upon in Druskin's and Schmemann's diary notes, this cultural context meant a lot in this regard. Thus, one of the most important matters Schmemann was concerned with was the destiny of modern Christianity as a religion, its links with the Church as social institution and trust as an inherent human need. Besides, he contemplates considerably about Russian immigration, Western and Soviet societies, the global problems of today—the political, in particular. It should be noted that many of his ideas and concepts sound quite relevant nowadays. As for Druskin, due to the mere facts of life, he as deprived of the chance to observe and analyze "global" events. Nevertheless, his reflections on religious subjects, no matter how odd they are, are much deeper than Schmemann's. He considers seriously the following matters: freedom of choice and trust; immortality of spirit and eternity; love (for God Almighty and your neighbor) and sin, etc. Amazingly, he used to exist as if in a parallel world (vs. Soviet reality), in an endless dialogue with the Supreme Creator: "I keep on experiencing this kind of eternal living . . . I live within God's sight slanted at me."[7] With this constant description of one's intellectual experiences, it looks as if Druskin belongs to the existentialist tradition.

4. Druskin, *Dnevniki*, 11.

5. Vayl' and Genis, *60-e. Mir sovetskogo cheloveka*, 233.

6. Pomerants, "Poiski podlinnogo."

7. Druskin, *Pered prinadlezhnostyami*, 201.

If you wish to comprehend Druskin's and Schmemann's outlook deeper, it is worth asking yourself: why on earth did two really different philosophers used to make their diary notes for many years; both them expressed their basic thoughts in other works, didn't they? The two of them had different motives. Druskin kept on writing due to a profound need for recital in writing, as simple as that: "I do not write for someone's sake or a certain others sake, I just can't help it."[8] At the same time, he feared that the discourse in his diary might sound too literary[9] and, simultaneously, was gravely concerned because of the inability of full-scale creative self-actualization: "I buried my talent in the ground, instead of augmenting it."[10] And that is not just his personal tragedy: this is the fate of all the intellectuals and creative people who decided to remain in the USSR and lived there.

As for Schmemann's notes, he used to write them in order to maintain a certain self-contact, it was not "a desire to record everything, but an encounter with inner self, 'a visit,' even rather brief one. Are you here? Yes. Well, Thank God!" Then comes the attempt at "preserving everything in my soul, without focusing on something special only: 'dean of Saint Vladimir's Orthodox Theological Seminary,' 'liturgist,' etc."[11] This is a need for reflection, in a frank self-dialogue; this is the way not to disappear amidst the routine of endless tasks, in a whirl of masks, which we are all supposed to put on, while performing a variety of social parts. Schmemann's notes contain so many features typical for the diary genre: the description of exciting life events, one's own cares and feelings, the descriptions of Mother Nature, quotations from books read, etc. His philosophical discourse is closely linked with the actual events of his lifetime whereas Druskin practically does not mention in his diaries any "external" facts.

Comparing their views on the phenomena of time is a matter of special interest. As it was noted before, each and every second of his lifetime Druskin used to live feeling God's sight aimed at him. He did not care too much about the immediate aspects of life; he perceived it as rather something elusive, as a certain prelude for the Eternal Life. Any of its manifestations—say, his mother's death, or toothache, disputes with friends, everyday troubles, and the like—become significant not at this particular moment, not in their momentary nature, but, in their correlation with Eternity. What is the extent of the immutable and Divine in those events? In this regard, Druskin's approach is incompatible with Proust's concept of time.

8. Ibid., 219.

9. Ibid., 200.

10. Ibid., 156.

11. Shmeman, *Dnevniki*, 73.

Schmemann, in his turn, remarked: "Proust is right: the mission of Art is to restore Time . . . Thirst for solitude, silence, liberty—this is the thirst for "liberating" Time from dead bodies, encumbering it; to transform it into what it is supposed to be, i.e., a receptacle of eternity."[12]

It looks as if Schmemann tried in his diary notes "to outsmart" the elusiveness of time, to record the pulsating beat of "life itself;" he believed that only in vibrant life can one perceive the Divine presence, (not in some deeds or thoughts) and encounter the Eternity. Such was his comprehension of religious life as an inseparable relationship with all of the environment, as a whole, in the spiritual oneness of Nature.

In general, Druskin and Schmemann have only a few common subjects. A certain topic may seem most crucial for one of them, while the one may disregard it completely. Nevertheless, it is worthwhile underlining a few more important "overlaps." Schmemann was sure that "any religion *without Christ* (even Christianity, even the Orthodox Church) is definitely negative and even awesome; the fact of contact with such religion is a menace."[13] He believed that within the core of our trust, should be Christ and nobody else; he is the Judge, first and foremost in the sphere of religion and Church. Christ is the one and only Savior for us all. At the same time, most likely, Schmemann was an adherent of ecumenism. Druskin, in his turn, without denying the greatness of Christ, remarks that "any religion is Divine; whenever a pagan believer is praying to one's deity and doing it with all the fervor of his heart, then this is the case of *latria*."[14] This statement sounds rather daring, I would rather call it "radical." Obviously, any appreciable variation of their views in this matter is predetermined by the difference of the contexts themselves. Schmemann, despite his critical attitude towards the modern church and religion, was an Orthodox priest by all means. Surely, this fact had a certain limiting impact on considering various matters of religion. Since he conscientiously adopted the "thought itself," all he had to do was just follow the established rules, and it's only natural, since a man truly wishes to follow his world perception integrity. Druskin, on the contrary, rather by his own accord was absolutely outside any religious mentality: he was never baptized, or attended church liturgy, even though in the 1960s it was undoubtedly possible.

It is noteworthy that sometimes they mean quite opposite things while discussing one and the same notion. Thus, while speculating about *sobornost'* (collegiality) Druskin actually implied, that this notion means:

12. Ibid., 186.

13. Ibid., 66.

14. Druskin, *Pered prinadlezhnostyami*, 245.

"together overjoy and fear of the name of our glorious and frightful name of our God Almigty."[15] He was very anxious about the fundamental impossibility of its translation into life and, reproached himself for his "egoistic-solipstic constraint."[16] Whereas Schmemann confirms that an individual oneself "is 'collegial,' is capable and must do functioning within oneself and combine divided by 'natures;' theoretically speaking there's no bound to this 'collegiality,' or, to be precise, its comprehensiveness is in Jesus Christ, God-man, the one who combines within himself *everything*."[17]

Evidently, this is also stipulated by the difference of circumstances. As for the "collegiality" notion, each of the two thinkers contributed the thing which supposedly was missing for the sense of completeness of their religious life. Druskin was a very lonely and reserved person. Despite the fact that he did have supporters to discuss theological matters, he did still lack the *compatibility* in religious matters. Schmemann, on the contrary, was in continuous dialogue with the outside world, other people, including official representatives of the clergy, and, at the same time, he felt an acute need for internal dialogue.

So, we have examined just some of the religious and philosophic topics touched upon in diaries of Druskin and Schmemann, as well as in the circumstances of their lives. The views of these thinkers do not contradict each other, it seems that they are in opposite planes, which do not actually cross with each other, but this does not mean they have nothing in common. Both thinkers had literary talent and were perfect men-of-letters. Both of them were deeply concerned about reality and thought about it; hence, all everyday life private events, all the numerous impressions and evaluations are elevated towards the main, the supreme sense, which was inherited in God's creation from the outset. Suppose we consider the two diaries alongside one another; one might say that the two texts are mutually complementary, since they present an integrally whole representation of religious and philosophic spiritual quests of the mid- and second part of the twentieth century. Doubtlessly, Schmemann is an extrovert personality, and the scope of matters touched upon in his diary notes is really enormous. First comes his discourse on the fate of Russia, Russian immigration and the West; then comes religion, church and trust. His political correctness enabled him to see things unavailable for most people. Druskin is an introvert type, his texts do impress with the *depth* of his apprehension of religious matters. "Being isolated from his Western colleagues, he was the creator of an existential

15. Ibid., 130.

16. Ibid., 145.

17. Shmeman, *Dnevniki*, 148.

philosophical doctrine, partly similar to Kierkegaard and Husserl."[18] Besides, he perceives the world through the "iron curtain," a kind of perception from the "inside" unavailable for Schmemann, who never lived in Russia. Both thinkers were totally free in terms of inner freedom; ironically, Druskin's sense of freedom was stronger.

It looks as if further investigation of Druskin's and Schmemann's diaries is a very promising analytical activity. Studying their ideas is not merely a historical and philosophical review of national thought in retrospect, but also the desire for an apprehension of the various ways of the development of original and unique Russian philosophy nowadays.

## Bibliography

Bibikhin, Vladimir V., et al. *Dnevnik sovremennogo filosofa*. Moscow: Izdatel'stvo MGIU, 2009.

Druskin, Yakov S. *Dnevniki*. St. Petersburg: Akademicheskiy proyekt, 1999.

———. *Pered prinadlezhnostyami chego-libo: Dnevniki, 1963–1979*. St. Petersburg: Akademicheskiy proyekt, 2001.

Jaccard, Jean-Philippe. *Daniil Harms et la fin de l'avant-garde russe*. Bern: Peter Lang, 1991.

Kobrinskiy, Aleksandr A. *Poetika "OBERIU" v kontekste russkogo literaturnogo avangarda*. St. Petersburg: Svoye izdatel'stvo, 2013.

Kozyrev, Aleksey. "Filosof iz zazerkal'ya." *Novyy Mir* 4 (1997). http://magazines.russ.ru/novyi_mi/1997/4/obz104-p.html.

Lyubimov, Boris. "Pravoslavnyy protestant?" *Novyy Mir* 7 (2006). http://magazines.russ.ru/novyi_mi/2006/7/lu13.html.

Parfenov, Filipp. "Na nas nadvigayetsya novoye srednevekov'ye." *Kontinent* 132 (2007). http://magazines.russ.ru/continent/2007/132/pa16.html.

Pomerants, Grigoriy. "Inkvizitor v odezhdakh struktur i sistem." *Vestnik Evropy* 21 (2007). http://magazines.russ.ru/vestnik/2007/21/po21.html.

———. "Poiski podlinnogo." *Kontinent* 135 (2008). http://magazines.russ.ru/continent/2008/135/po21.html.

Roberts, Graham. *The Last Soviet Avant-Garde: OBERIU—Fact, Fiction, Metafiction*. Cambridge: Cambridge University Press, 1997.

Shmeman, Aleksandr. *Dnevniki, 1973–1983*. Moscow: Russkiy put', 2005.

Vayl', Petr, and Aleksandr Genis. *60-e. Mir sovetskogo cheloveka*. Moscow: AST, 2013.

18. Kozyrev, "Filosof iz zazerkal'ya."

# 19

# The Symphonic Unity of Traditions

*Sergey Horujy's Synergetic Anthropology and the Interpretation of*
*History*

—Roman Turowski

THOSE INTERESTED IN MODERN Russian thought associate Sergey Horujy's name not with philosophy alone, but also with research in quantum theory and the translation of *Ulysses* by James Joyce into Russian.[1] Having degrees as a Doctor of Science in Physics and Mathematics, a recognized figure in the field of literary translation and the history of Russian philosophy,[2] in philosophy proper Horujy is known primarily as the author of the so-called Synergetic Anthropology.

Synergetic Anthropology is a serious attempt to create a new anthropology, an alternative to the classic European version, that grows out of the philosophy of Aristotle, Descartes and Kant.[3] Firstly, in contrast with latter, Horujy takes his basic concepts of anthropology from the tradition of orthodox asceticism—Hesychasm,[4] which formed cut and dried inside eastern Christianity's *oikoumene* during the fourth to the fourteenth cen-

---

1. See Khoruzhiy, *Vvedeniye*, and Dzhoys, *Uliss.*
2. Khoruzhiy, *Posle pereryva.*
3. Khoruzhiy, *Fonar' Diogena*, 11–220.
4. Horujy, "Man's Three Far-Away Kingdoms."

187

tury. Here the author of the new anthropology fits into the tradition of the theological philosophy of the Neo-Patristic synthesis, at the base of which stood Georges Florovsky.[5] Secondly, Horujy follows European phenomenology in many aspects, especially writers like Edmund Husserl, Martin Heidegger and Michel Foucault.[6] Besides focusing on existential moments of philosophical discourse, the Russian philosopher puts himself in line with the philosophizing style proposed by Søren Kierkegaard.[7] Horujy, through his anthropological concept, seeks above all to rethink metamorphoses through which a human being comes today, those anthropological changes for which, in his opinion, modern philosophical discourse has not yet developed adequate tools of analysis and interpretational keys. Moreover, Horujy presents his Synergetic Anthropology not as a branch of philosophy, but rather as a new discipline of humanities, which would eventually become the new foundation for the whole of humanistic knowledge.[8] Horujy's version of anthropology is now developing rapidly as a discipline, its new applications appearing in such areas as literature, psychology, and even psychotherapy.[9]

This paper focuses on one of such applications of Synergetic Anthropology: an original interpretation of the logic of cultural and civilizational processes. Horujy in numerous articles, as well as at public lectures,[10] introduced a strict conceptual apparatus which, I believe, can be successfully and creatively applied for both understanding history in general, and for the interpretation of contemporary life in particular. The concept presented below could be a useful tool for historians, specialists in cultural studies and political scientists.

In its most general form, Horujy considers history not as a complex of facts, but rather as a sequence of cultural and civilizational formations. Moreover, all major categories of his concept are taken from the discourse relating to the description of the structures of consciousness. The philosopher analyzes the historical process not so much in the context of sociology, economics or political science as from the perspective of anthropology.[11]

---

5. Khoruzhiy, *O starom i novom.*

6. Khoruzhiy, *Fonar' Diogena*, 492–599.

7. Ibid., 221–375.

8. Khoruzhiy, "Novaya antropologiya."

9. See Khoruzhiy, *Fonar' Diogena.*

10. See Khoruzhiy, "Dukhovnaya i kul'turnyye traditsii v Rossii."

11. This approach to history fits well with the general tendency towards "anthropologizing" history, which has become increasingly popular during the past half a century. As an example, one can recall the trend in academic history known as "La Nouvelle Histoire."

The anthropological level is considered here as the basis for the analysis of each historical formation. In his study Horujy constantly makes transitions from the structures of human consciousness to the structures of history. Apart from Synergetic Anthropology itself, the basic concept of his historio-sophical concept is "tradition." Herewith, the key idea is that the historical dynamics itself is the result of the interaction of various traditions, especially the Spiritual and the Cultural.

In the following, I will first define tradition as it is understood by Horujy, and present the classification of different traditions proposed by him. I will also briefly describe the essence of Synergetic Anthropology to the extent necessary for the coverage of the given subject. Then I will introduce several basic types of tradition and show how they interact with each other and form a historical reality.

## The Concept of Tradition

The Russian author treats the concept of tradition in a special way, drawing it from the more general concept of transmission (*translyatsiya*). According to Horujy, everything in the time-space continuum is "transmitted." This primarily refers to material good but, by analogy to them, the same can be said about the senses, thoughts, emotions, about everything that in the language of the philosopher comprises an "anthropological space."[12]

Tradition as it is, is a transmission that has three key predicates:

1. *Memory*. Contents transmitted in tradition keep unity in time. Such unity is achieved within and through appropriate institutions and communities.

2. *Value*. Contents transmitted within the tradition must represent a certain objective value.

3. *Coherence*. Contents transmitted within the tradition are integral.

In the context of the three criteria set above, some transmissions are usually understood as traditions but in fact are not. This applies, for example, to stereotypes, gossip, fashion or behavioral conventions. All these transmissions, despite having unity in time (the memory predicate), are of dubious objective value (value predicate) and they rather do not possess integrity (coherence predicate). So, behavioral conventions often persist rather by virtue of a certain inertia than by their perceived usefulness. For example, traditionalist societies are imbued with such conventions and

12. Khoruzhiy, "Dukhovnaya i kul'turnyye traditsii v Rossii," Lecture 2, November 13, 2013.

stereotypes, but the question here is rather about a certain historical value in itself than about a cultural value.

Horujy introduces his own classification of traditions based on the following two parameters:

1. Type of transmitted contents in a given tradition. Such contents may be of the essential (formal) nature or of an energetic one (not formalized).[13] To the former, Horujy refers to the scientific or theological tradition, traditions, crafts or techniques. The latter is about the transmission of certain aspirations, emotions, cognitive arrangements.

2. Way of content transmissions in a given tradition. You can talk, for example, about verbal/non-verbal, oral/written, pedagogical methods of broadcasting.

Horujy lists the following classes of basic traditions: Spiritual, Religious, Cultural and Folk. Following this, he distinguishes three possible ways of the coexistence of the traditions mentioned above: the relation of complementarity, the relation of mutual exclusion and the hierarchical relation.[14]

Summing up, it is worth saying what, according to Horujy, tradition is not about. First, the concept of tradition is not a synonym of traditionalism. On the contrary, from Horujy's point of view the existence of tradition requires creativity on the part of its adepts.[15] Secondly, the tradition is not

13. The dichotomy of the essential and energetic is one of the basic concepts of Synergetic Anthropology. So Horujy talks about essential (*sushchnostnyy*) and energetic (*energiynyy*) discourse, understood as the most common cognitive patterns. More narrowly, the meaning of such a separation will be revealed further in the paper.

14. According to Horujy, the medieval era of the Kievan Rus (tenth–thirteenth century) was characterized by the domination of Religious Traditions, that grew primarily from the Spiritual Tradition. The later period of Muscovite Russia (seventeenth century) was characterized by an opposition between the Spiritual Tradition and Believing in rituals (*obryadoveriye*), which took place within one Orthodox Religious Tradition. In turn, since the era of Peter the Great (eighteenth century) Spiritual, Religious and Cultural traditions have evolved largely independently of one other. The situation changed only in the age of Pushkin and Seraphim of Sarov (nineteenth century). Then the creative interpenetration of the Spiritual and Cultural traditions served as a powerful impetus for creative development. Nevertheless, from the beginning of the next century, a contradiction which had been smoldering between Spiritual, Religious and Cultural traditions ever since the Split became visible. That resulted in a tragic experience for Russia, which was revolutions. See Khoruzhiy, "Evolyutsiya."

15. For Horujy, decomposition of the tradition begins at the moment when the content of the energetic character becomes stored and transmitted by means adequate for the transmission of the content plan. As an example, the philosopher refers to Orthodoxy in which, since its adoption in Russia, coexisted a tendency towards development of ascetic practice's tradition (the energetic content) with purely pagan tendencies towards sacralization and believing in ritual (essential content).

confined to the social sphere. Sources of traditions must be looked after not at the social, cultural, or even religious level, but rather at the anthropological. It is formed as a result of the functioning of the most general principles of reality mastered by human consciousness.

Now let me proceed to outline each of these traditions more carefully.

## Spiritual Tradition

This tradition is not identical with the Religious, although it is a basic element forming part of the latter. The Spiritual Tradition grows from a particular kind of personal experience that is issued in a coherent discourse within this tradition. Horujy calls it Spiritual Practice and this is the core and main subject of the given Spiritual Tradition. Spiritual Practice and Spiritual Tradition form a certain binary system. Thus the field of the application of the former is individuality, the latter is community. According to Horujy, "Spiritual Practice is a mechanism of anthropological unlocking (*samorazmykaniye*) experience towards the ontological Other (*Inobytiye*). It contains specific individual experiences, a mystical act."[16]

Horujy describes Spiritual Practice in terms of his Synergetic Anthropology in which a person is considered from the point of view of two key concepts: the Energy and the Border. He analyzes the human being as some kind of energetic formation, not in terms of its essence (an essentialistic approach), but rather in terms of personal aspirations and inner impulses, various human manifestations (an energetic approach). Such a methodological perspective, according to the philosopher, allows him to avoid reductionism in the descriptions and the need to postulate the presence of some unchanging entities in human beings and, therefore, to introduce a coherent system of definitions. Among all anthropological manifestations, the key ones are those, in which the person does not appear as closed, but rather as an open system. Horujy associates such manifestations with the so-called Anthropological Border (*Granichnyye proyavleniya*). Unlocking himself, a person is confronted with something completely different in the broadest sense, thus stating his own identity.[17]

16. Khoruzhiy, "Evolyutsiya."

17. The model of three basic mechanisms or topics of anthropological unlocking is introduced in Synergic Anthropology: (a) ontological topic: man as a living being realized in existence, unlocking himself to another horizon of Being, to the ontological Other; (b) ontical topic: man, as a creature possessing consciousness, unlocking to the Other, perceived as reality located beyond the horizon of consciousness; (c) virtual topic: not quite actualized manifestations. There is no virtual self unlocking towards the Other in "virtual" practices. But it is also a manifestation of the human boundary. All

Spiritual Practice is a specific strategy which aims to achieve the onto-logical Other. We are talking about self-unlocking in an ontological sense, here the person tends to develop a certain vertical vector in himself. Spiritual Practice is a practice alternative to all other anthropological practices. It aims to achieve a meta-empirical, trans-empirical goal, a Telos. Within Spiritual Practice, individual (energetic) contents are transmitted. It is based on the stairs paradigm, at each regular stage of which the complexity of the anthropological structure increases. Such a practice generates the corresponding instruction, its own Organon, which serves as the organizer of spiritual experience, its implementation, verification and further transition. Spiritual Practice persists within a certain community, which contributes to its implementation, and it is church-related. At the same time, such a practice has an individual dimension. For Horujy, Spiritual Practice plays a crucial role in shaping the Spiritual Tradition, which, in turn, is the key tradition in the ensemble of basic traditional classes—Cultural, Religious, Artistic, Scientific, etc. Spiritual Tradition itself exists, in fact, in order to store and transmit the Spiritual Practice.

## Religious Tradition

The Religious Tradition stems from the respective Spiritual Tradition. It creates a certain universe in which man is able to fulfill himself entirely. Within the Religious Traditions, heterogeneous in its nature, Horujy identifies several formative sub-traditions: Spiritual Tradition (serves to aid the organization, preservation and transmission of practice), Material Tradition (sacred architecture), Cultural Traditions (sacred music), Social Traditions (schools), Intellectual Traditions (doctrine), and Folk Tradition (rites, beliefs, customs). The whole ensemble serves to preserve the Spiritual Tradition which, in turn, is a tool for creating, verifying, broadcasting and saving a certain key to personal self-realization experience.

Analyzing the internal structure of Religious Tradition, Horujy says about its projections, speaking in mathematical terms, that there are three inextricably linked aspects connected with and affecting one other:

1. Aspect of experience. Religious Tradition as a mechanism for the transmission of personal (non-formalized, energetic) content through personal communication;

---

the three classes of boundary human manifestations mentioned above together form the so-called Anthropological Border. It should be noted that we are not talking here about the geometric understanding of the border but rather about the ontological one. See: Horujy, "Man's Three Far-away Kingdoms," 3–7.

2. Aspect of the institution. Religious Tradition as a mechanism for transmitting impersonal (formalizied, essential) content. Mechanism used here for transmission has rather essential than energetic character;

3. Aspect of doctrine. Transmitting mechanism and the nature of transmitted content is similar to the previous, institutional aspect.

The crucial and formative aspect of Religious Tradition is the aspect of experience. For Horujy, institutional and doctrinal aspects play an auxiliary role in it, helping to create the conditions for the emergence of relevant experience, its verification, preservation and transmission through time.[18]

Thus, Horujy obtains another tool for analyzing a particular historical formation. For such a study you need firstly to trace the dynamics of the institutional, spiritual (experienced) and doctrinal changes in aspects of the given Religious Tradition. Then you need to analyze the nature of their interaction, yielding a clear holistic image of the given cultural and civilizational reality.

For Horujy, one can talk about coexistence in some eras, of two parallel Religious Traditions—the Minor (*Malaya*) and Major (*Bol'shaya*). A Minor Religious Tradition consists of a non-reflected complex of content, sets of images and beliefs. It is strictly separated from the rational, intellectual and cultural spheres of the anthropological reality. The Minor Religious Tradition is an integral part of the Folk Tradition, heterogeneous in nature. In the Major Religious Tradition, in turn, a key role is played by the corresponding Spiritual Practice, the aspect of experience.[19] This tradition also includes the doctrinal aspect it is engaged in and has a huge impact on the Cultural Tradition.

## Cultural and Folk Traditions

Cultural and Religious Traditions, consist of several sub-traditions: Spiritual, Material, Social, Intellectual, Artistic, etc. The content transmitted in it, usually by pedagogical methods, is essential and energetic. The Cultural Tradition is characterized by a variety of different institutions related to economic, legal, educational or artistic spheres.[20] In addition, the Cultural

18. Khoruzhiy, "Dukhovnaya i kul'turnyye traditsii v Rossii," Lecture 3, November 20, 2013.

19. An example of the coexistence of Minor and Major religious traditions would be that of Muscovy Rus. In its later period, its Religious Tradition was almost completely reduced to a Minor Religious Tradition. For Horujy, exactly such a position became one of the main causes of the historical dynamics of the Russian state.

20. Khoruzhiy, "Dukhovnaya i kul'turnyye traditsii v Rossii," Lecture 5, November 27, 2013.

Tradition, compared with the Religious one, is much more diverse in terms of the content of the conceptual (intellectual) plan.

In turn, the Folk Tradition transmits content which should be attributed to irrational layers of human existence—the myths, stereotypes, beliefs. Similar content of consciousness are ascribed a special status, they are perceived as a value which should be preserved as a guarantor of the integrity of the respective ethos.[21] According to Horujy, the Folk Tradition is a purely social phenomenon. There is no personal dimension itself, this dimension could even be harmful for the existence of the Folk Tradition. The philosopher believes that the Folk Tradition always acts as an alternative not only to the Religious Tradition, but also to the Cultural Tradition.[22]

## The Symphonic Unity of Traditions

To summarize, one needs to point out the exceptional role of the Spiritual Traditions for generating historical dynamics. Such exclusivity is the main thesis of this text, along with the thesis of the relentless interaction of Spiritual and Cultural Traditions, which, according to Horujy, duly determines the entire image of the historical process.

According to Horujy, one leading tradition in each historical formation can be selected besides dependent traditions which draw content and purpose from the main tradition. The latter, regardless of the specific historical formation, is highlighted by Horujy as the Spiritual Tradition.[23] Horujy sees at least three reasons for its uniqueness: Firstly, the Spiritual Tradition has an ontological and meta-anthropological nature which allows for the most complete personal self-realization. Secondly, the Spiritual Tradition has an individualistic, personal character which is the most representative feature of a person. Thirdly, the structures of personality and human identity are formed within the Spiritual Tradition, in the depths of spiritual practice.

Religious, Cultural and Folk Traditions primarily have a social, collective character. A human being is regarded here as a part of the Collective. But such processes play a crucial role in the cultural and civilizational dynamics at the individual, rather than the social level, for Horujy. Besides,

---

21. Nevertheless, it is difficult to rationalize what is objectively attributed to archaic folk value. According to Horujy, this can include only emotional value.

22. Khoruzhiy, "Dukhovnaya i kul'turnyye traditsii v Rossii," Lecture 5, November 27, 2013.

23. This thesis is not self-evident. Often Spiritual practices which underlie Spiritual Traditions, especially in secular traditions, are not valued highly, for example as a marginal phenomena associated with mental abnormalities.

such processes are responsible for the formation of a particular human identity. And, even if at a particular historical moment Spiritual Tradition occupies a marginal place in public life, there can always be an appropriate tradition adjacent to it, by which the Spiritual Tradition profoundly affects the entire cultural and civilizational process.[24]

In a situation when within any historical formation a decisive role is played by traditions other than the Spiritual, identity is not formed as a result of self-unlocking on the ontological Other (ontological topic). Such an identity which appears as a result of unlocking to the unconscious (ontical topic) or virtual (virtual topic) does not have, according to Horujy, some anthropological completeness. Therefore, the solution of the key problems of human existence within such a stripped-down identity becomes impossible. A person with such an identity is not able to realize his full anthropological potential. According to Horujy, at the moment when the leading tradition within a particular historical formation becomes one of the sub-traditions, such as the Folk Tradition, this formation loses its impetus and the creative vector looking to ontological Other. In fact, it is exactly in the latter that one should seek an inexhaustible source of the most profound contents and objectives for any cultural and civilizational formation, unless such a formation purports to be complete and universal.

## Bibliography

Dzhoys, Dzheyms. *Uliss. Roman.* Translated by Viktor Khinkis and Sergey Khoruzhiy. Moscow: Respublika, 1993.
Horujy, Sergey S. "Man's Three Far-away Kingdoms: Ascetic Experience as a Ground for a New Anthropology." http://synergia-isa.ru/english/download/lib/Eng4.doc.
Khoruzhiy, Sergey S. "Dukhovnaya i kul'turnyye traditsii v Rossii." Series of lectures delivered at the Moscow State University, November 6–December 13, 2013.
———. "Evolyutsiya kul'turno-istorichskikh form russkogo soznaniya." Lecture delivered at the Moscow State University, December 6, 2013.
———. *Fonar' Diogena. Kriticheskaya retrospektiva evropeyskoy antropologii.* Moscow: Institut sv. Fomy, 2010.
———. "Novaya antropologiya kak nauka nauk o cheloveke." Lecture delivered at the Pontifical University of John Paul II in Krakow, March 14, 2013. Online: http://synergia-isa.ru/wp-content/uploads/2013/05/horuzhy_talk_krakov_3_2013.pdf.

24. As an example of the harmonious coexistence Spiritual and Religious Tradition, Horujy gives the so-called Russian synthesis (*Russkiy sintez*) that took place in the nineteenth century. Just then, the classical Russian culture emerged, which would raise questions of enduring and universal value. We are talking primarily about classical Russian literature and it was influenced by the tradition of Hesychasm and, in recent years, this influence has been a frequent subject of research in cultural studies, literarature and anthropology.

———. *O starom i novom*. Saint Petersburg: Aleteyya, 2000.

———. *Posle pereryva. Puti russkoy filosofii*. Saint Petersburg: Aleteyya, 2000.

———. *Vvedeniye v algebraicheskuyu kvantovuyu teoriyu polya*. Moscow: Nauka, 1986.

# PART III

Religion, Politics, and Ecumenism

## 20

# The Roman Question in the History of Russian Culture in the Late Nineteenth and Early Twentieth Centuries

—Fr. Yury Orekhanov

THE FOCUS OF THIS paper is the concept of the Roman Question, which was first introduced in journalistic use by Fyodor Tyutchev in an article of the same title. By summarizing the content and extending the scope of the article by Tyutchev, under the concept of the Roman question we shall refer to those aspects of the presence of the Roman Catholic Church in Russian historical life that have had a significant impact on Russian culture and society. The influence of the Roman Catholic Church was manifested in a number of ways, including, but not limited to:

1. The history of the first Catholic missions in Russia, the legal status of the Roman Catholic Church, the formation of Catholic dioceses, and the particularities of the Russian legislation that regulated the structure and the legal status of Catholic institutions and Catholic clergy.

2. Jesuit activities in Russia, primarily educational and proselytizing, as well as the criticism thereof in the works of Russian public and Church figures.

3. The phenomenon that can be termed "Russian Catholicism." Here, researchers should be primarily interested in those factors that prompted

peoples' decisions to convert. We should also consider historical and philosophical studies (including works of Catholic apologetics) of famous Russian Catholics of the nineteenth century, such as Prince Ivan Gagarin, Vladimir Pecherin, Ivan Martynov and others, as well as their memoirs and correspondence.

4.  The question of dogmatic differences in the teachings of the Orthodox Church and the Roman Catholic Church. While this problem might appear to be merely theoretical, one aspect of it, namely, the reception of the First Vatican Council, has proved to be hugely significant for the overall perception of Catholicism in Russia.

5.  One of the consequences of the council, as is well-known, was the emergence of the Old Catholic movement. In this regard, contacts between representatives of the Russian Church, Russian theologians, philosophers and public figures, on the one hand, and the Old Catholics, on the other, became extremely important.

6.  Finally, the influence of Catholicism on Russian culture, especially on the culture of the "Silver Age."

This particular paper focuses on the Russian perception of the decisions of the First Vatican Council, where, on the July 18, 1870, the dogma of papal infallibility was proclaimed. Given the difficult situation in Europe and the growth of anti-clerical sentiment, the dogma was clearly perceived in liberal political circles as a challenge to progressive European public opinion.

How were the resolutions of the council perceived in Russia? This article summarizes the central "ideological beacons," those fundamental arguments that underlie the reception of the main decrees of the council in Russia, Russian theology and Russian culture in general. Chronologically the article will cover the period from the late 1860s until the first half of the twentieth century.

## Fyodor Tyutchev

It is well known that the Roman Question was first addressed to by Petere Chaadayev in his philosophical letters. However, until the early 1860s, censorship laws inhibited the dissemination of his views. That is why the article by Fyodor Tyutchev, "The Roman Question," published in January 1850 in the conservative Parisian magazine *Revue des Deux Mondes* acquired so much importance and immediately became quite famous in Europe.

For Tyutchev, Russia and the West were two different worlds, two "humanities" that historically flew "two different flags."[1] But, unlike Chaadaev, Tyutchev emphasized that Russia was "another Europe," which had preserved a Christianity for the world which had been historically distorted by Catholicism.

For Tyutchev, the Roman Question was the "root of the Western world," the crossroads of the contradictions of Western civilization. On the one hand, he explained, "everything that still remains of actual Christianity in the West is connected, either explicitly or by more or less evident congeniality, with Roman Catholicism."[2] On the other hand, although Rome "has not abolished the Christian focal point which is the Church," she has "absorb[ed] it the Roman ego,"[3] i.e significantly distorted the Christian idea in favor of purely political objectives and motivations. Tyutchev argued that the Reformation itself was a natural result of the development of the concept of the papacy in the Catholic Church: there was a "terrible, but undeniable bond through different times between the birth of Protestantism and the conquests of Rome." He continued, "The revolution, which is only the apotheosis of this same human *ego* come to its total and full flowering, has not failed to acknowledge as its own and to hail as its two glorious masters Luther as well as Gregory VII."[4]

Although Tyutchev's article appeared long before the beginning of preparations for the First Vatican Council, its consequences for further debates cannot be overestimated. The publication immediately provoked a strong reaction in Europe and *de facto* became the impetus for the discussion that was started by the Catholic publicist P. S. Laurence and led to Alexei Khomiakov's famous works, the arguments of which cannot be reviewed in detail here.

Let us, then, consider in more detail the question of the perception of the First Vatican Council in Russian theological and philosophical journalism.

## Russian Theology

In general, it can be argued that Russian theologians' reaction to the decisions of the First Vatican Council (both planned and actual) was negative.

1. Tyutchev, "Roman Question," 191.
2. Ibid., 188.
3. Ibid., 191.
4. Ibid., 192.

One of the foremost experts in this matter, Fr. Tarasiy Seredinskiy, emphasized that the doctrine of papal infallibility:

1. Did not have a distinct grounding in the Holy Scriptures;

2. Was refuted by the events of early Church history;

3. Was disputed by many Latin theologians, some popes and Western councils;

4. Was untenable due to the variability of distinguishing features and conditions of infallibility, and their overall vagueness.[5]

Seredinskii thus in an article written in 1870 formulated the basic arguments that were subsequently developed and more seriously conceptualized in various discussions. Perhaps one of the most prominent of these discussants was Vladimir Soloviev.

## Vladimir Soloviev

It is well known that Vladimir Soloviev's perception of Catholicism was constantly shifting; it was often contradictory and always complex. It should be pointed out that, until 1881 his views on Catholicism were in line with those of Fyodor Dostoevsky. However, after the death of the writer, the views of Soloviev began to change. We will focus on the period in which Soloviev demonstrated an overt sympathy towards Catholicism, a sympathy which would be altered by the end of the 1880s, after his Parisian experiences and the negative reaction of the Parisian Jesuits towards his writings.

In the first half of the 1880s, in journal articles and private correspondence, Soloviev made a strong apology not only for the decisions of the First Vatican Council, but in general, for the position of the Catholic Church in the history of the so-called "Great Schism." Already in 1882, in a letter to Ivan Aksakov Soloviev said that, from his point of view, the main cause of "interior disease" of the Russian Orthodox Church (meaning the schism of the Old Believers') is a "general weakening of the earthly organism of the visible Church,"[6] a gulf dug not by God's but by human hands.

In subsequent articles written during the eighties, the philosopher outlined a program with a series of resolutions, which he believed could bridge this gap. Characteristically, Soloviev pointed to the unity of the Western and Eastern Christians in the divine-human union of believers with Christ and the apostolic succession, and the unity of the faith and the sacraments.

5. Seredinskiy, "Nepogreshimost' rimskogo papy," 494.
6. Quoted after Strémooukhoff, *Vladimir Soloviev*, 145.

He tended to consider the contradictions which had emerged historically as minor episodes that had no fundamental significance in comparison with the existence of an absolute Church authority, a powerful doctrinal and administrative center (*centrum unitatis*) uniting all Christians. From Soloviev's point of view, Eastern Christianity had seriously underestimated the importance of this center and had been deceived by the temptation of so-called "Byzantinism." It is also important to emphasize that Soloviev distinguished between the concepts of the "Papacy" and "Popery." The "Papacy" was the expression of the full knowledge of divinely revealed truth in the personality of the Roman primate, while "Popery" was a term used to indicate the long record of historical abuse of this position.[7] Soloviev's thoughts reached their logical conclusion in the late 1880s in the context of his harsh criticism of the Russian Church.

It is well-known that in the nineteenth century the views of Vladimir Soloviev on Church unity were strongly criticized in the Russian press. That is why in one of his letters the philosopher called himself "the only defender of Catholicism"[8] in Russia. Without dwelling on the particulars of this criticism, let us consider the views of his opponents, namely, Nikolai Danilevsky, another famous Russian thinker.

In his criticism of Soloviev's position, Danilevsky raised a radical and substantial question: How should the Orthodox Church perceive the Catholic Church after the adoption of the latest decisions of the First Vatican Council, "is it [Roman Catholicism] going to be viewed as a heresy, schism, or as an integral part of the universal Church, separated from us only by an unfortunate misunderstanding?"[9]

From Danilevsky's point of view, the proclamation of the dogma of papal infallibility was the proclamation of an eighth sacrament, previously unknown to the Church, which was indicative of the triumph of Western rationalism. Realistically, we should speak about the difference "between the Orthodox concept of the infallibility of the Council and the Catholic concept of papal infallibility."[10] The first, "the infallibility of the Council"—is a manifestation of the infallibility of the Church itself, which is never granted to any council *a priori*, but is confirmed, perhaps, after a fairly long period of time, in the act of reception: a resolution of a council must undergo "a procedure" of *ecclesiastical recognition*.[11] This process is, in effect, rejected

7. See in particular Solov'yev, "Papstvo i papizm," 55.
8. Ibid., 77.
9. Danilevskiy, "Vladimir Solov'yev," 375.
10. Ibid., 368.
11. Ibid., 369.

by the wording of Council which states that the truth proclaimed by the Pope no longer requires Church sanctions. In this Danilevsky referred to the well-known *Encyclical of the Eastern Patriarchs* of May 6, 1848, which stressed that in the Orthodox Church, neither the patriarch nor the council had the right to introduce any dogmatic innovations without the sanction of the "people of the Church" i.e. the Church in its fullness.

Danilevsky also responded to the fundamental question of how the obstacles of communication between Orthodoxy and Catholicism, so obvious to Soloviev, should be overcome. He believed that it was necessary to "try to eliminate these barriers to communication, and not to turn a blind eye and not to make false representations to them, for we will then get the wrong message of the truth that we were communicated by the grace of God."[12]

As we turn to the twentieth century, it is only natural that we should focus on the works of Lev Karsavin, Fr. Sergey Bulgakov and Nikolai Arsenyev, three remarkable writers of the twentieth century who expressed a frank sympathy towards—or a great interest in—Catholicism.

## Lev Karsavin

In his small book *Catholicism*, published in 1918, Karsavin paid special attention to the question of papal infallibility. Karsavin was particularly interested in questions of Church unity and union of love in Christ, which, in his view, found their fullest expression precisely in Catholicism. He observed that the Catholic Church had always sought not only mystical, but also concrete, "visible" manifestations of this unity. Thus, there existed within the Catholic Church the idea of the depository of Tradition implemented through a specific *body* through apostolic succession. This body had the "mysterious power and authority of teaching, the power of interpretation of old truths and the finding of new ones."[13] The Papacy itself was actually such a body as it was "this very Tradition living by the apostolic spirit."[14]

Karsavin pointed out in his paper that the decisions of the First Vatican Council were the logical conclusion, not only of the tradition of Catholicism, but of the very Catholic idea: "Since there is apparently one true Church, and in it there is the true doctrine and the authority keeping it, it is necessary that the decisions and opinions of this body be infallible."[15]

12. Ibid., 373–74.

13. Karsavin, *Katolichestvo*, 28–29.

14. Ibid., 29.

15. Ibid., 40.

According to Karsavin, the dogma of papal infallibility gave to Catholicism an exceptional vitality and impetus for further development. Moreover, the philosopher considered the decisions of the council in this regard to be brilliant, and believed that most criticisms of the doctrine tended to focus on the "external and non-essential." In his view, "the dogma of the infallibility of the papacy solved the age-old problem of reasoning of the only Universal Church on earth."[16]

## Sergey Bulgakov

Father Sergey Bulgakov also demonstrated a marked interest in the dogma of papal infallibility. In the early 1920s, when he was already a priest, Bulgakov experienced a strong passion for Catholicism, as he wrote in his diary at the time. It is therefore important for us to discover how one of the most famous Russian theologians of the twentieth century understood the problem of papal doctrinal primacy.

Fr. Bulgakov's stance was outlined in his seminal article in the journal *Put'* in 1929. The conclusions of Fr. Sergey's article of 1929 can be summarized as follows:

1. The spirit of the conciliar movement in the fifteenth century in the Catholic Church (meaning primarily the Councils of Constance and Basel) clearly indicates that until a certain moment this doctrine was present in Catholicism as one of the possible points of view and was therefore open to discussion and exploration;

2. To the Eastern (i.e. Orthodox) Church consciousness, the idea of papal infallibility is unacceptable, as well as is the concept of absolute papal authority over the whole Church;[17]

3. Both historically and dogmatically, the major decision of the First Vatican Council had some serious defects, the most important of which was the fact that the dogma of papal infallibility, unlike earlier dogmatic definitions, did not belong to the *a priori* experience of the Church. On the contrary, it contradicted this experience, and therefore in no way could be declared by the Ecumenical Council itself;

4. Vatican dogma was the final and inevitable conclusion of "Church juridicism" and a symptom of the decay of Western Christianity, caused by the Reformation. The Vatican definition represented a serious shift

---

16. Ibid., 45.

17. Bulgakov, *Vatican Dogma*, 25.

in the balance of the ideal form of the "combination of Christian free-dom and ecclesiastical obedience."[18]

5. Bulgakov concludes with an argument of a "practical" nature: "So long as the Vatican dogma stands, it is for the Orthodox world an insuperable obstacle to a sincere and real striving for union with the Catholics."[19]

## Nikolai Arsenyev

Finally, Nikolai Arsenyev, the famous émigré theologian and philosopher, was deeply interested in the study of the Russian reception of "Vatican dog-ma." He treated the issue in great detail in the article "Orthodoxy, Catholi-cism, Protestantism" (1930). In the second edition of this text, published in 1947, after the Second World War, Arsenyev pointed out that, after the merciless, inhuman and brutal events of a war which had led to the destruc-tion of European culture, the Christian world had to seek unity in Christ with particular force. He insisted that his gaze was "directed toward what unites Christians—much more than toward what divides them."[20]

Nikolai Arsenyev indicated that the dogma of papal infallibility, from his point of view, was the highest manifestation of a legalistic understanding of grace, and of the very essence of Church life, and that, therefore it "clearly and definitely separates Rome from the Orthodox Faith."[21] In his opinion, the main problem with the dogma was that the burden of the freedom of Christ, the burden of the conciliar responsibility for the life of the Church, was replaced by the responsibility of one person, namely the Pope. Arsenyev emphasized that, although the theory of papal infallibility was really harmo-nious, it was also contrary to the essence of the Church, and demonstrated a clear desire to "concretize the truth of the Church in the person of the living pope."[22]

## General Conclusions

The discussions which arose over the controversial decisions of the First Vatican Council had an enormous historical and theological significance

18. Ibid., 68.
19. Ibid., 72.
20. Arsen'yev, "Pravoslaviye," 271–72.
21. Ibid., 294.
22. Ibid., 303.

not only for the Catholic Church, but also for Orthodoxy. These decisions challenged, not only Orthodox theology, but also Russian culture in general, conscious of itself as it was of being rooted in Orthodoxy.

In general, representatives of Russian theological science, philosophers and artists reacted negatively to the decisions of the First Vatican Council. This was primarily due to the fact that the dogma of papal infallibility, from the point of view of the Russian authors, did not comply with the principles of catholicity as they understood it. Indeed, the Eastern viewpoint emphasizes that the doctrinal infallibility of the Church does not belong to one person (the pope), and not even to one collective body (the council), but to the plentitude of the Church.

Most Russian authors of the nineteenth century were convinced that the resolutions of the First Vatican Council increased the divide between East and West, and created even greater obstacles to Christian unity. The only exceptions to this rule can be seen in the positions of Vladimir Soloviev and Lev Karsavin, who argued that the dogma of papal infallibility provided a sound basis for Church unity.

## Bibliography

Arsen'yev, Nikolay S. "Pravoslaviye, katolichestvo, protestantizm." In *Dusha Pravoslaviya. O zhizni preizbytochestvuyushchey. Pravoslaviye. Katolichestvo. Protestantizm.* Moscow: Khram Svyatoy muchenitsy Tatiany pri MGU, 2009.

Bulgakov, Sergius. *The Vatican Dogma.* Translated by Lev A. Zander. South Canaan, PA: St. Tikhon Press, 1959.

Danilevskiy, Nikolay Ya. "Vladimir Solov'yev o pravoslavii i katolitsizme." In *Gore pobeditelyam. Politicheskiye stat'i,* 338–39. Moscow: Alir," Oblizdat, 1998.

Karsavin, Lev P. *Katolichestvo.* Petrograd: Izdatel'stvo Ogni, 1918.

Seredinskiy, Tarasiy F. "Nepogreshimost' rimskogo papy v uchenii very i nravstvennosti khristianskoy pered sudom Svyashchennogo Pisaniya i Svyashchennogo Predaniya, tserkovnoy istorii, samikh episkopov rimskikh, latinskikh bogoslovov, zapadnykh soborov i zdravogo smysla." *Khristianskoye chteniye* 3 (1870) 488–529.

Solov'yev, Vladimir S. "Papstvo i papizm. Smysl protestantstva." In *O khristianskom edinstve.* Moscow: Rudomino, 1994.

Strémooukhoff, Dimitri. *Vladimir Soloviev and His Messianic Work.* Translated by Elizabeth Meyendorff. Belmont, MA: Nordland, 1980.

Tyutchev, Fyodor I. "The Roman Question." In *Poems and Political Letters of F. I. Tyutchev,* translated by Jesse Zeldin, 188–92. Knoxville: University of Tennessee Press, 1973.

# 21

# The Rotten West and the Holy Rus

*Ethical Aspects of the Anti-Occidentalism of the Contemporary Russian Orthodox Church*

—Fr. Marcin Składanowski

Russian anti-Occidentalism is by no means a new phenomenon. It can be traced back to the period during which the Russian state was formed and the Russian national identity began to emerge. Although Russian anti-Occidentalism is not only a consequence of the relationship between this identity and the Orthodox Church as such, the religious factor was of considerable importance for its development in Russia. It is mostly about the centuries-old conviction that there is only one Orthodox country (which is "truly Christian" as opposed to Western Christianity), which derives its strength from opposition to the influence of Western culture.

Post-Soviet Russia turned out to be particularly sensitive to Western cultural influences, which also manifested themselves in growing trends towards copying the socio-cultural changes taking place in the West. Astonishingly, however, while some Western trends are popular in Russian society (e.g. a consumer lifestyle), others have been definitely rejected (e.g. the possibility of accepting family life patterns that are alternatives to marriage between a man and a woman). Here, it should be noted that, although post-Soviet Russian society was left in a void in terms of values, it does not accept all ideas coming from the West uncritically. Since the end of the 1980s, there has been a revival of the Russian Orthodox Church, which has been very successful in the area of socio-cultural and, in a sense, also political activity.

The clash between the civilization and cultural influence of the West (which is sometimes called cultural imperialism) and the social situation in contemporary Russia leads to an incredibly strong resistance to certain ethical aspects of the Western lifestyle offered to Russians. The Russian Orthodox Church especially opposes an individualist concept of society which is connected with consumerism (the Church is not very successful in this area) as well as individual ethics (the Church's strong resistance to promoting homosexuality has been supported both by society and politicians). It has also combatted the aggressive secularization coming from the West (the Church's controversial response to the activity of the band Pussy Riot was met with widespread support despite strong pressure from Western pressure groups).

This paper is aimed at presenting the contemporary manifestations of anti-Occidentalism, as displayed in the activities of the Russian Orthodox Church—in Orthodox theological and popularized religious texts as well as in the socio-cultural and political actions it inspires or supports. In order to outline the main ethical aspects of the contemporary Russian anti-Occidentalism inspired by the Russian Orthodox Church, this article presents the sources and transformations of Russian anti-Occidentalism and discusses the situation of post-Soviet Russia in the context of cultural and social trends coming from the West.[1] Then it shows the contemporary aspects of the opposition to the ethical postulates related to the cultural influence of the West, as inspired by the Russian Orthodox Church, and finally it presents conclusions about the possible directions of the development of the Russian Orthodox Church's attitude towards the West.

## The Sources and Transformations of Russian Anti-Occidentalism

Russian anti-Occidentalism which is understood as a resistance to the influence of Western culture, as broadly defined, is a wide-ranging phenomenon. It includes a contestation of basic values that govern social life,[2] which is mostly manifested in, for example, rejecting Western individualism or personalism that gives priority to a subject, or person, over the community.[3] The opposition to the culture of the West is manifested in the criticism of

1. Zyablitsev, "Ecumenical Problem," 104.

2. Zinov'yev, *Zapad*, 9.

3. Osipov, "Theological Conceptions," 43.

Western political reality, in particular of the version of democracy that prevails in the West as well as of the associated patterns of relations between political power, the media, and business, especially in countries with a well-established democratic system. Russian anti-Occidentalism also affects religious life, which is most evident in the rejection of the Catholic Church and in the frequent questioning of the Christian identity of Protestant communities[4] as well as in a lack of acceptance of contemporary Western models of relations between the state and the Church.[5]

Anti-Occidentalism, so broadly understood, has its origins in history and culture, and, to a certain extent, in religion. As for the historical and cultural dimensions of this phenomenon, it should first be noted that Moscow had a role in its development since it undertook the task of "gathering the lands of Rus" as its historical mission. Russia's rivalry with the Polish-Lithuanian Commonwealth, which was located along the European border between the West and the East, led Russia to base its own identity and separateness on becoming increasingly different from the West.[6] One should also mention that it is Russia that turned out to be more effective and, finally, to have won the centuries-old competition. It can therefore be assumed that Russia's policy of developing independence and strengthening its statehood in constant opposition to the West produced results.

Religion was a vital element separating Russia from the West and an important part of its self-definition virtually until the outbreak of the October Revolution. The fall of the Byzantine Empire made it possible for Russia to build its own identity as the only Orthodox state, which was sometimes manifested as the state- and religion-related idea of "Moscow as the Third Rome."[7] The fact that Russian identity became bound up with the Orthodox Church led to clear anti-Catholic and anti-Protestant sentiments which culminated in the emergence of the Slavophile movement in the nineteenth century.[8] These tendencies are perfectly evident in Fyodor Dostoevsky's writings[9] which are deeply religious and yet imbued with a hate for Catholicism.

Although the imperial and religious motives behind Russian anti-Occidentalism ceased to be supported by the state's policy when the October

4. Ibid., 35, 38.

5. Knox, *Russian Society*, 105, 108; Garrand and Garrand, *Russian Orthodoxy Resurgent*, 130–31.

6. Papadakis and Meyyendorf, *Khristianskiy Vostok*, 512–14.

7. Lanne, "Three Romes," 10–11.

8. Osipov, "Theological Conceptions," 35.

9. Knox, *Russian Society*, 158.

Revolution broke out in 1917, the collapse of the idea of world revolution and the consolidation of the Soviet Union as a model communist country and the "homeland of the proletariat" were another factor fuelling anti-Western sentiment. The Soviet Union wanted to be perceived as the opposite of the West which was full of social injustice and which oppressed the working class. It is from the Soviet Union that ideas and models were to spread, which could give the exploited people of the West true freedom.

The political changes of the 1990s challenged the reasonableness of the communist motivation behind Russian anti-Occidentalism. In today's Russian Federation, which is a multi-ethnic and multi-religious country, one cannot identify Russianness with the Orthodox faith to such an extent as it was done before the Bolshevik Revolution. Anti-Occidentalism, which is still alive, also constantly takes different forms. Although it is still manifested in significant anti-Western political gestures (for example, connected with the conflict in Georgia or Russia's military response to US plans to build an "anti-missile shield" in Central Europe) or economic ones (for example, in using the issues of natural gas and of economic exchange as a means of pressure on Ukraine aimed to hinder its rapprochement with the European Union). It seems, however, that Russian anti-Occidentalism is shifting its focus to a civilization-related dispute in which ethical issues are becoming increasingly important.

## Contemporary Russia's Attitude toward the Cultural Influence of the West

The causes of the Russian Orthodox Church's strong opposition to the ethical consequences of the cultural influence of the West are related to the specific situation in which contemporary Russian society has found itself. Whilst disintegration processes are taking place in Western societies, Russia is still looking for factors that could integrate and rebuild society. Furthermore, while a profound secularization of both public and private life is taking place in Western countries, which are sometimes referred to as post-Christian, a strong Orthodox Church in Russia is an indicator of a strong Russian identity and historical roots.[10] Finally, while Western societies have been accused of being in ethical chaos, the Russian Orthodox Church emphasises that contemporary Russia needs genuine and unquestionable values in order to survive and develop.[11]

---

10. Ibid., 106; Strickland, *Making of Holy Russia*, 27–32.

11. Knox, *Russian Society*, 99–100.

Today there is no doubt that the wounds that Russian society has suffered during the communist period are still quite deep, although the generation which grew up after the fall of communism is already beginning to live
independently. Russia is still facing the challenge of integrating society, as
well as of finding and strengthening values that would allow this diverse,
multi-ethnic and multi-religious society to unite behind a common goal
of building a modern state which would not agree to the loss of its status
as a superpower with a key role not only in the region, but also globally.[12]
The ideas of modernization that are directed toward the above-mentioned
issues, which are evident in Vladimir Putin's and Dmitry Medvedev's policy,
are faced with opposite cultural and moral trends coming to Russia from the
West, mainly due to popular culture. These trends are consistent with the
general pattern of civilization-related changes in the West which transform
social life through an emphasis placed on the individual's autonomy and
various activities aimed at protecting minority groups, as well as marginal-
ising traditional values and standards of conduct, especially those that are
based on the Christian religion.[13]

Western culture exerts an influence on Russian society in mainly three
areas, i.e. political and economic life, family life (or alternative forms of
expressing one's sexuality), and the very foundations of socially accepted
ethical norms.

In the first domain, the West influences Russian society in two ways.
First, Western countries demand that Russia adopt Western models of the
relationship between politics and economy. It is common for Western opin-
ion-makers to criticise the Russian economic system for being oligarchic
and dependent on the government as well as for subordinating economic
activity to the political interests of the state that are identified with the political and economic interests of people in power.[14] However, representatives
of the West are not free from hypocrisy when they promote the Western
model of the relationship between politics and economy: they point to the
pathologies of political and economic life in Russia and, at the same time,
they have no qualms about engaging in economic cooperation with Russia
whenever this can be of benefit to them. The former German Chancellor
Gerhard Schröder's decision to start working for the Russian state-owned
Gazprom after the end of his tenure was an exceptionally vivid example of
such an attitude—his ethical concerns did not preclude him from doing so.
One must, however, admit that the Russian Orthodox Church has still not

12. Ledeneva, *Can Russia Modernise?*, 2–4; Knox, *Russian Society*, 17.

13. Papkova, *Orthodox Church*, 8–9, 29–30.

14. Knox, *Russian Society*, 106–8.

developed a comprehensive conception of the ethics of social and political life which would be able to inspire an effective response to the often insincere allegations made by the West.

The second way in which Western countries exert a cultural influence on Russia with respect to political and economic life is consumerism, which is widespread in the West and understood as a kind of cult of material values. In the context of the contestation of religious values and the atomization of societies, i.e. rejection of values that create and unite a national community, material values sometimes even play the role of the only authentic and sought after values. The discourse of consumerism, which is present in the products of Western popular culture and aimed at young people, is clearly opposed to the Russian tradition of community involvement and of subordinating the individual's interests to the well-being of society and the state.[15] What is more, it can be noticed that the discourse leads to an actual lack of interest on the part of many young citizens in their country's fate. In this regard, from the perspective of a Russian social ethics which is deeply rooted in the Christian view which emphasizes the importance of human community, the discourse of consumerism is profoundly destructive because it is individualistic, egoistic, and thus also anti-national and anti-social.

The second area influenced by the West is related to the principles of family life. Today, it is more about the destruction of family that is based on marriage between a man and a woman as well as about promoting different kinds of non-stereotypical sexual behavior, which is what granting sexual minorities subsequent privileges in Western law leads to.[16] The destruction of the family, which is progressing in the West and which results especially in an increasingly lower birth rate, is also seen in Russia. At the same time, this country is going through a demographic crisis for other reasons, i.e. mainly because of the deep-rooted pathologies of social and individual life. However, Russian society does not seem to be willing to welcome the attempts to accept non-standard or alternative behavior (such as extending the concept of marriage to include same-sex relationships), which is definitely evaluated negatively by public opinion, in accordance with the Orthodox Church's clear teachings. In response to extensive political and cultural pressure from the West in this regard, in 2013 the State Duma passed a law banning the spread of propaganda of non-traditional sexual relationships among children, which was clearly perceived as resistance to homosexual indoctrination and, as such, had the full support of society.

15. Zinov'yev, *Zapad*, 51.
16. Papkova, *Orthodox Church*, 140.

The foundations of the socially accepted system of values constitute the third of the identified areas in Russia that are influenced by the West. Regardless of the actual religious crisis in Russia, which is a legacy from the period of decades of official communist atheism, there is the sacred sphere in Russian cultural space—it is mainly manifested in the existence of churches and monasteries.[17] Icons have played a special role in this cultural space for centuries.[18] These are understood not so much as a form of religious painting as a mystical, ineffable presence of God among people. Meanwhile, the concept of the sacred or of sacral space has disappeared completely, due to the impact of secularization and the self-destruction of the Catholic Church, as well as of Protestant communities, which has been clearly progressing since the second half of the twentieth century. This is evidenced by iconoclastic artistic projects or modern works of art which make use of Christian themes and distort them in many ways. From the perspective of Russia, such tendencies that have appeared in Western culture are an expression of seeking to cut off from Christian roots.[19] In Russia, especially after the destruction and desecration of churches in the communist era, such tendencies are not associated with freedom of artistic expression but with violence, as well as disrespect and contempt for values on which European civilization was built. Therefore, Western iconoclasm, which is part of a broader secular trend, cannot be accepted by the majority of Russian society and is rather interpreted as aggression against what is most precious in Russian culture.[20]

## The Response of the Orthodox Church to the Ethical Challenges Posed by the West

In light of the above, it is not surprising that the activities undertaken with regard to Russia by various progressive and pro-democratic organizations acting for human rights are not met with a more positive reaction. This is especially true of the socio-cultural domain. To the surprise of many Western observers, such activities have been almost unanimously rejected by Russian society. The Russian Orthodox Church has contributed significantly to the development of such attitudes—although its situation changed over the twentieth century, it also wants to play a role in rebuilding and preserving

17. Kotelnikov, "Primacy of Monastic Spirituality," 28–29.

18. Garrand and Garrand, *Russian Orthodoxy*, 7.

19. Papkova, *Orthodox Church*, 38.

20. Ibid., 145–46.

Russian society's axiological foundations and in protecting this society from the destructive, and sometimes even nihilistic, influence of the West.[21]

As one can indeed notice, the Russian Church's social teaching has been developed and disseminated enough to be able to exert an effective influence on contemporary political and economic life in Russia. Furthermore, there is no doubt that the Russian Orthodox Church is making an effort to combat the selfishness and consumerism coming from the West which breaks the unity of Russian society.[22] Even if the battle has not been resolved yet, it would be difficult not to notice the role that the revival of monastic life, as well as reconstruction of churches and monasteries in Russia, which began in the 1990s, has played in it—these changes are a clear sign of the other world for Russia which is being modernized.[23] The increased interest in Christianity among young Russians is undoubtedly the result of the Church's presence in public life. Unlike in the West, this presence does not only mean that the Church takes actions that are modelled on activities carried out by social or political organizations (which sometimes makes the Western churches lose their identity by placing them among the many charitable organizations), but it is also a kind of message to the contemporary world and humankind.

The Russian Church acts even more strongly and definitely more effectively against Western ideas that destroy the Christian vision of the family and promote alternative forms of expressing human sexuality. The Church's strong opposition both to changes in the definition of marriage and to the presence of sexual minorities in public life, which is based on the Christian vision of the human being, is almost totally supported by today's Russian society.[24]

Moreover, the Russian Church opposes the kind of Western secularization that is focused on destroying Christianity in the name of artistic freedom or freedom of speech.[25] As the Church sees the numerous examples of anti-Christian Western art as evidence of the spiritual collapse of the West, it resists similar attempts in Russia. The controversy surrounding the performance given by the scandalous Pussy Riot band in Moscow's Cathedral of Christ the Savior is a good example of the Church's attitude. What was seen as an innocent artistic show or a justified form of political protest against Vladimir Putin's policy by Western defenders of freedom and

21. Knox, *Russian Society*, 116.

22. Papkova, *Orthodox Church*, 42.

23. Garrand and Garrand, *Russian Orthodoxy*, 70.

24. Papkova, *Orthodox Church*, 37–38.

25. Ibid., 147–48.

democracy, Russians perceived as an unscrupulous desecration of temple church which, destroyed by Stalin and rebuilt in the 1990s, is a symbol of the revival of Russian Christianity and the freedom that the Church enjoys in Russia today. What is more, the numerous voices of Western defenders of human rights only strengthened Russian convictions that the West is collapsing if it sees the current destruction of its own religious tradition[26] as a manifestation of the legitimate freedom of human beings. This Western position has been definitely rejected by the Russian Church, which is supported both by the authorities and society.

## Conclusions

Over centuries of political, cultural and religious relations between Russia and Western Europe, Russian anti-Occidentalism has been accompanied by a lack of understanding of the unique nature of Russia in the West. Anti-Western sentiments in Russia as well as the West's lack of understanding of Russia's situation and problems were, to a certain extent, mutually conditioned. Unfortunately, it should be noted that this is also characteristic of the contemporary relations between Russia and the West. Western cultural imperialism, which is manifested in imposing Western norms as well as behavioral and conceptual patterns on other countries and societies, is still accompanied by a lack of understanding of the uniqueness of Russian culture and civilization. At the same time, the directions of socio-cultural development in today's West and Russia are different. While in the West, traditional society is disintegrating and the norms and values it is built on are being destroyed, Russian society must become more integrated. While the Western Churches often accept their own marginalization or even extinction, in Russia the Orthodox Church is incredibly aware of its own social and cultural role, which becomes noticeable especially when Russia and Russians have to be protected against the destructive influence of contemporary Western culture, which is full of selfishness and individualism. For this reason, it is not surprising that the deepening ethical discrepancies, especially with regard to the view of the basic values in people's social and individual life, lead to the consolidation of negative stereotypes of the West, which is often perceived as the epicenter of moral corruption or even of human self-destruction.

26. See Kozlov, *Zapadnoye khristianstvo*, 531.

# Bibliography

Garrand, John, and Carol Garrand. *Russian Orthodoxy Resurgent: Faith and Power in the New Russia*. Princeton: Princeton University Press, 2008.

Knox, Zoe. *Russian Society and the Orthodox Church: Religion in Russia after Communism*. London: Routledge, 2005.

Kotelnikov, Vladimir. "The Primacy of Monastic Spirituality." *Concilium* 6 (1996) 21–32.

Kozlov, Maksim. *Zapadnoye khristianstvo: vzglyad s Vostoka*. Moscow: Izdatel'stvo Sretenskogo monastyrya, 2009.

Lanne, Emmanuel. "The Three Romes." *Concilium* 6 (1996) 10–18.

Ledeneva, Alena V. *Can Russia Modernise? Sistema, Power Networks and Informal Governance*. Cambridge: Cambridge University Press, 2013.

Osipov, Aleksi I. "The Theological Conceptions of the Slavophiles." *Concilium* 6 (1996) 33–48.

Papadakis, Aristidis, and Ioann Meyyendorf. *Khristianskiy Vostok i vozvysheniye papstva. Tserkov' v 1071–1453 godakh*. Translated by A. V. Levitskiy et al. Moscow: Izdatel'stvo Pravoslavnogo Svyato-Tikhonovskogo Gumanitarnogo Universiteta, 2010.

Papkova, Irina. *The Orthodox Church and Russian Politics*. Oxford: Oxford University Press, 2011.

Strickland, John. *The Making of Holy Russia: The Orthodox Church and Russian Nationalism before the Revolution*. New York: Holy Trinity Publications, 2013.

Zyablitsev, Georgy. "The Ecumenical Problem in the Russian Orthodox Church in Relation to the 1994 Synod." *Concilium* 6 (1996) 101–9.

Zinov'yev, Aleksandr A. *Zapad*. Moscow: Algoritm, Eksmo, 2007.

# 22

# The Universalism of Catholicity (*Sobornost'*)

*Metaphysical and Existential Foundations for Interdenominational Dialogue in the Philosophy of Semen Frank*

—Gennadi Aliaiev

The historical plurality and multiplicity of religions poses not only a challenge to the faith of any religious conscience (especially monotheistic), but also a serious academic, philosophical and ideological problem. This is equally true for those which have emerged (at least relatively) independently of one another, as well as those which coexist within the framework of a cultural and civilizational area. This is especially true of those that in a sense represent a whole, since their faithful believe in one God, although, at the same time, they represent themselves as independent (if not hostile) confessions (churches, communities). Each religious community accepts this challenge to faith—being more or less aware of it or even fanatical about it—as a call for an embodiment of the Truth, recognising any other community, in the best case, as a temporal (although, possibly, honest) error (about the worst cases we would rather not speak at all). In the case of academic and philosophical study, the most important question is about the causes of such a state of affairs (obviously, historically conditioned) and its possible consequences and perspectives. Yet this problem becomes more urgent for the religious philosopher, whose task is either to find an algorithm to marry the truth of philosophy with that of religion or to justify his own belief with means of philosophy, or to find in his faith the mystical source of philo-sophical knowledge.

For Semen Frank, the problem of the plurality and multiplicity of re-ligions was not merely a theoretical one. It was an existential problem, as his spiritual way had been marked not only with "an epoch of unbelieving youth" and thereafter with a period of the *reinvention* of faith, but also with the inner tension of *conversion to new faith*, the shift to the other confession. However, that inner tension played a rather constructive than destructive role—Semen Frank himself wrote about it: "I have always been conscious of the fact that my Christian belief is an accomplishment of my Jewish one, the natural development of the religious life of my childhood."[1] Therefore it was quite important for him, who believed in one God (of both the Jews as well as the Christians), to find theoretical ways explaining interdenominational differences, and yet much more important to formulate the ideological and metaphysical foundations for the unity (universality) of religious faith.

In this context, it is natural enough that the problem of correlation be-tween Christianity and Judaism was of great importance for him although I can hardly say that he stresses the issue much in his works—it is rather on the contrary. Some approaches to the problem can be found in Semen Frank's review of Franz Rosenzweig's book *Der Stern der Erloesung* (*The Star of Redemption*). This little text contains the general principle which may be called Semen Frank's guideline in his relation to "heterodox" philosophical and theological works: the theological and confessional context of the book is of no importance if we deal with "the mystical philosophy, teaching on the substance of God, world, man, and the sense of human life which comes from religious experience."[2] Certainly, it does not mean any unreserved ac-ceptance of such a teaching or the religion either with which it is connected. In this case, Semen Frank supposes that Rosenzweig's mystical construction reveals "the gravest sin of Judaism," "*rupture between God and man*," "*ig-norance of God-manhood.*"[3] Simultaneously he states—logically (or mysti-cally!) but contradictorily—the immanence of the realm of this world and the Kingdom of God, the "cult of completely earthly, worldly, natural holi-ness" which searches for salvation in "tribal life of Israel" as of the "chosen people."[4] Although, from the other hand, the understanding of these "eter-nal dissonances of Jewish soul" does not lead to the unreserved rejection of such—religiously alien—constructions. It is much more important for

1. Frank, "Predsmertnoye," 44.

2. Frank, "Misticheskaya filosofiya Rozentsveyga," 139.

3. Ibid., 146.

4. Ibid., 147.

Frank that despite "the whole book is hostile towards Christianity, simultaneously, there is some unconscious craving for it"—that "in many places throughout the book Rosenzweig comes right to the threshold of Christian truths, stating them often with startling profundity and spontaneity."[5] As a Christian, Semen Frank accepts this (as any other) religious and philosophical teaching in the light of the Truth of the Christian faith. Meanwhile, dealing with the issue as a philosopher, Semen Frank takes for his starting point the idea of the universality of the Truth—not as a rationally and theologically proven (or, moreover, enforced from outside, with compulsion) priority, but merely as an acceptance of the immediate revelation, the true religious experience. In this case the limitation or even falsity of Rosenzweig's mystical metaphysics comes from the "disintegration, division and distort of the mystical experience, laying in its very foundation." It is said not even about personal experience as such, but about the necessity "to empathise"—Plotinus as well as the mystics of Christianity—the Eastern and the Western, Kabbalah as well as Jewish and Arabic Platonism.[6] Thus, the truth of Christianity is not only the truth of the Christian religion (or of any particular Christian denomination)—it is universal (more concrete: interdenominational), otherwise it is not truth, but superstition.

As it has already been said, the problem of the correlation between Judaism and Christianity, and especially the one of the conversion of a Jew to Christianity was for Semen Frank a deeply personal, existentially empathized issue—it is the reason why his philosophical reflections on this topic are of interest to us. Unfortunately, Semen Frank's article "On Jewish Conversion to Christianity" is still remain unpublished,[7] but there is another one—"Die religiöse Tragödie des Judentums" (The Religious Tragedy of Jews), in which the issue is discussed almost with a burning (if we consider the place and time it was written: Germany, 1934) sharpness.[8] On the one hand, we can perceive here an unavoidable compromise—for the sake of being printed—to the hopeless political situation (right up to the mention—in even a metaphysical and excusatory sense!—of the infamous "'Aryan paragraph' of the new German legislation"[9]), on the other hand, Semen Frank's analysis is not a political prognostication (or, even lesser, a justification) of

---

5. Ibid., 146.

6. Ibid.

7. Boobbyer, *Frank*, 262.

8. The article was published in the journal *Eine heilige Kirche* (the publishing of the Lutheran movement High Church, which was headed by a well-known Marburg theologian, Friedrich Heiler) anonymously, with the subtitle "Von einem Judenchristen" (Of a Jew-Christian).

9. Frank, "Religioznaya tragediya," 291.

the coming catastrophe, but a metaphysical reflection and interpretation of the religious tragedy of the Jewish people and the ways of his—as well as Christian nations—salvation.

It is worthy of notice that in considering the issue of the problem of the correlation between religions, Semen Frank is rather taking an interest not in the outward (temporal and possibly occasional) circumstances, but in the inner spiritual destiny of the people. His point is not in outward suffering (though, of course, it does not mean he is indifferent to them). The point of his interest is "the sufferings caused by acting in human soul . . . pitiless collisions of antagonistic spiritual and ideal powers."[10] In this case, Frank is saying not only about a religious destiny of the people, the example of which "reveals destructive consequences of indissoluble union and identification of religion with a feeling of nation,"[11] but about the destiny of concrete people—the Jews who converted to Christianity.

However, from the point of our subject, the most important thing in the text is Semen Frank's statement that the truth of Christianity is not a mere prerogative of the earthly Christian church. If it was so, religious contempt to other denominations might easily flow from it, and especially to that one, which openly and consciously rejected the truth. Semen Frank is courageous enough (let us remind ourselves again of the circumstances of the place and time), underlining that "Christianity is the divine revelation in Israel and through Israel," that "it was born from the ultimate depths of the Jewish religious spirit."[12] Furthermore, Frank explains the religious tragedy of the Jewish people with the tragedy of historical Christianity—it is namely in that Christianity was transformed into the dominant religion, and along with relatively positive aftereffects of Christianization, "it has also brought with itself the peril of secularization and have often become the cause of great religious losses." "The Christian church—dominant, quietly and comfortably existing in this world—yet, in some way, it betrayed its vocation, which is the representation of God's Kingdom that is 'not of the world.'"[13] Secular power, as well as the rest of secular temptations, just as the religious blessing of nationality (national (ethnic) identity and national messianism) are, according to Frank, the main and interconnected obstacles standing before us on the way to salvation. Although, Semen Frank speaks about the historical guilt of Christendom, which is partly a share of the religious sin of the Jews, to stress that the main difference between people is not defined with confes-

10. Ibid., 285.
11. Ibid., 289–290.
12. Ibid., 286.
13. Ibid., 290.

sional, ethnic, or national identity, but with the measure of profundity of their religious faith—the profundity which overruns the narrow bounds of earthly communities. This is the "difference between those, who are truly religious, having their ultimate and the most profound center in God and in their being—in the beyond-national idea of the Kingdom of God (which, of course, does not hinder them from loving and serving their people and their fatherland), and people, for whom state and the nation have the absolute, and eventually the highest, ultimate, defining significance."[14] Facing state anti-Semitism, nationalism and racism, which became obvious enough in the first years of Hitler's regime, as well as some other expressions of national and denominational arrogance or isolationism, Semen Frank states the general idea of Christian universalism, defining its basic preconditions: social—"rejection of any forms of worldly power, Church endures suffering in the world," and existential—"religious deepening, true and self-denying life in God." All this "is an unavoidable prerequisite of the reunification of denominations in one Church of Christ, which every true Christian strives for."[15] About this—rather inward than outward—Church Frank writes in the mentioned review, deepening Franz Rosenzweig's thought, making it more precise: "The true approach of the Kingdom of God is attainable only for a human unity reconciled in the face of God– 'the Church'" (in Rosenzweig's text the words "the Church," certainly, do not appear but for Frank their necessity is obvious: "God grants his salvation through the Church").[16]

The foundations of Semen Frank's position are simultaneously common to all Christians and metaphysical ones. By the way, in this also—not only in his metaphysical constructions—he treads in Nicolas of Cusa's footsteps, who, being a representative of the high Roman Catholic hierarchy, openly stood up not only for Christian unity to overcome the Great schism between the Christian West and East, but also for the principle of religious tolerance in its totality. He proceeded from the idea of one God of all religions ("religio una in rituum varietate," in the tract De pace fidei), understanding well that any religion in its manifestation "fluctuates inconstantly between spirituality and temporality."[17]

The Metropolitan Antony of Sourozh, who knew Semen Frank in the last month of his life, recollected that "he was in a sense a universal Christian, who belonged to the Orthodox Church"—"theologically" fully belonging to Orthodoxy, in his "daily life," he was open to other denominations. He

14. Ibid., 292.

15. Ibid.

16. Frank, "Misticheskaya filosofiya Rozentsveyga," 144.

17. Nicolas Cusanus, "De coniecturis," 240.

would not cause strife with a Roman Catholic or a Protestant just because they were Roman Catholic or Protestant. In any discussion, the only important thing for him was the quest for truth. The quest must not be founded upon mere rational arguments, but upon the true profundity of faith. The Metropolitan Antony retells Frank's words: "You must remember that the intellect is a servant. It must be attentive to the heart—here I speak of course not about emotions, but about the whole 'interior'—and find an expression for it."[18]

Metaphysical foundation for Semen Frank's position of spiritual tolerance is the principle of antinomic monodualism—"the transrational unity of unity and duality, identity and difference, indivisible wholeness and separateness,"[19]—which is, in its turn, founded upon the principle of *coicidentia oppositorum*,[20] postulated by Nicolas of Cusa. In addition to that, for Frank it is not merely "the only legitimate *logical theory*," but also "the only adequate *spiritual* state, the only state which is adequate to the essence of reality as all-embracing fullness."[21] This spiritual state is the perception of "the deep harmony and reconciliation in the fullness of all-embracing unity of all that is mutually antagonistic and empirically incompatible, the perception of the relativeness of all mutual antagonism, all disharmony in being."[22] In other words, it is spiritual intention on love and catholicity (*sobornost'*).

The ontological, as well as the social and anthropological, features of the concept of "catholicity" (*sobornost'*) (in the opinion of Alexei Khomiakov, "the Creed of the Church of Christ can contain such base definitions"[23]) were actively studied by many Russian thinkers in the nineteenth and early twentieth centuries. The scholars underlined the fact that the ideas of catholicity and individuality (personalism) are not contradictory a number of times, but mutually contribute and complement each other. On the other hand, the catholicity (*sobornost'*) of the Orthodox Church was often put in opposition to the other defining features of other Christians denominations (yet Khomiakov put it in opposition to individualism in Protestantism and the outward organization in the Roman Catholic Church), turning out to be some exclusive confessional feature. It is obvious that under such

18. Mitropolit Antoniy, "Beseda."

19. Frank, *Unknowable*, 97–98.

20. By the way, Frank finds in the works of Cusanus yet more satisfying than this commonplace term: *unitas* or *complicatio contrariorum*, i.e. not a "coincidence," but "unity" or "reduction" of opposition, and also *non aliud*—"no other." Frank, *Predmet znaniya*, 204–5.

21. Frank, *Unknowable*, 85.

22. Ibid.

23. Khomiakov, "Letter to the Editor," 137.

an approach, catholicity (*sobornost'*) is rather interpreted not as an inner mystical unity, but as "an enclosed area" the entrance to which is strictly forbidden for those, who is unable to prove his/her denominational—outer, not inner—orthodoxy.

Semen Frank's philosophy represents the idea of catholicity (*sobornost'*) in its ontological, social and moral, as well as interdenominational dimensions with an exceeding depth. Catholicity, according to Frank, is an inner organization of social life, as opposed to outward organization ("publicity," "public life"). Frank makes a distinction between "the inward" and "the outward" sections of society, and ultimately its "empirical reality" and "metaphysical substance." Although catholicity is not a "whole and homogenous all-unity," it is also not a mere "unity of 'we are'" either, but it is a "connection of every 'I' with this primary unity of 'we are.'"[24] The content of each human being, each personality reveals itself in the life-forms of catholicity (family, Church, people)—insoluble unity of "I am" and "you are," which comes from the prime unity of "we are." "The unity of catholicity is the free life, as a spiritual capital that nourishes and enriches the life of its members."[25]

Semen Frank combines the catholicity of the Orthodox Church with the recognition of "rights" of other denominations, which are (on his opinion) quite just forms of expression for the same divine truth, as much as they consistently combine individual and collective religious experience. Being in agreement with Schleiermacher, Frank states that "the singularity of each religious form is the only token for the authenticity of a religion, as an indefinite community witness only the lack of a mature religion."[26]

The last years of Semen Frank's life were marked with an unconditional enhancement of religious universalism. He recognized not only the truth of different Christian sects, but also that of the other religions—Judaism, Islam, Buddhism, etc. "Moses and the Hebrew prophets, Buddha and the author of Upanishads, Laotze, the sages of ancient Greece and Mahomet can, and ought to be, our teachers in so far as they have adequately given expression to the voice of God."[27] Acceptance of the truth of one religion is not a rejection of the relative truth of the others—the Russian philosopher draws attention towards the relativity of *truth*, not *errors* of different religions.

24. Frank, *Dukhovnyye osnovy obshchestva*, 98.

25. Ibid., 114.

26. Frank, "Lichnost' i mirovozzreniye Shleyyrrmakhera," 21.

27. Frank, *God with Us*, 24–25.

However, Frank's religious universalism does not turn into religious indifferentism. According to his conception of love, and understanding of Christianity as a religion of love, it is possible to love not an abstract humanity or an abstract human being, but only a concrete person in all his/her unique individuality. Christ's demand for *love for people* should be understood solely as the "love for *every man* as unique and individual."[28] The same is true in relation to nations and religions. Love for the entire human race, in which any national differences are eliminated, has in this philosophy incomparably lesser value than that "the loving breadth of spirit in virtue of which a man recognizes, respects, and loves all nations with their individual peculiarities."[29] Certainly, religious indifferentism[30] completely loses its value in the face of the "approach to the individual types of religious life and thought in the true spirit of love. Following the great words of Christ: 'In my Father's house are many mansions,' they see in the peculiar character of each something of value, lacking in others and complementary to them."[31]

This position was not simply a logical conclusion, but came from Semen Frank's personal experience. He himself experienced conversion to another religion, with a feeling of deep and vital importance for holding a concrete and lively connection with a confession. He maintained universality and tolerance towards others, assuming an attitude of toleration towards the conversion of his own son Victor to Roman Catholicism (dissuading, but not forbidding), as well as towards the similar conversion of the philosopher Vyacheslav Ivanov.[32] The letters and papers of the last years of his life contain the words: "I am an Orthodox as well as a Roman Catholic or a Protestant, but none of them apart, in isolation," and "that is because personally I believe I may consider myself a member of One and Indivisible Universal Church, and therefore I share the same confession with the Western Church."[33] However, these confessions do not mean the loss of connection with the Orthodox Church, which he remained faithful to the end. It is possible only to say that the love and catholicity common to all Christians (and, to some extent, universal) dominated Semen Frank's philosophy, as

---

28. Ibid., 170.

29. Ibid.

30. Or, rather, a reductionism that rejects any confessional differences as superfluous, endeavouring to keep faith in only one God in all its abstractness and lifelessness

31. Frank, *God with Us*, 171.

32. Boobbyer, *Frank*, 194–96.

33. Ibid., 194, 198.

well his life, but his understanding of universalism remains Christian, and his Christianity, Orthodox at its foundation and creative core.

## Bibliography

Antoniy, Mitropolit. "Vidnyye deyateli russkoy emigratsii. Beseda s mitropolitom Antoniyem." September 8, 1999. http://masarchive.org/Sites/texts/1999–09-08–1-R-R-C-EM00–001.html.

Boobbyer, Philip. *S. L. Frank: The Life and Work of a Russian Philosopher, 1877–1950.* Athens: Ohio University Press, 1995.

Frank, Semen L. *Dukhovnyye osnovy obshchestva. Vvedeniye v sotsial'nuyu filosofiyu.* New York: Posev, 1988.

———. *God with Us: Three Meditations.* Translated by Natalie Duddington. London: J. Cape, 1946.

———. "Lichnost' i mirovozzreniye Fr. Shleyyrrmakhera." *Russkaya mysl'* 9 (1911) 1–28.

———. "Misticheskaya filosofiya Rozentsveyga." *Put'* 2 (1926) 139–48.

———. *Predmet znaniya. Dusha cheloveka,* 35–416. St. Petersburg: Nauka, 1995.

———. "Predsmertnoye. Vospominaniya i mysli." In *Russkoye mirovozzreniye,* 39–58. St. Petersburg: Nauka, 1996.

———. "Religioznaya tragediya evreyskogo naroda. Napisano evreyem-khristianinom." Translated by O. Nazarova. *Vtoraya navigatsiya: Al'manakh* 5 (2005) 285–92.

———. *The Unknowable: An Ontological Introduction to the Philosophy of Religion.* Translated by Boris Jakim. Athens: Ohio University Press, 1983.

Khomiakov, Aleksei. "Letter to the Editor of 'L'Union Chrétienne' on the Occasion of a Discourse by Father Gagarin, Jesuit." In *Aleksei Khomiakov and Ivan Kireevsky, On Spiritual Unity: A Slavophile Reader,* edited and translated by Boris Jakim and Robert Bird. Hudson, NY: Lindisfarne, 1998.

Nicolas Cusanus. "De coniecturis." In *Metaphysical Speculations: Six Latin Texts,* translated by Jasper Hopkins, 2:163–297. Minneapolis: A. J. Banning, 2000.

# 23

# Local Civilizations and the Russian World

*Nikolai Danilevsky and the Russian Orthodox Church of the Moscow Patriarchate*

—Olga Shimanskaya

The doctrine of local civilizations by Nikolai Danilevsky is a turning point in the historiosophy of Slavophilism. Early Slavophiles argued that a young and strong Russia was called upon to accomplish the next step in the rise of the global civilization after taking the leading role away from Europe that was already incapable of further development and both mired in a severe crisis and shaken by revolutions and wars. In this context, the Slavophiles called for the preservation of the distinctive Russian foundations among which they stressed especially: Russian orthodoxy, Russian autocracy and the Russian people. It is hardly surprising that the Slavophiles' position towards the reforms implemented by Peter I was a complicated one. While admitting them to be historically inevitable, they affirmed that Peter, focusing on Western European models while applying decisive and violent methods, altered the way of Russian life: "The turning point Peter accomplished was not much of an evolution, but rather a breaking of our nation; not much of an internal success, but rather an innovation from the outside."[1] As a result, Russia entered into a prolonged and severe crisis. While admitting that Peter

---

1. Kireyevskiy, *Polnoye sobraniye sochineniy*, 1:48.

I had done a lot for Russia's greatness, the Slavophiles presumed: This did not happen thanks to his reformatory activities, but despite them. Peter's Russia was victorious and became one of the world's largest empires thanks to the forces of pre-Petrine Russia, harnessing and exhausting its potential completely. The Slavophiles were convinced that imitating Western Europe destroyed the prospect of a distinctive historical development for Russia, plunging it into a systemic crisis and undermining the concept of her great destiny on a global scale. They realized, however, that the way Russia had to follow was not a return to the old times before Peter, but the way of the pre-Petrine Rus. Returning to concrete forms of a former life could only lead to an exacerbation of the crisis. The Slavophiles were not against the accomplishments of European culture, but against bowing like slaves before the West, plunging Russia into an irreversible crisis which could only end in disaster.

In his work *Russia and Europe: A Look at the Cultural and Political Position of the Slavic World Towards the Germanic-Roman world* (1869) the main representative of Neoslavophilism Nikolai Danilevsky focuses his criticism when defining the causes of Russia's crisis on eurocentrism. He writes that when Peter I got to know Europe he "fell in love with it and wanted at all costs turn Russia into Europe."[2] As a result, "the Russian way of life was by force turned around to match the foreign fashion."[3] Russia fell gravely ill with the disease of "mimicking Europe." Russia needs to process Western borrowings, lest it turns into Europe's cultural appendage leading a miserable existence. At the same time, Danilevsky totally shares the early Slavophile idea of a "West in a state of decay." With regard to the problem of Russia's and Europe's interrelations he asserts that "Europe" does not have a geographical but a historiocultural sense. "Europe is the field of the Germanic-Roman civilization . . . Europe is this very Germanic-Roman civilization. These two words are synonyms,"[4] he declares.

According to Danilevsky's conviction, it is dangerous to regard Europe's fate as equivalent to the fate of the whole of humanity. He strove to propose the ideal way to unite the Slavic world to help it endure in its resistance against the aggressive West and become an independent historiocultural kind of its own. Slavic peoples must become active in the fight against Europe. Our thinker did not believe in reconciliation between Europe and the Slavic peoples, but in their struggle, which was to trigger a "salvational

---

2. Danilevskiy, *Rossiya i Evropa*, 224.

3. Ibid., 225.

4. Ibid., 48.

alienation" from the values of the European civilization and a turn toward the distinctive Slavic culture.

For Danilevsky, the European and Slavic civilizations developed on completely different historical and religious foundations: "The heirs of Rome were the ancient Germans, the heirs of the Byzantine Empire were the Slavs."[5] Hence here is the dichotomy of Europe and Russia, brute force and tolerance, Orthodoxy's truth and Catholicism's lies. Europe does not recognize Russia, stated Danilevsky, and does not welcome it in the family of its peoples because it sees enmity in it since Russia does not give in to assimilation. It is impossible to deprive it of its independent distinctive life. The Russian people "has the gift of marvellous political sense," is ready to sacrifice its personal good for the state, the community dominates over individualism. Most importantly, the genuine interest of Russian people expresses itself only in Orthodoxy, together with other Slavs and the Greek they are the keepers of religious truth.

Danilevsky was a practising biologist who, when positive knowledge gained in influence, based his religious viewpoints on a positivistic argumentation. Therefore, Novikova and Sizemskaya's conclusion is convincing, that the pursuit of a scientific approach "after all made Danilevsky a different kind of man compared to the Slavophiles,"[6] he maintained an empirical approach not only in science, but also in philosophy.

In his opinion, history is the development of separate, closed historiocultural types—complete aggregates of characteristic elements of an ethnos' spiritual and material life, which become evident in religion, socioeconomistic, political and other relations. Each historiocultural type is an archetype built according to an original plan. To prove this, the thinker combines the empiricism typical for positivists with romantic conservatism. Based on pre-darwinist ideas about biology, he affirms that, given the absence of universal rules for nature's development, there cannot be a single concept for the development of a society either. The life cycles which different ethnic groups go through are analogous to the main phases of life of any given living organism and given to it at the basis of the global historical process. Danilevsky declared that the division of the world's history into ancient, medieval and recent does not cover its entire content, because all historical people had their own ancient, medieval and recent history, so they "underwent their phases of development."[7] At the same time, civilization is the completion of a historiocultural type of life. Each historiocultural type

5. Ibid., 260.

6. Novikova and Sizemskaya, *Russkaya filosofiya istorii*, 169.

7. Danilevskiy, *Rossiya i Evropa*, 69.

undergoes three stages: ethnographical, state and civilization stages, a life cycle lasting about fifteen hundred years before it turns into "apathy of despair" or "apathy of complacency" and falls.

According to Danilevsky, in the second half of the nineteenth century the Roman-Germanic historiocultural type reached its apogee—civilization. Afterwards, Europe's fall was inevitable. Furthermore, the contradiction between Europe and Russia does not lie in the struggle between progress and stagnation, but in the opposition of waning age and growing youth. Progress and stagnation are age-related characteristics when a mature civilization bears fruit. Humanity's progress does not manifest itself in the accumulation of material and spiritual values, but in the diversity of the human mind's expressions. The Slavic historiocultural type appears four centuries after the European one and its chief accomplishments are yet to come. No historiocultural type can progress in an unlimited manner: "Progress," the author of *Russia and Europe* writes, "does not mean that everybody goes into the same direction, but that the field of humanity's historical activity is to be covered in different directions, since this is exactly the way it has presented itself up to now."[8] An advancing historical development means opening up new ways of socio-natural creation and a subsequent change of civilizations.

Danilevsky regards synchronic and diachronic intercultural interaction as a socio-cultural system's exit out of a state of crisis. Categorizing civilizations into isolated and successive ones, the philosopher mentions three kinds of interaction between successive civilizations: transfer, inoculation, and enrichment. Transfer occurs through colonization when the distinctive culture of colonized peoples perishes. An inoculated people turn into material for an alien civilization. Only enrichment promotes the development of distinctive spiritual foundations of the enriched people. The contradiction of Danilevsky's positions lies in the attempt of a synthesis of crisis and stabilization awareness in the doctrine of local civilizations. He gives the reason for the societal crisis in Russia and suggests a possible solution. In his bio-organismic theory, the naturalist's optimism which is ready to reshape the world based on reason coincides with Christian optimism which is convinced of future salvation. According to his logic, however, from a historical point of view this salvation is possible on earth, if the Russians realise their providential mission and, together with other Orthodox peoples, create a Slavic historiocultural type.

Danilevsky is convinced that Russia cannot regard itself as integral part of Europe, neither by origin, nor by adoption: "It has only two options:

8. Ibid., 73.

to create a special, independent cultural unit with other Slavs, or to deprive itself of any historiocultural type meaning whatsoever—to be nothing."[9] Russians have the capacity of self-denial taught by Orthodoxy; together with a strong statehood and a freed peasantry a Slavic historiocultural type has to be created. Previous civilizations opened one aspect of cultural creation, the European type found two, so the Slavic type will be able to unlock all four aspects: religious, cultural, political and socio-economic, predicts Danilevsky, seeing in accomplishing this mission the way out of the crisis not only for Russia, but also the potential for future historiocultural types to develop.

In his opinion, the ideal model of a Slavic civilization is a federation, which depending on the degree of external threats can take "the form of a union state, of a union of states or simply of a political system."[10] In accordance with the laws determining the formation of historiocultural types, diversity and a complete life are attained by ethnically heterogeneous types, such as Europe. Danilevsky highlights incessantly: "for the greatness and cultural importance of the family of the Slavic peoples it is necessary, that the Slavic world does not take the form of Slavic streams flowing into the Russian sea, as Pushkin put it, but rather the form of a wide ocean with distinctive though united and subordinated elements, that is seas und deep bays."[11] Only a federation preserves the distinctive culture of every people in it. In Danilevsky's opinion, it is possible to create a pan-Slavic civilization and a universal civilization which is to replace the European one that pretends to be universal, but in fact is not. Criticizing eurocentrism in a devastating manner, he replaces it in a familiar way with slavocentricism. He finishes his book with a prophecy of fully corresponding opinions of early Slavophiles, whom he criticizes throughout the book for trying to solve a universal problem according to which the theory of historiocultural types does not exist.

The fate of Danilevsky's ideological legacy is paradoxical. There was an almost complete lack of understanding on the contemporaries' side that alternated with heated discussions about his theories, then oblivion at home and a prominence in the West that is rare for a Russian thinker. Nowadays he is one of the most acclaimed philosophers in Russia. This is not surprising since it was he who coined the fundamental tenets of a local civilization's crisis and, furthermore, indicated what a solution might look like. Thinkers about social issues of any kind draw on his work. Contemporary Orthodox

9. Ibid., 337.
10. Ibid., 191.
11. Ibid., 329.

theologians pay attention to Danilevsky as a thinker who argued for the uniqueness of Russian Orthodox civilization, as the warrior against the West and pan-Slavist without always paying attention to positivism, cyclical developments, discreteness and co-evolutionary approach to history in his constructions. The doctrine of local civilizations find itself again in the center of socio-political polemics linked to the Russian Orthodox Church's growing authority in the public space.

Russia's contemporary civilization is in a state of systemic civilizational crisis and the search for solutions. The Church witnesses a crisis as well:

> Tension and anxiety which can be seen all over the world and which are caused by the consequences of humanity's spiritual and moral crisis are evident also in the lives of the countries inside the canonical space of the Moscow Patriarchate. First of all, this becomes visible in society's disintegration and a widespread disappointment in those values which for twenty years had given rise to hope for a happy future when the countries of the historical Rus tried to find a new vector of their societal development[12]

—generalized the Church primate with regards to the opinion of religious people on the liberal reforms after the fall of the USSR in 1991.

The growing role of religious organizations as institutions of a modern society and their increasing authority is due to Russian citizens' firm belief in their capacity of "healing" "social wounds" and their opinion that they are the only pillars of morality and spiritual life. This is what Patriarch Kirill permanently talks about: "In the current order of our earthly existence's system the church, alongside the secular power and the civil society, is a fundamental and system-defining structure. If, however, secular power and society provide stability, self-development and security of human social life, than religion gives it supreme content and everlasting sense."[13]

In an interview for the *Journal of the Moscow Patriarchate*, the famous sociologist of religion Yulia Sinelina commented, based on many sociological studies, on how firmly Orthodox values sit in the consciousness of our contemporaries:

> A tenth of Russia's inhabitants account for the religious core of society which constantly participates in religious life and has well assimilated the articles of faith. It is surrounded by a periphery of religious part of the population making up 25–30% Russian citizens. These are people who, in one way or another,

12. Kirill, "Iz doklada Svyateyshego Patriarkha," 46.
13. Kirill, "Aktual'nyye voprosy," 28.

are connected with parishes and think religion to be a vital and
integral part of their lives. For the rest the positioning of themselves towards Orthodoxy takes place on a cultural level.[14]

Belonging to the church is connected with participation in religious practices. A certain part of society hopes for a religious revolution as a way of
Russia's development. What has the Russian Orthodox Church, the pri-
orities of which always were spiritual, moral and ideological functions and
which actively demonstrates its mission on the world, to offer Russia's society today? There are various ideas about the models for the country's further
development in the thinking of society, one of the most popular being the
concept of a Russian world or Russian civilization which theologians and
hierarchs of the Russian Orthodox church elaborate.

The Russian world is a model of a community beyond the state level in
the entire post-soviet space, which is united through belonging to Russian
culture and language. It also stands for a single civilizational, cultural and
societal space mainly located in the territory of the CIS countries and en-
compassing about 250 million speakers of Russian, who feature the spiritual
and mental traits of Russianness and are not indifferent to Russia's fate and
place in the world. Appeals to recreate the Russian world can permanently
be heard in speeches of the Russian Orthodox Church on various public
fora. For instance, at the Russian World Assembly, Patriarch Kirill declared
that

> the idea of a Russian world stipulates the preservation and de-
> velopment of those cultural accomplishments that are common
> to different people guided by the Russian Orthodox Church.
> This understanding takes us away from a narrow ethnic percep-
> tion and the very Russian Church. In this context the Russian
> Church is a church of a multi-ethnic Russian world, not of the
> Russian ethnos.[15]

This is rather a statement by a conservative politician, than by a pastor. The
soft power strategy delivers results, the position and the authority of the
Russian Orthodox Church is strong in former Soviet republics, despite the
emergence of various independent churches. In Ukraine, believers in the
East and the South maintain strong ties to the Moscow Patriarchate. Even
in the absence of diplomatic contact between Russia and Georgia after the
war in August 2008, the dialogue between the Russian and the Georgian

---

14. Sinelina, "Naskol'ko pravoslavny," 81.
15. Kirill, "Vystupleniye."

church was not interrupted. It is therefore safe to say that the idea of a single cultural and civilizational space has the right to exist.

Orthodox theology elaborates its version of a national idea based on anti-communism, anti-westernism, Russian messianism, the state idea, political patriotism, prioritizing spiritual values over materialistic ones etc. The concept Russian civilization or Russian world is not merely turned towards a post-imperial image, but also a unifying idea which is indispensable in a multi-confessional state with a history of thousands of years. In its foundation these are ideas of the philosophy of the history of the Russian conservative thinking, rethinking of the neoslavophile doctrine of local civilizations. In Danilevsky's doctrine, the Orthodox theology found the form more appealing than the essence; this is why the concept of the Russian world, which is being elaborated, is a version of a retrospective utopia.

## Bibliography

Danilevskiy, Nikolay Ya. *Rossiya i Evropa: Vzglyad na kul'turnyye i politicheskiye otnosheniya Slavyanskogo mira k Germano-Romanskomu.* St. Petersburg: Izdatel'stvo Sankt-Peterburgskogo universiteta, Izdatel'stvo Glagol,' 1995.

Kireyevskiy, Ivan V. *Polnoye sobraniye sochineniy.* Moscow: Izdatel'stvo Put,' 1911.

Kirill, Patriarkh Moskovskiy i Vseya Rusi. "Aktual'nyye voprosy tserkovnoy zhizni." *Zhurnal Moskovskoy Patriarkhii* 2 (2011) 28–38.

———. "Aktual'nyye voprosy tserkovnoy zhizni. Iz doklada Svyateyshego Patriarkha Moskovskogo i vseya Rusi Kirilla na Eparkhial'nom sobranii g. Moskvy." *Zhurnal Moskovskoy Patriarkhii* 2 (2012) 44–66.

———. "Vystupleniye Svyateyshego Patriarkha Kirilla na torzhestvennom otkrytii III assamblei Russkogo mira." November 3, 2009. http://www.patriarchia.ru/db/text/928446.html.

Novikova, Lyudmila I., and Irina N. Sizemskaya. *Russkaya filosofiya istorii.* Moscow: Izdatel'stvo Magistr, 1997.

Sinelina, Yuliya Yu. "Naskol'ko pravoslavny nashi pravoslavnyye." *Zhurnal Moskovskoy Patriarkhii* 8 (2012) 78–81.

# 24

# The Idea of the Antichrist in Russia

*From Religious to Political Narration*

—Magda Dolińska-Rydzek

Russia has always been some kind of a puzzle, not only for the Western world but also for its own sake. There is a popular maxim taken from the poem of Fyodor Tyutchev that it is impossible to grasp Russia with one's mind. According to a Polish researcher of Russian philosophy, Marian Broda, all questions about Russia could be the subject of complementary analysis—anthropological, cultural, political, psychological, ideological, and even theological.[1] The main purpose of this article is to give a short overview of the idea of the Antichrist as a kind of metaphor whose meaning has changed over the centuries. The Antichrist was used as a means of threatening people, not only in Russian literature and historiosophy, but also in different contexts—religious and political.

There has always been a strong connection between religion and politics. Religion is not only one of the most important factors forming the identity of individuals and nations, but also the way of peddling and entrenching a certain world-view in the society. Religious ideas could also shape political systems, the functioning of the state and its way of defying international relations. Although religion was thought to have been gradually eliminated from social life after the Second World War, at the turn of

1. Broda, *Zrozumieć Rosję*, 7–27.

twentieth and twenty first century it appeared to be a very important tool of state policy, especially because of its consolidating and identifying role in the creation of national postmodern identity.[2]

The Orthodox Church, understood as the medium of Orthodox Civilization, always had a strong influence on the formation process of national identity in Russia. According to Alicja Curanović, the political system in Russia cannot be indifferent to religion, as it is one of the most important components of the national idea. As a result, many attributes of Orthodox Church tradition strongly influence politics.[3] Russian power has a tendency towards antinomies and eschatological thinking, anti-Occidentalism and belief in the exceptional historical role of Russia. Moreover, since its baptism in 988, messianic ideas such as Moscow being the incarnation of the Third Rome or the Kingdom of God, where the Antichrist will be defeated, have been extremely vivid in Russian historiosophy and comprised a significant part of the *Russian Idea*.[4]

During the times of the USSR, the communist authorities tried to transform Russian society into an atheistic one, replacing sacral ideas with those connected with Marxist ideology. There was also an attempt to create the *new type of citizen, homo sovieticus*, which should be characterized by features such as atheism, allegiance to the Communist Party and collectivism.[5] After the fall of the Soviet Union, when almost all of the previous values defining the Russian nation lost their meaning, the Orthodox Church started to play a significant role in redefining Russian modern identity. Religion took an important place not only in the social but also the political life of the Russian Federation. Trying to fulfil an axiological vacuum, the Kremlin authorities created a kind of *ideological hybrid* composed of political and religious symbols and concepts. This *confession diplomacy* was an endeavour to find a new formula of national identification and a try of defining the place of the Russian Federation on the international arena.[6]

Another religious aspect characteristic of Russian culture which I mentioned above is the existence of the *Russian Idea*, strongly connected to the Orthodox Church tradition. It is not only the conception of Russia, its fate and destiny, but also the concept of Russia as a bearer of the true idea of God and its mission to accomplish it in the whole world.[7] Components of

---

2. Curanović, *Czynnik*, 9–14.

3. Ibid., 312–37.

4. Lazari, *Czy Moskwa*, 9–17.

5. Zinoviev, *Homo Sovieticus*.

6. Curanović, *Czynnik*.

7. Lazari et al., *Idei v Rossii*, 3:174–86.

*Russian idea* such as the Russian-Christ, *narod-bogonosets* (God-embodying nation), the Third Rome and holy places (such as Bielyevody and Kitezh, where people would be saved from the power of the Antichrist) decide about the unique character of the Russian idea. All of them were used in numerous historiosophical and political conceptions, for example by the Panslavists, the Slavophile movement or Eurasians. Their idea derives from the interwar geopolitical doctrine created by such thinkers as Lev Gumilev and became a very important ideological power in contemporary Russia because of Alexander Dugin's activity.[8]

A very idiosyncratic place in Russian discourse is taken by the concept of the Antichrist, which is used as a constant historical threat. According to the *Lexicon of Ideas in Russia*, the Antichrist is understood not only as the embodiment of Satan but also the false Messiah—the usurper, just like tsar Dmitry during the years of the Russian Time of Troubles. Moreover there are two main aspects of his nature which have been distinguished—*dukhovnost'* (spiritual perception) and *chuvstvennost'* (tangible perception).[9]

According to Vardan Korolev, the Antichrist in Russia is a kind of ideo-myth, whose main role is to conceptualize the way of a state's historical progress. The scholar claims that every epoch of Russian historiosophy created its own Antichrist, who has very little in common with the beast from the Book of Revelation, and was seen as a very current problem. There was an assumption that if the Russian Orthodox Church is the embodiment of God, there should exist its opposition—the Church of Satan's worshippers.[10] As a result, ideological and political antagonists were often considered to be the Antichrist, whose only intention is to destroy Russia.

Russians believed that AD 1000 was the year when Devil was unlocked and the power of the Antichrist started to rule in the temporal world. The Catholic world and the Pope, seen as the *metaphysical antipodes* of Orthodox Church, where considered to be the Kingdom of the Antichrist after the East-West Schism in 1054. Such a conception was popularized in nineteenth century by Fyodor Dostoevsky, who claimed that the Catholic Church is the misrepresentation of Christian ideas and values. As the great Russian writer stated, the main proof that the Western Church became the Antichrist is the acceptance of the dogma of Papal infallibility.[11]

The idea of the Antichrist and his rule in Russia was also very vivid in the seventeenth century among Old-Believers in the Orthodox Church.

---

8. Gołąbek, *Lew Gumilow*, 7–20.

9. Lazari et al., *Idei v Rossii*, 1:58–69.

10. Korolev, "Obraz Antikhrista."

11. Ubrankowski, *Dostojewski*, 252–58.

They claimed that Patriarch Nikon's attempt to establish uniformity between Greek and Russian practices was in order to implement a cult. As a result, they did not accept his reforms, leading to the *Raskol* that still exists in the Orthodox Church.[12] Russian Old-Believers interpreted the reforms of Nikon as the beginning of the Antichrist's spiritual rule that was to precede his tangible arrival. In the fear of an imminent End of the World and fleeing from persecutions, *starovery* established colonies in the most distant territories of Imperial Russia.[13]

Although Old-Believers considered Peter the Great as the Antichrist, also other individuals, for example Ivan the Terrible, Rasputin or Lenin were claimed to be the legates of Satan. Over the years, *starovery* started to perceive the Antichrist not as an individual but as the forces of the evil ruling in Russian Empire. The other aspect of manifesting the idea of Antichrist in Russian discourse is the phenomenon of transferring it from the historiosophical to psychological sphere. In the late nineteenth century, under the influence of Friedrich Nietzsche's philosophy concluded in his book *The Antichrist*, Russians started to look for a source of evil in human nature. In this way of perception significantly pervaded Russian philosophy in the times of religious renaissance—Dmitry Merezhkovsky believed that Tsarist autocracy (*tsarskoye samoderzhaviye*) stemmed from the power of the Antichrist.[14] The opposite theory was represented by Konstantin Leontiev, who claimed that the Antichrist is delivered by liberal-democratic values and is strongly connected to mass culture. In his opinion, Russian's destiny is to create and defeat the Antichrist that would be born in a Russian Jewish environment.[15]

The idea of the Antichrist also appeared in the works of other Russian thinkers, for example Fyodor Dostoevsky—in his works one can find two different incarnations of fiendish powers. This Russian writer understood the Antichrist not only as a false Messiah personified by the *Grand Inquisitor*, who preached Christian values detached from God, but also as the evil existing in every man. Examples of that understanding could be Rodion Raskolnikov or Stavrogin, who rationalized their crimes with the *sverkhideya* of liberty and equality. Movements such as communism, socialism and revolution were also understood by Dostoevsky as the Antichrist's work.[16]

12. Korolev, "Obraz Antikhrista."

13. Crummey, *Old Believers*, xi–xviii.

14. Korolev, "Obraz Antikhrista."

15. Kantor, "Antikhrist."

16. Korolev, "Obraz Antikhrista."

The other great thinkers of the Russian religious renaissance that dealt with the concept of the Antichrist were Nikolai Berdyaev, Dmitry Merezhkovsky and Vladimir Soloviev. While Berdyaev and Merezhkovsky equated evil powers with authorities (the tsar or the Bolsheviks), Soloviev described his metaphysical vision of Antichrist as the ideal of seductive leader. Just like the Grand Inquisitor, his Antichrist was to be a pacifist, humanist and philanthropist that came to Earth to save humankind. However, his true aim was to lead to the fall of Europe and its values. In "A Short Tale of the Antichrist" Soloviev not only referred to Dostoevsky's conception, but also transferred it to the reality—his idea of the Antichrist devolved from the Apocalypse to a historical plan and became canonical.[17]

At the turn of twentieth and twenty-first centuries, the idea of Antichrist in Russia left the walls of Orthodox Church and transferred to political discourse by the Alexandr Dugin affair. After the fall of the Soviet Union, in the time of lack of an imperative idea that would root the multi-ethnic and multi-religious society of Russian Federation, his project of revived Eurasianism, which was at first just an intellectual concept, become an important part of the Kremlin's internal as well as foreign policy.[18] The idea of new Eurasianism as a geopolitical conception that blends different political, cultural and religious values is meant to implement new identical discourse in Russia—it should not only define the national identity but also determine the place of Russia on the international arena.[19]

Eurasianism was the idea that arose within the Russian émigré community in 1920 and established Russia as a completely distinct civilization which should not be described with European or Asian categories. Using the conception from the beginning of twentieth century, by archetypization and reference to toposes and ideo-myths characteristic for Russian Orthodox civilization, Alexander Dugin created a Neo-Eurasianism which harks back to such messianic ideas as Panslavism or the Slavophile movement.[20] The central role in that conception is taken by religion, which is an indispensable factor for the moral revival and main instrument of realization of the Eurasian geopolitical project, in which Russia should take the leading role.[21]

In his sacral geography, Dugin made use of the *Russian Idea* that perceived Moscow as the Third Rome—the place where, thanks to the Orthodox Church, the Antichrist will be permanently defeated. Yet, in his conception,

17. Kantor, "Antikhrist."

18. Curanović, *Czynnik*, 312–17.

19. Gołąbek, *Lew Gumilow*, 7–20.

20. Ibid., 121–48.

21. Curanović, *Czynnik*, 312–37.

the embodiment of Satan is not only a religious idea but a real enemy striving for the destruction of the Russian Federation—it is the United States.[22] Considering the fact that the existence of a common enemy helps to root a society and is very important for the construction of national identity, Alexander Dugin used the anti-American atmosphere that had been very strong in Russia since Soviet times. The disappointment in the American system of values, common consumerism and dollar fetishization made equating the United States with a satanic power very easy for Russian society. Dugin claims that the American Antichrist in twenty first century, along the lines of Grand Inquisitor, tempts people with the illusion of equality, liberty and prosperity, popularizing democracy and the free market in order to conquer the world. Only Russia, where true Christian values are still living, is able to oppose the destructive power of the United States' hegemony. According to Andrzej de Lazari, the gnostic division of the world and peculiar political mythology offered by the idea of Eurasianism, could easily inseminate the mass imagination, especially in the times of crisis and intensification of nationalist moods.[23]

The idea of Eurasianism popularized by Dugin, who is one of Vladimir Putin's greatest supporters, recently became very vivid in Russian political discourse. During his presidency, Putin not only was favourable towards the phenomenon of Orthodox Church revival, but also courted propitious relations between state and church. Moreover, the elements of Eurasianism ideology could be noticed in the Kremlin's diplomacy. In the recent Concept of the Russian Federation Foreign Policy (February, 2013), Putin accentuated the striving for multidimensional order in the world and attenuating American hegemony. According to this conception, the Western world appears as the source of the crisis and growing destabilization of international system. In such circumstances, the main aim of Russia is to establish a Eurasian Economic Union and to keep influences to the "near abroad."[24]

## Bibliography

Broda, Marian. *Zrozumieć Rosję. O rosyjskiej zagadce-tajemnicy.* Łódź: Ibidem, 2011.
Crummey, Robert O. *The Old Believers and the World of Antichrist.* Madison: University of Wisconsin Press, 1970.
Curanović, Alicja. *Czynnik religijny w polityce zagranicznej Federacji Rosyjskiej.* Warsaw: Wydawnictwo Uniwersytetu Warszawskiego, 2010.

22. Ibid., 312–17.
23. Lazari, "Skąd nadchodzi Antychryst."
24. Rodkiewicz, "Koncepcja polityki."

Gołąbek, Bartosz. *Lew Gumilow i Aleksander Dugin. O dwóch obliczach eurazjatyzmu w Rosji po 1991 roku*. Krakow: Wydawnictwo Uniwersytetu Jagielllońskiego, 2012.

Kantor, Vladimir. "Antikhrist ili vrazhda k Evrope: stanovleniye totalitarizma." *Oktyabr'* 1 (2001). http://pravaya.ru/faith/11/74?print=1.

Korolev, Vardan B. "Obraz Antikhrista v russkoy istoriosofskoy mysli." January 19, 2003. http://pravaya.ru/faith/11/74?print=1.

Lazari, Andrzej de. *Czy Moskwa będzie Trzecim Rzymem?* Katowice: Śląsk, 1996.

———. "Skąd nadchodzi Antychryst? Kategoria Zachodu w nacjonalistycznej myśli rosyjskiej." In *Skąd przychodzi Antychryst? Kontakty i konflikty etniczne w Europie Środkowej i Południowej*, edited by Tomasz Falęcki, 139–44. Krakow: Wydawnictwo Akademii Pedagogicznej, 2004.

Lazari, Andrzej de, et al., eds. *Idei v Rossii. Idee w Rosji. Ideas In Russia. Leksykon rosyjsko-polsko-angielski*. 3 vols. Warsaw, Łódź: Semper, Ibidem, 1999–2000.

Rodkiewicz, Witold. "Koncepcja polityki zagranicznej Federacji Rosyjskiej." February 2, 2013. http://www.osw.waw.pl/pl/publikacje/analizy/2013-02-20/koncepcja-polityki-zagranicznej-federacji-rosyjskiej.

Urbankowski, Bohdan. *Dostojewski: dramat humanizmów*. Warsaw: Alfa, 1994.

Zinoviev, Alexander. *Homo Sovieticus*. Translated by Charles Janson. Boston: Atlantic Monthly, 1986.

www.ingramcontent.com/pod-product-compliance
Lightning Source LLC
Chambersburg PA
CBHW070400270326
41926CB00014B/2634